TRAVELS WITH A 2CV

NICKY EARWAKER

INTRODUCTION

At 6.45 a.m. the alarm clock suffered a severe blow which sent it crashing to the floor and an unwilling body struggled out of bed in the darkness and tripped over it. At 7.35, in the dreary half-light of that February morning, the same body fled from the house and leaped into the old brown Saab which Ashley, the body's half-conscious husband, was coaxing into reluctant action. 7.36 saw them set off for the station at full choke and five minutes later the car had rumbled into the forecourt, husband had ejected wife from the passenger seat and trundled off homewards to have his breakfast. All around the station, in contrast, wives were imprinting the routine, daily kisses on the cheeks of their parting husbands, before shooting back to pack the children off to school and feed the dog.

Amidst a dark swarm of briefcases, suits and umbrellas I was swept up the station steps onto the platform and at 7.42 precisely... the London train failed to arrive. It was not unusual for it to be late. Every so often, on the other hand, and on the very mornings I found myself delayed, its adherence to the timetable would catch me out. Driven, like so many others, by this constant fear of the punctuality of the '7.42', I had followed the same terrorised routine for nearly two years since we were married.

Today, however, there was one difference: I was carrying to work a letter of resignation and with it the glorious knowledge that my rail-commuting days were numbered. When the train finally arrived to ensnare me, for once I felt strangely insulated from the howling draughts in the luggage van, where many of us were forced to stand; and I emerged from the inter-platform crush at East Croydon and the final, forcible extrusion at Victoria, feeling abnormally close to the shape that God had intended for me. Hope can be a wonderful cushion.

If I was yearning to escape from the role of a crushed commuter, one might well wonder (and many have) what made us choose to squeeze ourselves into a little Citroën 2CV and embark on a journey of thousands of hot and potentially uncomfortable miles - surely this was something to be avoided at all cost? Discomfort, however, is an inescapable ingredient of all travels. The significant difference between daily commuting to a London office and the expedition we had planned was the vital element of unpredictability. It was this prospect of the unknown which provided the attraction and the challenge of our journey - an adventure for which we had been longing for some years - in fact ever since we had returned to Britain after working abroad.

We had met in Oman five years earlier, both of us employed as geophysicists with different companies there. When I had moved to a new job in Aberdeen, Ashley had remained in the Sultanate for another year, after which he and two friends drove back to England in an old Range-Rover - an experience I would have loved to have shared. The nearest I had come to a major overland adventure was travelling in the back of a lorry on a week's camping trip from Nairobi to Lake Turkana. Itchy feet are incurable, however, and, if living in Oman for barely fourteen months had whetted my appetite for overseas travel, Ashley, having worked abroad for four and a half years and travelled with a friend for several months through India and South-East Asia, not only yearned for more but filled me with enthusiasm for the places he had visited too.

We had few reservations about leaving our jobs: although we both enjoyed our work, there were certain disadvantages, such as those already outlined. In addition, Ashley's employers had jumped on the redundancy bandwagon and he was eager to leave before the choice no longer existed. As for finding similar new jobs in oil and gas exploration on our expected return a year later, we were both optimistic - foolishly so, it transpired, for little did we realise that the oil price would drop so dramatically, squeezing exploration budgets and compelling geophysicists to turn their hands to other skills.

We have failed to agree on the exact date of our decision to make the overland journey but certainly the winter of 1984-1985 found us trudging through deep snow to look at second-hand Land-Rovers and then listing the pros and cons of taking a vehicle at all, or carrying minimal possessions on our backs and trusting to public transport. From then on the plan gradually evolved. By necessity, it was never cut and dried, even after we had decided on the 2CV - after all, the trip was intended to have as flexible a timetable as possible.

Naturally, there was a great deal to organise in terms of things to be left behind and those to be taken with us, and the first part of the journey was forced to fit a rough schedule in order for visas and car documents to be valid for the correct periods. Beyond these requirements and the aim to be back in about twelve months we intentionally left the route and time-planning as open as we reasonably could. This would give us the freedom to stay longer in places which we found interesting and the time to overcome the anticipated events of a less desirable nature, such as breakdowns in remote areas or bureaucratic delays - not that we lacked faith in our French travelling companion or doubted the smooth-running of the whole of Asia's governmental machinery, of course. It was simply that, like most sensible pessimists, we preferred to predict disasters in order to gain extra pleasure when they failed to strike. The journey was bound to be memorable but we wanted it to be enjoyable too.

'For my part, I travel not to go anywhere but to go. I travel for travel's sake. The great affair is to move.'
Robert Louis Stevenson, from *Travels with a Donkey*

CHAPTER 1

On 13 August 1985, we had left our home in Kent to catch a night ferry from Dover. It was an undistinguished beginning: nobody who passed a little lay-by outside Dunkirk in the early hours of the following morning could have guessed that the parked white Deux Chevaux and its two dormant occupants, contorted uncomfortably in the front seats, were intending to drive to India. We could hardly believe it ourselves after the whirlwind of last minute activity which had preceded our departure. Nothing short of sheer exhaustion could have extinguished our intense excitement and relief at the end of months of preparation when we finally set out.

If the two drivers looked alarmingly jaded only hours after leaving home and with ten thousand miles to go, it was fortunate that the young car was in shining health.

Admittedly it could hardly be described as a perfectly conventional 2CV: in fact with all its modifications we felt as though we were travelling in a lightweight tank rather than a standard roadrunner. The engine itself was unchanged - air-cooled, 602 cc and just two cylinders - but very little else had escaped unscathed from the adaptation. In the interests of security we had fitted extra door-locks, bolted a lockable steel chest to the floor (having dispensed with the back seat) and riveted aluminium bars across the front windows and as a rigid lattice across the roof. The latter was an eleventh-hour improvisation after all hope had failed of receiving the fibre-glass roof which we had ordered from France several months earlier. We could not prevent someone from slashing the soft hood with a knife but at least we had made it difficult for him to get into the car or lift anything out without the aid of a hacksaw and a good deal of determination. We had also retained the facility for open-top driving, even though when the soft roof was rolled back and we looked up at the sky through a mesh of metal we did feel like a couple of caged canaries.

Before embarking on the adventure we subjected the car to 5,600 miles of British roads, including taking it up to Aberdeen one week to accustom it to being a long way from home. We had fitted certain special 'P.O.' (Pays d'Outre-mer) Citroën parts, designed predominantly for use in African countries: improved air filter, sump guard, fuel-tank guard and strong front bumper, ideal for warding off wart-hogs or other large obstacles. The car's further modifications included cut-off rear wheel-arches, strengthened suspension arms (filled with epoxy resin via pre-drilled holes), reinforced steering arms (with sleeves made of electrician's conduit), displacement of the coil to a less vulnerable position on top of the bell-housing, and fitting Firestone Winter Traction tyres. We also added an extra horn (and a switch for the passenger) and fitted spotlights, a reversing light, a home-made bull-bar and protective grilles. I could continue for pages to detail the preparatory treatment inflicted on the car - Ashley spent so much time performing all these operations that our neighbours began to wonder where the evolution of the increasingly strange vehicle was going to end.

Ashley was well qualified for the journey, having driven a Range Rover from Oman to England four years earlier and with a history of rallying Saabs in Britain. I was to be chief cook and diary-keeper, driving when allowed!

I had never hoped to acquire Ashley's skill of travelling light, but confronted with a car already bursting with essential spare parts and jerry cans, overflowing with anti-malaria tablets and pots of Marmite, I had little choice but to squeeze my personal survival kit into a small rucksack. The car's load was crucial to its performance and we had to list and weigh every item of baggage contents to ensure that the total was below the statutory limit. The stark truth was that whatever we put inside the car had to add up to less than 700lb. Having deducted 270lb for our bodyweights, 67lb for the vital tools, fire extinguisher and spare parts, and allowed 180lb for petrol and water (should all our jerry cans and plastic containers be full), we had less than 200lb to play with for camping gear, food, books, maps, medical equipment, cameras and films, radio, cassettes, water-filter, cooking stove, binoculars and clothes. For months before our departure we amused ourselves repeatedly by going through the list, juggling with the weights, deleting an extra paperback and a tin-opener here in order to slot another camera lens in there, eliminating the cool-box as an unnecessary luxury and squeezing in more dried milk and soya meals instead.

By the time we left we had reduced our personal

allowance to 25lb each (including shoes and snorkels) and were wondering how we had had the audacity to give ourselves 50lb in the first place. When we packed the car on 13 August our total payload was 500lb which allowed another 140lb for our maximum fuel and water capacity and left us remarkably with 60lb to spare. Everything in the car had been carefully selected for our planned year of travel.

We had bought the new car in March, perplexing a number of friends and relations who firmly believed in Ashley's unstinting loyalty to Saabs (old ones in particular); they regarded our purchase of a B-registration Citroën with trepidation, interpreting it as the first sign of madness. It was when they discovered that we had bought an export car (one that had to be taken out of Britain within a year) and when we were forced to let the cat out of the bag about our intended journey that their worst fears were confirmed.

'Give up your jobs to go travelling round the world for a year? You must be crazy!'

'Only a small part of the world, really. Just a bit of Asia and a fraction of Africa.'

'But, in *that*? Why don't you take a real car?'

'Like a Saab, you mean? It would be too difficult to find spare parts. The 2CV is ideal for our trip anyway. It's been tried and tested in Africa under all conditions. It's simple, air-cooled, cheap and can last for days without refuelling - like a camel in many ways. That's why it will be so good for crossing the Sahara ... '

'Sahara? You can't be serious!'

'Don't worry, it's been done before in 2CVs.' As it transpired, however, we were causing them unnecessary alarm - although we had planned initially to drive across the Sahara from Morocco to Nigeria and then through Central Africa to reach Tanzania, we eventually abandoned the idea as needless masochism. It was not the desert section which worried us: provided we stuck to the winter months, took plenty of food, water and sand ladders and followed the main road where possible, there was little danger - it is a well travelled route these days. It was at the thought of spending weeks, if not months, thrashing our way through the equatorial jungles of the Central African Republic and Zaire, up to our ears in mud and in constant fear of running out of fuel, that we finally quailed. After all, our journey was intended to be an enjoyable experience, not a commando course writing the car off before we had even done its 10,000 miles service. Judging by the advice of some friends who had made this African journey in a Land-Rover some years earlier and whose tales consisted largely of civil war, bribery, blood-sucking insects and the barter of visas for diesel, and whose photographs of main roads showed tracks with ruts three feet deep and dense jungle on either side, it was probably an adventure we could do without.

If the luggage list had been subjected to a thousand alterations, our route plan must have undergone at least a million. The final version was to drive overland to India and Nepal, ship the car from Bombay to East Africa to visit relations in Tanzania, and then to return via Egypt to Britain. India and Tanzania, being our major targets, were almost the only constant factors during the formulation of our itinerary. For months all the other countries on our proposed routes were repeatedly uprooted and tossed together by a tornado of climatic factors, politics, shipping lines and road conditions. For example, could we drive back from Tanzania via Kenya and Sudan to Egypt? There were only a few months in the year when the floodwaters of the Nile in southern Sudan subsided sufficiently to allow a passage by road, but it was possible: the overland holiday companies did it. On the

Queuing to cross border at the Loibl Pass

'Keep cool!' said Ashley, after a good deal of sighing over the state of Austrian holiday traffic. 'Remember we've got all the time in the world - well, twelve months anyway.' With that he swung the car round as violently as was possible without actually using the handbrake.

'Yugoslavia, here we come!'

Leaving the tourists to their strüdels and their lederhosen we yodelled off into the mountains, or rather a dense mass of clouds which rested like a giant, grey bolster on its bed of pine forests. As though electrified by the storm, the contrasting greens of the dark trees and the fresh meadows were vivid beneath the threatening sky. The scene was charged with colour: the golden wood of massive farm buildings, each an agglomeration of house, barn, garage and cattle-byre; wooden balconies overflowing with bright, wet geraniums in rich reds and pinks. After the dreariness of the grey autobahns, we felt exhilarated and cheerful: we had wiped the rain from our view, learning to see through it and to focus our eyes instead on the beauty beyond. It was to be a useful exercise - few scenes are ever perfect.

The next day was dry and sunny and the entire car-owning population of northern Europe was on its way to Yugoslavia - or so it appeared to us as we sat in a long, snaking queue on the steep Austrian approach to the Loibl Pass. With the roof rolled back and the warmth of the sun lifting our spirits, we were not worried now by a few hours' delay. Soon the queue was moving haltingly through the Loibl Tunnel and we felt as though we were crawling inside the ribcage of a buried dinosaur, with the overhead string of fluorescent lights marking its spine and a series of arc-like drainage pipes curving across the roof like ribs. In any case we were glad to see daylight again, even though it only meant more queuing: this time at the border post where everyone was after his share of Yugoslavian petrol coupons - understandably, since they entitle visitors to 10 per cent discount.

One of the first things which struck us as odd as we strolled around the centre of Postojna that evening was the paucity of shops. While the town was crowded with young soldiers drinking beer at the open-air bars and with German and Italian tourists returning from their visits to the Postojna caverns and pouring out of coaches or lapping up ice-creams, it was remarkably free of the normal clutter of high street enterprises. In fact the scattering of little shops was more reminiscent of small, forgotten towns in the Welsh borderland than of a typical European holiday centre. Admittedly it was Sunday but Postojna's shop windows showed every sign of being perennially dingy and undressed. There was a tiny one containing stacked boxes of outdated 'fashion' shoes alongside strong farmers' boots. Another displayed essential tools and basic hardware, while the grocer's window showed a sparse and unappetising selection of tinned food with long-faded labels. Postojna, we soon realised, was not peculiar in this regard - it was simply that in the Socialist Federal Republic of Yugoslavia, private enterprise did not flourish.

Meanwhile, on the outskirts of the town, local children were competing in some junior track events at Postojna's little stadium. It seemed an intensely serious affair. While we sat in the warm sun watching one race, half a dozen more unsmiling schoolchildren were flexing and stretching in smart tracksuits, preparing themselves like international athletes for their big moment. After all, medals were at stake, not to mention honour among classmates. Just outside the perimeter fence three little urchins aged between six and nine were holding their own events, marking a start line on the dusty path and running no more than a few yards across some gravel before one of them had tripped and was rubbing grazed knees and the race had to restart. Even the real track was small but its loudspeakers, like the competitors, had delusions of grandeur and insisted on blasting their messages with a volume which would have penetrated the furthest reaches of any Olympic stadium. Each time there was a prize-giving ceremony we put our hands to our ears to avoid irreparable damage, as we watched another medal-adorned threesome solemnly standing to attention, the national anthem booming around them. Fearing for the integrity of our eardrums, we abandoned our ringside seats for the more peaceful environment of Postojna's campsite, where the loudest noises were the attempts to hammer tent pegs into solid limestone and the vociferous reactions of campers failing to do so.

It is the limestone which has imprinted Postojna firmly on the tourist maps: the soluble rock has been fashioned by nature into some of the most spectacular caverns in the world, with underground passages whose total length is said to be 23 kilometres. Certainly it was the scale of the caves which so impressed us: the great 'Concert Hall' chamber, for example, could have seated thousands of people and, judging by the number of visitors who flocked down for the guided tours, there were times when it probably needed to. We had chosen the first tour of the morning, at 8.30, thinking mistakenly that we should avoid the crowds. Instead we queued for half an hour with hundreds of other tourists, were piled into little wooden railway trucks and went hurtling down the steep and winding tunnel at hair-raising speed, accompanied by a symphony of rattles and screams which reached an alarming crescendo at every bend in the overloaded track. It was like rushing down a bob-sleigh run in semi-darkness, and feeling compelled to keep ducking continually beneath a low roof, which in reality was just high enough not to endanger the scalp of even the tallest man on the train. When we landed at the buffers at the bottom end and flopped onto the platform like lumps of quivering jelly, most of the passengers had been reduced to nervous wrecks, children were screaming in terror or clamouring for another ride, families of noisy Italians were hugging one another emotionally as though they had just survived a holocaust, and somebody's small dog was quietly being sick.

It had felt like a journey to the centre of the earth (and maybe these caverns inspired Jules Verne to write his book) but in fact we were only 200 metres below the surface and already in a strange world inhabited by *Proteus anguinus,* a pale, blind salamander which swims in the underground streams and can apparently survive for up to six months without food. At Postojna there is now a special pool for them. For the purposes of the tour we were segregated into language groups whose relative sizes confirmed our belief that Postojna was overrun by Italians and Germans and which placed us in a quiet party of camera-happy Japanese.

The chambers were magnificent, with stalagmites like sturdy sculptures, brown with iron or grey with manganese, and delicate ribbon stalactites hanging like rippled curtains from roof cracks or fissures. They were beautifully illuminated like a series of elaborate stage sets for *Aladdin* and we praised the power of electricity, imagining the first visitors one hundred and sixty years before struggling about in the gloom with their lanterns, unaware of the latent, unlit beauty all around them. Then we thought of the last caves we had visited in southern France, the Grottes des Desmoiselles, where the electric train had taken us *up* inside the hill because the system was a fossil one, long-since dry. There the garrulous guide had hardly given us a chance to let our imagination wander but had deluged us with already-labelled formations such as 'Madonna and Child', the 'Pink Elephant' and other titles in that vein. Here we could play at choosing our own titles for the weird and wonderful shapes which glistened before our eyes. The Yugoslavian guide, on the other hand, was concerned with the less romantic side of things, such as the fact that prisoners of two world wars had built the paths and bridges which we were walking on and that the next little section was going to be exceedingly wet and slippery and would we please proceed with caution.

The first thing we did on reaching the surface was to remove about three layers of surplus clothing. Then we pottered down to the coast which we followed as far as Jurjevo. The road, winding in and out and up and down, would have seemed rather tedious had it not been for the stupendous view of limestone hills slicing down into clear blue sea. We camped by a small rocky inlet near Jurjevo for a couple of tranquil days, visiting the pretty little fishing village in the evening to eat at the terrace restaurant overlooking the harbour. We ordered two beers to celebrate England's victory in the 5th Test against Australia. Inexplicably, fish was the most expensive dish on the menu so we chose omelettes, watching a couple of boys who were sitting on the harbour wall nonchalantly casting their lines in the water and landing fish with enviable regularity. Meanwhile the waitress trotted across the concrete patio in her laced white ankle boots which reminded us of the surgical variety but had a hole cut out of each above the heel, creating a sling-back effect which seemed to be fashionable among the Yugoslavian ladies. She had probably bought them at the dingy little village store which appeared to sell everything from sausages to paint stripper but with a bias towards the inedible, judging by our own purchase of a nail brush and a brick of brown bread.

We spent the days swimming, snorkelling (carefully avoiding sea-urchins) and grovelling under the car to adjust the suspension. The nights were not quite so peaceful. On the first we were woken by a thunderous rumbling which we took to be the warning of another storm, until the ground started to tremble beneath us, giving us the impression that we had pitched our tent above a subterranean railway. Then the truth struck our vibrating brains: Poseidon, not Zeus, had come to torment us - this was an earth tremor! Ashley had felt one before in New Guinea. For me it was a new experience; it seemed to last for several unforgettable minutes, although it was probably only a few seconds before all was restored to stillness. On the second night we felt as though two hundred electric hair dryers were being aimed in our direction as a hot, gale-force wind buffeted the tent sides relentlessly from midnight onwards, forcing us to dispense with our thick, down sleeping bags and guaranteeing us hours of restlessness. Only after nights such as these comes true appreciation of the dawn, and we greeted that particular sunrise as though it were our first sight of land after months on a storm-tossed sea.

'Time to get up!' called Ashley in an unprecedented burst of enthusiasm for such an early hour and, before I could be sure that I was not dreaming, he had unzipped the tent flaps, cried 'Breakfast!' and poked his head through the gap. Within a second he was back inside, frantically zipping up the opening against the wind, choking and complaining that a mouthful of dust was not what he had had in mind. I was laughing so much that our eyes were soon streaming in unison. Little did we suspect just then how forlorn the car was feeling. During the night, some practical joker from the campsite had delved under the bonnet, fished out the heater hoses (flimsy great tubes of corrugated cardboard) and stuck one on each of the wing mirrors so that the poor vehicle looked like a reindeer with collapsing antlers.

Having reassembled it, we set off along the gusty road high above the gleaming, turquoise sea, gazing down at the islands of limestone which seemed to float like slim, white ships anchored parallel to the coast. A few hours later, in a cloud of white dust, we were bouncing our way inland along a rocky track and I was being blamed for poor navigation - as usual, quite unfairly. The surfaced road (which came in the category of 'other tourist roads' on our map) had simply come to an abrupt end, miles from anywhere, with an apologetic sign reading 'Asphalt' but ominously slashed by a black diagonal line. It was hardly my fault that the car was encountering its first 'off-road' test and in any case I suspected that Ashley was secretly enjoying this little reminder of his stage-rallying days, beneath his half-hearted 'Whose idea was it to go to Knin anyway?' jibes. As a matter of fact it was my idea to leave the coast for a spell and visit this particular castle. The karst scenery we crossed alternated between barren aridity and lush greenery. Even in the harshest-looking environment the farmers had managed to scrape together their little domed haystacks and raise a few thin sheep on little more than small blue thistles. But in the valleys and the poljes (oasis-like areas several kilometres across, where underground water had reached the surface) there were vineyards, orchards and rich fields of maize and vegetables. Every little uvala (a large swallow-hole but smaller than a polje) was a green island of cultivation enclosed by dry-stone walls.

In Knin there was no sign directing visitors to the castle, but then it was hardly necessary to point out its prominent hilltop position and pretty optimistic to expect many visitors anyway, judging by the attendance that day. We climbed a steep path in the hot sun, and panting, crossed the drawbridge. It was so quiet and eerie that we looked up at the walls uneasily for signs of spying eyes, wondering whether, when we reached the portcullis, we should be drenched in boiling tar. We woke the caretaker who sold us tickets for about fifteen pence each and then slumped back into his peaceful slumber amongst the museum's plaster casts, while we conducted ourselves round the ruined ramparts. These great walls of limestone went marching across the hillside as though the ancient Chinese had had a hand in their building, but within this series of battlements there was little remaining of the castle itself. The most memorable features of Knin were the spectacular view over the Krka Valley towards the Dinaric Alps to the east, and the prodigious quantity of arrow slits incised in the upper ramparts - perhaps a job creation scheme for unemployed archers.

Later that afternoon we parked in the centre of Sinj, next to a magazine booth displaying surprisingly pornographic front covers, and strolled along the empty cobbled streets. It was like a ghost town - no vehicles, but old houses with shutters closed. The only sign of life was a handful of young soldiers ambling across the square.

Two hours later we might have been in a different town. As we sat outside the busy little cafe, the pedestrianised centre was humming with activity: the house martins were swarming above us in the fading light, the shutters were thrown back and the entire population of Sinj was shopping, socialising and milling around us in a casual and friendly atmosphere. The shops, very small and dimly lit with inconspicuous signs above their doors, were old-fashioned general stores, packed with everything from cheese to galvanised buckets. You could have tossed out a few of the more trendily dressed youngsters and used the remaining scene as a 1940s film set. We discovered the modern face of Sinj just around the corner, concentrated in a small, dark pizza bar crowded with young people and resounding with the strains of Bob Dylan. Yugoslavian youth was doing its best to pull the country into the second half of the twentieth century.

Not far down the coast from Split we stayed in a guest-house with a family for two days - with granny and grandpa, their son, Ivo, and his wife and two small boys. There was not much space between the steep hills and the sea - just enough to squeeze a narrow pebbly beach, the road and a row of houses with small, terraced back gardens which ran amok with pumpkins, melons, tomatoes and chickens. On the second morning granny assailed us on our way to the beach for breakfast, lurched towards us with breast-stroke movements of her arms and raised her eyebrows questioningly. We nodded to indicate that we were indeed going to the beach to swim but she proceeded to the edge of the balcony and started shouting, 'eave-'o! 'eave-o!' ostensibly to some

Woman gardening near Split

'fishermen at the water's edge. When we went down to the shore the significance of her actions suddenly became clear, for there was Ivo offering us a ride in his little wooden boat. We accepted eagerly, the engine eventually spluttered into life and we pottered down the coast and back with Ivo and his adoring sons who, at the grand ages of four and six, took turns to cling proudly to the tiller and directed appealing eyes upwards for paternal approbation.

That evening we sat at the table on their concrete balcony, enjoying an arm-waving conversation with the family over glasses of iced home-made red wine. Ivo, whose schoolboy's English was a great success, not only kept the pension and took guests out on boat excursions at the weekends, but also ran a welding business from a workshop below the house and worked as a mechanic from 6 a.m. until 2 p.m. at an ore-processing plant at Dugi Rat. There, he explained, minerals from Gabon, Australia and Albania are separated electrolytically to produce chromium for the North American market. Despite his string of occupations, Ivo maintained that the wages were too low to contemplate affording a house of his own and that he was compelled to stay here with his parents. Nevertheless they seemed to be a happy enough family and we were sad to leave them the next morning after granny, hospitable to the last, had forced us to have some strong coffee, for a 'Good *strada'*, as she put it.

Our *strada* took us to Dubrovnik to explore the old fortified town, whose walls are as much as five metres thick in places. Within its maze of alleyways and streets paved with limestone and smooth-polished by centuries of passing feet, tourists flocked to see the Sponza Palace, the churches and the old pharmacy. But life for the inhabitants went on regardless: children and cats were playing in the alleys, old women gossiped at doorways, washing hung like bunting from lines running from window to shuttered window, and stonemasons were at work on the old buildings.

In stark contrast, Kotor, once a similar walled town, further down the coast, was the last link in a chain of devastation: we had passed hillsides scarred by forest fires which had recently swept through the region, burning and blackening as they roared, sparing only the tops of the tallest firs, now left like green helmets on an

Earthquake ruins, Kotor

army of charred skeletons. Kotor's disaster, no less serious than this holocaust, had been an earthquake in April 1979 which caused destruction on such a scale that most of the inhabitants had to be rehoused and the restoration of its buildings was destined to continue into the twenty-first century. We found it a forlorn place - stray cats scavenged from rubbish piles in cracked, deserted houses or in rifted alleys; telephone wires and guttering dangled from fissured stonework; and the glory of a once-proud town lay smashed and buried beneath the jumble of its fallen masonry.

It was not a place in which to linger, so we pressed on to a campsite at Sveti Stefan, where we daubed ourselves liberally with Mijex and pitched the tent in a welcoming cloud of mosquitoes. This was the end of the Yugoslavian coast for us: it was impossible to carry on much further without running into Albania. The next day we turned inland towards Titograd, ascending steeply from the sea via hairpin bends while the rubbery smell of overheated brakes wafted in through the open windows in the wake of descending lorries. Once over the hilltop, we were gliding down towards Skadarsko Jezero, a large lake which extends to the Albanian border. In the summer it is somewhat shrunken and there were broad areas of marshland around its shores.

Having paused briefly to buy some pears and fresh figs from a roadside fruit stall, we continued through the busy, modern city of Titograd and, following the Moraca River northwards, looked down longingly from the hot car at the beautiful, deep gorge and the cool, blue water. Soon the temptation proved too great: we stopped the car and scrambled down the steep side about two hundred feet to the river. The reward was an afternoon of sheer delight - the tranquil gorge was the most beautiful place we came across in Yugoslavia. The sun was warm, but a cool and pleasant breeze stroked the valley as we sat on a white pebble beach with the water-bottle cooling in the water and ate our lunch. The river had sliced down through the limestone forming precipitous canyon walls, and lying in the riverbed were great boulders of conglomerate the size of cars, cemented mounds of motley pebbles. The water was shallow and fast-flowing, tumbling over smooth stones in chilled, white splashes, but we found a deep, calm pool for bathing and dipped our startled bodies into the icy water. Tiny fish darted away and a brown patterned eel slithered beneath a rock. It was pure joy to emerge from the freshness of the water and feel the heat of the sun drying and penetrating our skin as we sat lazily on the warm pebbles. It was such a haven of peace after the busy coast that we had to tear ourselves away in order to reach Ivangrad that evening.

The route was painfully slow as we wriggled along the gorge, in and out of tunnels, struggled up steep hills and were caught repeatedly behind sluggish lorries. The campsite was in the grounds of Ivangrad's hotel and we shared it with a German VW campervan and a couple of lean Dutchmen who had just driven through Hungary and Romania and spoke of scarcity of food and of border searches for guns and religious literature. Then four gregarious Italians arrived and, with all the room in the world, chose sociably to set up camp just a few feet from our tent.

Had it not been for the campsite we would not have stopped at Ivangrad. It was not an attractive town, having grown up around a huge plastics factory which employed about five thousand people but also spewed out its foul-looking effluents into the River Lim, polluting it horribly. There was something depressing too about the way hordes of young people congregated expectantly, and yet hopelessly, in the town centre that evening. It was as though for days they had been awaiting a carnival procession or were hoping forlornly that someone would open some magic doors and an exciting new club would spring up before their eyes; but there was nothing - not a bar, nor cafe; no meeting-place save the pavements and a solitary little ice-cream shop which was doing a roaring trade.

The following morning, light rain soon developed into a cracking thunderstorm as we left our eastern trail from Ivangrad to Titova-Mitrovica, and turned south towards Skopje and Greece. It had been a pleasant start, driving between gentle, grassy slopes with small herds of cows, fields of maize and orchards. Little red-roofed chalets nestled like dolls' houses amongst the pastures, their lovable families of haystacks like clusters of upturned acorn-cups, each with a central pole rising proud of its domed rick. Tiny, bubble-shaped Zastava cars went bumbling by, bulging with large families and roof-racks piled high.

By the time we reached Pristina the thunder and

lightning flashes were in full swing, following one another like an unending series of drum rolls and cymbal clashes. The rain sluiced down the windscreen by the bucket load, so that we could hardly make out the struggling wipers, let alone the slippery road ahead. Not wanting to join the fully laden bus which had already toppled into the ditch, nor the three cars which had slid into one another, we decided to stop in a field and wait for the storm to pass. As is his wont, Ashley rolled up his trousers, donned a waterproof jacket and leaped out of the car into a puddle in his eagerness to sponge the loosened dirt from the car.

'Perfect car-washing weather!' he grinned, jumping back inside the now outwardly gleaming vehicle and drenching me with his dripping, discarded anorak as I watched a pool of muddy water collecting on the floor around his feet.

'Lovely.' I agreed with less than total conviction.

After lunch the weather quietened and, wiping the condensation from the windows, we revealed a beautiful landscape of vast, dark, peaty fields sprinkled with the yellows of maize, sunflowers and harvested corn. There were other changes as we travelled through this southern region: an outbreak of mosques and of men in white Moslem caps, of women wearing billowing, baggy, bright trousers; and there was a dangerous predominance of horses and carts on the roads. We were well away from the 'Zimmer' (Rooms) and 'Turist Biro' (Tourist Office) signs. Here, as in Sinj, the older generation did their best to ignore change. The small peasant farmer travelling to his fields by donkey was apparently oblivious of the giant cement lorries rumbling past him to the local factory. We passed an old man and his little grandson squatting under a plum tree, minding their sheep in the greater shadow of a colossal pylon.

The summer had shrivelled the Lepenac River to a stream which trickled towards Skopje along the valley's gravelly wasteland, between acres of dry, withered grassland. The outskirts of Skopje, with their dismal blocks of flats, looked equally desolate and poor. At some red traffic lights four boys rushed up to clean our windscreen with dirty rags, demanding money and cigarettes. Then, displeased at their less than welcoming reception, they kindly spat on our windows and ran off to their next victims.

Having joined the major E5 route from Hungary and Belgrade, we spent the night in a dreary motel near Gradsko. The tariff was astronomical, the facilities were abominable and the unpalatability of the omelettes for dinner was surpassed only by that of breakfast the following morning. After a wonderful week, it was an unfortunate choice for our last stop in Yugoslavia.

We were only in Greece for a couple of days - just passing along its eastern limb between the Rhodope Mountains of Bulgaria and the Aegean Sea. Thessalonika was a nightmare, a sentiment subsequently endorsed by other Turkey-bound travellers. The traffic was chaotic, the signposts were atrocious and a pestilential thunderstorm had turned the sloping side streets into rivers which poured their contents into shallow lakes, once main roads, where we were practically afloat. Rain bounced in through our leaking windows, splashing us to saturation point. We missed the crucial turning announced vaguely as 'Bulgaria' and spent a further hour in extricating ourselves from the muddled city.

No sooner had Ashley again performed his rain-and-sponge routine on the car than we ran into a stretch of recently resurfaced road where overtaking lorries delighted in tearing up the sticky top layer and redistributing it all over our car, spraying us with a protective coating of mud and diesel. Only repetitive scrubbing and half a packet of washing powder eventually removed most of this glutinous mess but the remaining dark patches clung stubbornly for several months, providing a standard of rust-proofing probably matched by few products on the market today.

Kavalla was wet too, the Hotel Panorama had no view, being one street back from the harbour, and as we tried to drown our lukewarm moussaka in retsina, the restaurateur and a drunken customer fought a running battle over a clove or two of garlic which the latter had pinched from an arguably decorative string on the wall. In the morning we breakfasted in the 'Fast Food' cafe on hot dogs and fried eggs accompanied by plastic cups in which Tetley's teabags had been flung into a sea of milk and warmish water and now floated lifelessly. Ashley insisted that he and Adrian and Bob, his companions in the Range Rover, had found Kavalla a pleasant little port when they spent one night there previously - which just goes to show that you should not judge a place by an isolated visit, particularly when you have been subjected to sequential showers of rain, diesel and cloves of garlic.

When we left Kavalla the sun came out and we drove past fields of rather stunted, drought-stricken crops of sugar beet, tobacco, cotton, maize, sunflowers, grapes, tomatoes, olives and almonds - the variety was incredible - all clearly unimpressed by yesterday's downpour. With the regularity of post-boxes in Britain, little wayside shrines with icons and offerings appeared along the road. Then a trail of squashed tomatoes warned us that we were about to be caught behind several tractor-loads of the ripe, red beauties on their way to the canning factory. On the top of a nearby telegraph pole perched a huge stork's nest, a great mass of straw and large sticks which looked so precarious that the stork who built it must have possessed the poise of a trapeze artist to balance on it.

We paused briefly in Komotini, a quiet little town as pretty as its name, to visit its modern museum, well laid out with a variety of relics of ancient Thrace, from gravestones to delicate gold filigree jewellery.

On the road to Alexandroupolis there were white-washed villages with mosques and men in white pill-box caps who stared in as much amazement as we did at a Frenchman plodding along the road and pulling a handcart whose sticker read 'Bordeaux - Istanbul'. (Give us a 2CV any day, we thought.)

That evening we camped near the sandy beach at Alexandroupolis and swam in the sea - briefly, for the strong wind was cold now. It was a well organised site but the tap water was brackish and unpleasant to drink. Suffering a plague of salt, we found that what we thought was a Yugoslavian packet of dried soup and had casually tossed into our boiling rice was in fact some kind of concentrated vegetable extract which rendered the whole mess inedible, even to Ashley. We made do with bread to accompany our sardines, polished off a mound of grapes and then completed the meal with mugs of distinctly saline coffee.

It was Turkey's Victory Day, 30 August, when we reached the border to find a queue of lorries held up by three days of celebratory 'Go slow' imposed by the local customs men. Fortunately we were not subject to the same delay but a British victim (a student of video and film art, now specialising intriguingly in 'inflatable design'), who had hitched a lift with a lorry all the way from Cologne and was now stymied, pleaded with us to take him on board. Exactly where in our tightly packed car we were supposed to install a hitch-hiker, especially one with designs on inflation, was beyond our imagination, unless possibly he was thinking of strapping himself to the boot lid and doubling as a spare tyre. Reluctantly, we left him looking for an emptier car and ploughed along a straight road between undulating fields of yellow stubble and brown, wilting sunflowers until we reached Tekirdag and the deep blue Sea of Marmara. A strong southerly wind churned big waves relentlessly against the shore, but not sufficiently to keep determined Turkish bathers out of the water. The traffic became heavier as we approached Istanbul along the sea's northern coast. Fields of sunflowers and stalls of bright yellow melons alternated with seaside resorts where holiday-makers were packed together with great canvas tents reminiscent of medieval battle camps, but soon they gave way to high-rise flats and then we were passing through the Topkapi Gates to enter the hurly-burly of the old city.

CHAPTER 2

Ataturk bust, Bosphorus

For four days we pounded the pavements of Istanbul, sightseeing, preparing for the next stage of our journey, and abandoning hope of obtaining Saudi Arabian visas in Turkey. On the fifth our feet were complaining and we took a ferry trip up the Bosphorus, idly watching the banks glide by, feeling the cool breeze on the aft-deck gently soothing away the dust and heat of the city. Cargo vessels chugged lazily by, fishing boats lay patiently in midstream, their vast red nets spilling into the grey-blue water and smaller craft simply bobbed about at moorings beneath white, shuttered villas - Henley-on-Thames transposed. We passed, on the western bank, a splendid castle with perfectly crenellated walls called Rumeli Hisar which, as we were informed by a young American woman on the boat, 'Ol' Mehmet II put up in a couple o' weeks on his way down the Bosphorus to take Istanbul.' She was not far off the mark: the castle was built in 1452 in just a few months, by the famous Ottoman sultan known as the Conqueror, who went on to capture Constantinople the following year, thereby putting an end to the Byzantine Empire. The woman, with her husband and two children, had been travelling in Europe and had undergone an interesting experience on crossing the Yugoslavian-Greek border by train. It had been held up for several hours while passengers were obliged to lob their passports into an official rubbish-sack, wait for them to be checked and then catch them as they were hurled back one by one through the carriage windows. It sounded an exceptionally haphazard method of immigration control and yet, miraculously, every passport had been restored to its rightful holder.

The ferry dropped us at a fishing village on the European side where we had a couple of hours to spend before the 'express' boat back. We walked up narrow cobbled streets where children were playing and women were carrying pails of water from public taps, until the cobbles gave way to a dusty track which wound up the hillside between brightly painted houses and hedges strewn with drying laundry. Three small children shouted excitedly 'Photo, photo!' skipping out from sun-baked gardens where fig trees, beans and tomatoes struggled for survival. We obliged and then a smiling mother called in her brood for lunch. We refilled our water bottle, bought

Bosporus

some bread, goat's cheese and a cucumber, and sat on the sunny quay for our picnic. Wafting past our nostrils came the smells of fish from the grills of the local restaurant and from the tall, wooden drying racks on the quay where row upon row of kipper-like bodies lay stiffening in the heat. A man wheeled his trolley of wafers and bread rolls for sale and a cow wandered incongruously up and down, delving in waste-bins for discarded melon skins but fortunately expressing no interest in our cucumber. (Perhaps she was a reincarnated Io, of Greek mythology, whom Zeus transformed into a heifer and who swam across this strait on her wanderings towards Egypt, thus bequeathing the name of Bosporus or 'ox-ford'.)

The fish-markets of Istanbul were far less tranquil. Down by the Sea of Marmara on a Sunday afternoon, boisterous fishermen stood in a row of colourful little boats displaying bowls of radially arranged fish, gleaming with frequent sluicings of seawater. They shouted up to their 'sales agents' and their customers fifteen feet above them on the quay, bargaining loudly and tossing up bags

Frying fish, Galata Bridge - Istanbul

of their shining, fresh harvest whenever a deal was struck. Hundreds of opportunist seagulls circled noisily overhead while little boys, touting glasses of ice-cold water, competed with street-vendors offering sandwiches and sesame buns, shaped like ring-doughnuts, to Sunday strollers. We mingled with the crowd for some time, eager to forget the dead horse we had just passed on the way back from Yedikule, the city's Byzantine castle. Such were the varied delights of the city.

A visit to Istanbul is rather like a day at Disneyland: packed with fairy-tale sights (such as the magical Blue Mosque and the fist-sized emeralds of Topkapi) and with people trying to sell you things - every conceivable item from grapes to carpets but predominantly, for the tourists anyway, *carpets*. There is no need to look for them, nor to walk through the covered passages of the Grand Bazaar to be invited into one of the myriad of its carpet shops: every citizen of Istanbul either owns one or has a relation, friend or friend of a friend who does, and most will go out of their way to tell you about it.

'Where are you from?' Ashley was asked in typical

fashion, as we emerged from the Blue Mosque one afternoon.

'England.'

'What is your name, sir?'

'Popeye. What is yours?'

'Ah, here is my card. Look, you see my brother has this shop with beautiful carpets. He will give you very good price. Come, come and see, sir . . .'

'No, thank you. We have already bought carpets' - which in fact was true since Ashley had stuffed a couple of them into the back of the Range Rover on his way back from Oman. Now, short of carrying them demonstratively on our backs throughout our Istanbul wanderings, we saw no simple way of convincing these insistent salesmen that we were not interested and that even if we were, there was no available corner of a 2CV for souvenirs of such mammoth proportions.

When it came to something we earnestly did want to buy, of course we could find no one able to sell it to us. That something was methylated spirit for our cooking stove and we spent many an entertaining hour scouring the shops and souks for the merest whiff of the precious liquid. Ashley became quite adept at miming a cigarette-lighter action, at enunciating with dramatic emphasis key words such as *alkol* and *ispirito,* and at persuading various bewildered paintshop owners to let him sniff the contents of some of their more likely-looking bottles - but all to no avail. The only thing we seemed to be achieving was the instigation of a popular belief that I had an alcoholic husband.

Paint thinner might do,' suggested Ashley, his nose in another bottle. 'It would burn beautifully.'

'So would dynamite.' I was beginning to lose my trust in his sweeping assurance that meths was a universally available commodity. If we could not lay our hands on it in Istanbul what chance did we have, I wondered, of brewing a cup of coffee in the remoter reaches of the Anatolian Plateau?

Fortunately we had less difficulty in extending the car's insurance cover. After half an hour in a little office near Taksim Square the combined efforts of four employees of a small insurance company had produced a certificate of third party cover which cost us 180 lira (about 20 pence) and was probably worth still less. In any case, the general opinion was that we were being unnecessarily pessimistic in taking such precautions at all. We began to wonder whether additional medical insurance might have been more appropriate, after repeated wrestles with the hotel bathroom: it was a broom cupboard of a room where a basin, toilet and shower had been flung together with little regard to plumbing. In the floor was a drain which fancied itself as some sort of polluted spring, emitting dirty water and cockroaches with equal reliability, while the shower cascading from the toilet's cistern was more effective than the genuine apparatus which fell into the cracked lavatory bowl with monotonous regularity.

There were certain advantages in driving one's own travelling 'hotel', we had to admit, as we talked to a British couple from Milton Keynes whose VW campervan was parked in the shadow of Theodosius' granite obelisk in the Hippodrome, near the Blue Mosque. It was one of a number of similar touring vehicles staying overnight in the street.

'Don't the police object to your staying here?' we asked.

'Oh, no. Provided we cause no disturbance, they just leave us in peace. We get more pestering from the shoe-shine boys than the bobbies.'

It seemed remarkable. It was like setting up camp

outside Westminster Abbey or on Venice's Piazza San Marco and being told to make oneself at home. If only we had bought a campervan instead of a car, we thought momentarily, we could have been so much more independent; but we had been through such arguments many times before in our quest for the elusive, ideal vehicle - weighing up the relative advantages of sleeping accommodation, four-wheel drive, low fuel consumption, an air-cooled engine, a fridge, luggage space, economy, availability of spare parts, ease of maintenance and cost of shipping, and ending up with our little white compromise. After months of consideration, our mental scrap-heap was piled high not only with campervans but with Land-Rovers, Range Rovers, assorted Japanese jeeps and one or two of the older Saabs. It was too late to change our minds.

It wasn't until our last evening in Istanbul that a little puzzle of ours was solved. On our meths trail we had been intrigued by the windows of several children's clothes shops, cluttered with what looked like circus-wear or some form of popular fancy dress for boys. There were fur-trimmed cloaks, white satin shirts and trousers with braid stripes, red bow-ties and pill-box hats. Were Istanbul's young males being trained as lion tamers or was it fashionable to dress them up as drum majors? The answer was neither. At a rendezvous with some English friends, coincidentally on holiday in the city, they told us at dinner that they had been up to the Eyup Mosque that day and accidentally encountered a circumcision festival, where the young so-called *mashallah* boys were dressed in these extravagant costumes for the occasion. Such glorious attire is clearly reserved for the sons of wealthy families, rather than the average Turkish boy.

It felt strange to have slipped into another continent

without entering a new country, but that is precisely what happened when we drove across the Bosphorus road-bridge into Asia the following day. We contemplated unlikely parallels such as crossing the Mersey to find ourselves in Africa or taking a ferry from Mallaig and disembarking in Skye, USA. The ferry we actually took ran from Kartal to Yalova, on the southern side of the Sea of Marmara. It was a leisurely crossing of nearly two hours, during which we sat up on the foredeck's wooden benches drinking glasses of *çay* for twopence a go, while the sun and wind, in league with the tea-boy, endeavoured to ensure that our thirst was never quenched. Half the touts of Istanbul seemed to have come for the ride - we were successively entreated to buy cola, *ayran* (a delicious yoghurt drink), watches, sandwiches and toys or to have our flip-flops cleaned by enterprising shoe-shine boys! Everyone was cheerful, with the wind on their cheeks and the blue waves splashing and rolling around the old boat. Even the overweight lorry-driver who had climbed on top of his cab and lay snoring in the sun, his body bulging out of vest and trousers and his head shaded by an old towel, seemed to ooze contentment, like a well-fed cat.

From Yalova we wound our way up a dry hillside and then down through scattered olive trees towards a small lake, Iznikgölu, in a valley which was lush with maize, sunflowers, tomatoes and orchards. Skirting the centre of Bursa, we were soon out in the open again and our mouths were watering at the sight of roadside stalls heaped with peaches and melons. Now we beetled westwards over flattish country of vast, brown fields - acres of drooping sunflower heads begging to be harvested. Then there were onion fields where earth-brown women squatted, collecting the dry, crackly-coated vegetables into piles before loading them into sacks and carts. Mound after mound of giant melons lined the roadside until we could resist the yellow footballs no longer and stopped to buy one for 50 lire (six pence!). Later a red carpet, like autumn leaves, had been rolled out along the old road which ran parallel to ours. We were puzzled: it may have been the beginning of autumn but there was not a tree in sight, let alone one with scarlet foliage. What was this bright layer stretching away into the distance? We stopped to look: it was a covering of large, red chilli peppers, drying in the sun - mile upon mile of them gradually cracking and disintegrating to form a river of hot, rusty-coloured powder. This was what we had been sprinkling on our meatballs in Istanbul.

Some of it had also made its way into the spicy meat topping on the *pide* (pizza) which we devoured hungrily and washed down with pints of *ayran* that evening, working on the principle that when in Susurluk's transport café, do as the Turkish lorry drivers. Susurluk is a small town on a busy route which connects Istanbul to Izmir, on the Aegean coast, and we had stopped simply because it was getting dark and we had seen a hotel sign. £2.50 a night may not have bought hot water or breakfast but it was ridiculously good value after Istanbul's room rates.

We breakfasted like kings, gorging ourselves on half our melon each and following it by a few rounds of bread and cheese. Then, after a thorough search of Susurluk's shops and having unintentionally enlisted the help of most of its school-age inhabitants, we miraculously discovered a supply of meths. It was hidden at the back of a grocery store behind a healthy assortment of sacks and boxes from which we also bought a kilo of olives. Everyone seemed equally overjoyed that our fuel-hunt was over and a chorus of *'Ispirito! Ispirito!'* rang through the shop, confirming once and for all the vital word. Outside, as if in celebration, a local band began to play disharmoniously in the square and a small troop of soldiers, lamentably out of step, marched along the street; but our attempts to find the real cause of the local festivities were as unsuccessful as our Turkish was limited.

The road to Balikesir was good and we sped across the dry hills where sunflowers alone had survived the ravages of the summer drought. Horse-drawn carts provided us with the rare experience of superior speed and a wealth of exciting overtaking opportunities, unparalleled in the history of our 602cc engine. All advantage was promptly dissipated in the town centre however, where most of the local vehicles of a genuine one-CV nature had contrived to arrive before us and were causing severe congestion. When Balikesir's grip finally released us the wind came roaring in from the sea, causing the soft roof to billow alarmingly and forcing already-disfigured olive trees to lean still further in submission. Just to the north of our route lay Edremit, not surprisingly one of Turkey's most renowned olive-oil centres, for the countryside was a mass of olive groves. Only on the coastal plain was the agricultural monopoly broken by crops of cotton and tobacco and fields of stubble.

Two German 2CVs rattled by with much waving, tooting and flashing of lights and were swiftly succeeded by the hurricane of a passing lorry which deftly ripped a vital piece of metal from our car. Although it was not beyond the bounds of possibility to imagine one of the bolt-on components such as a wing or bumper hurtling off in the wake of a speedy juggernaut, this time it was nothing as large as that which parted company - in fact it took us a few minutes to find the little wind-tossed victim which had come to rest in the middle of the road. There it lay, a scrap of bent metal to the uninitiated but a specially fashioned piece of coathanger to drivers of 2CVs - a do-it-yourself answer to the problem of how to hold the windows ajar rather than bow to the basic options provided by the manufacturer, namely *ouverte ou fermée.* Meanwhile, two camels tethered to a nearby tree regarded us disdainfully and three women dressed in bright *salvar* (baggy trousers) and blouses pulled their white shawls further over their heads and hurried away down the road to their white-washed dwellings.

What little we saw of modern Bergama was bustling with tourists and touts and well stocked with carpets, tomatoes, postcards and kebabs. We skirted the town centre and climbed up to the Acropolis to have a picnic on the windswept summit. There was dust everywhere: it blew into our hair and our eyes, grains stuck to the cheese and the cucumber, embedded themselves in the bread and clung obstinately to our hard-boiled eggs. For a moment we even considered joining the coach parties for a grit-free lunch at the local *lokanta,* but then we should not have enjoyed the same view down there. From the dry hilltop we could look down on what was, over two thousand years ago, the ancient kingdom of Pergamon which stretched away across the plains as far as the Aegean Sea to the west and to Tuz Gölü, near Ankara, to the east. From this strategic site the Attalid dynasty held power and influence during the third and second centuries BC until King Attalus III died in 133 BC and, much to everyone's surprise, bequeathed his state to Rome.

The dynasty was founded by a Greek called Philetaeus, who was succeeded by an alternating series of Eumenes and Attalus. In the words of our tourist guide-book,

'The founder of the nation is the grandson of a greek who is called Evmenes Attalos the first. When he died,

Attalos the first succeeded him, who was the grandson of his uncle. And then the members of this kingdom spread from this family tree'

- which only leaves me to conclude that, amid such relative confusion, Attalos seems aptly named.

Excavation of the site began over a century ago after the accidental discovery... but the guide-book's version is far more interesting:

'The giggins in Akropolis happened to be. Engineer Hunan who was constructing a road in the vicinity of Bergamon in 1878 saw a relief of marble in the cart of a farmer, and bought it at one, and sent it to library. Upon this Berlin Museums sent the necessary instruments and devices in order to make digging on the top of Pergamon castle.'

A century later German archaeologists were still 'making digging', although the giant crane with which they were heaving great blocks of stone across the Temple of Trajan and the loud drill employed to gouge holes down the centre of columns prior to their re-erection, were certainly not the 'instruments and devices' of Hunan's day.

From the arsenal, originally a wooden building now reduced to an outline of overgrown foundations, is a spectacular view to the north-west over Pergamon's solution to its water supply problem. Parts of an old aqueduct are visible and the route of the original lead pipeline is marked by a ditch striking across a series of low hills like Offa's Dike. It leads from the source a few miles away, on a hilltop only marginally higher than the Acropolis. It is difficult to imagine a more staggering sight, however, than that which confronted us as we arrived at the top of the Great Theatre. We had just emerged from a covered passage which leads from the famous library, built by Eumenes II and said to have consisted of 200,000 books - that is, before Mark Antony made off with a large number of them to restore Cleopatra's collection which had been lost in the Alexandria library fire. We found ourselves on the brink of a slope so steep that from the top it felt like a precipice. No doubt it is a good deal less than 45 degrees, but such rigid facts cannot convey the feeling of dizziness which overcame me, standing on the back row of eighty tiers of seats which appeared to fall away vertically several hundred feet to the stage below. Not only is the theatre's natural structure dramatic but also the view beyond it, as the hillside drops still further to the plains, provides an incomparable backcloth to the stage.

The Great Theatre at Ephesus which we visited the following day was no less impressive. What it lacked in comparative steepness it made up for in sheer size, seating 24,000, almost twice as many as Pergamon's theatre. As our guide-book explained:

'The outlook of that marble building, with seats for audiences of 145 m in width and 30 m in height, should be very magnificient and impressious in Roman Age.'

These dazzling adjectives refer to the view along the Arcadian Way, a broad colonnade leading westwards from the theatre to what was the city's harbour but is now a patch of fertile land about three miles from the Aegean Sea. The sediment of the Cayster River, whose valley provided Ephesus with an important trade route into Asia, was responsible for the harbour's demise. The Romans struggled to maintain a sea channel to their harbour, well to the west of the Greek one, but in Byzantine times even the Roman harbour became too silted for use. The great port soon declined to a small marshland town and its population diminished as fast as the malarial mosquitoes multiplied.

'It's still a bit marshy for my liking,' said Ashley, as

we scrambled through a dense undergrowth of reeds and bulrushes on our way to the old baths and gymnasia. To the north of the Arcadian Way they cover a vast area, largely unexcavated, although we did stumble across a stray Austrian archaeologist examining some bovine carvings on what looked like a large stone bath. The rest of his team were up at the *agora* (market-place), engaged in some rather more conspicuous restoration work not far from the popular ruins of the ancient brothel. Down by the harbour we were beyond the penetration zone of the guided tours. Monolithic remnants of gymnasium walls towered above the fig trees; lizards slithered over the hot brickwork and swallowtails danced amongst a profusion of brambles and wild vines. We tried a few of their grapes but each was small and disappointing - sour skin enveloping a couple of enormous pips, which left little space for anything edible.

Ephesus is not far down the coast from Pergamon. Izmir, Turkey's third city and a major port, happens to lie between the two but we hadn't let that hinder us. We had camped not far from Pergamon, in the company of a Turkish family and about two dozen playful kittens, on an otherwise deserted site by the sea and driven to Ephesus the next morning. Crossing the flat, fertile valleys we saw expansive cotton fields, colourful with women picking bolls into large sacks. Bright, painted open lorries with precarious loads rattled past us at high speeds and one lay crumpled in the ditch, its crates of grapes crushed and splattered around the wreck, its fate bemoaned but not improved by hordes of policemen and armies of bewildered onlookers. Like many of the Turkish main roads, this stretch was built on an embankment with a narrow strip of rubbly hard shoulder sloping steeply away on each side. Lorries were in constant danger of catching a wheel or two on these slopes and toppling off the road.

Having 'done' two ruined cities in as many days, we recuperated for a third on the sandy beach of a 'Mocamp' near Kusadasi, the busy seaside resort a few miles south of Ephesus. We felt like old hands at the sunbathing game by now, watching with pity a Scottish couple who spread their lilywhite bodies like fresh linen across the sand that morning and slunk away at four o'clock, like a pair of sorely embarrassed lobsters, their beach bag cluttered with empty bottles of sun-tan lotion.

The River Meander, whose broad, flat valley we were crossing all the way from Söke (south-east of Kusadasi) to the lake called Bafa Gölü - a distance of nearly twenty miles - does not owe its name to its wandering habit. On the contrary, it is the river which gave its name to describe the characteristic feature of 'meandering' waterways. True to form, the Meander itself has switched courses many times, leaving little signatures of oxbow lakes and stranding former population centres, such as the ancient city of Priene, once a port, now eight miles from the river. Sunflowers, cotton, corn and beautiful soft-eyed cattle, like dark Jerseys, thrived on the rich soil of the valley but as we wound our way up into the dry hills to the south only olive trees and herds of black goats clung to the rocky slopes and, higher still, forests had been ravaged by recent fires. Some soldiers, we heard on the radio, had lost their lives trying to fight the flames of other forest fires in western Turkey - it was the cost of an exceptionally dry summer.

There was a medieval air about Milas, a pretty little town of timber-framed, jettied houses and famous for its carpets, which are characteristically patterned in mellow shades of brown. It was a Sunday, however, and the looms were laid to rest, the shops had disappeared behind closed shutters and not a rug could be seen.

Nearby, the village of Koru was just as sleepy. Groups of men sat in the shade of fruit trees playing cards or *tavla* (backgammon), while small children were washed in the yards of tiny, one-roomed houses. Between villages, igloo-like stone shelters with doorways but no windows stood at intervals along the roadside, while in the fields three-sided, oblong huts of wood and rush-matting provided midday shelter for farmers.

The road which zigzagged along to Bodrum could have been in Yugoslavia: the rocks dived into the sea on our right and pine-clad hills soared on our left. Bodrum however had a quite individual character - a blend of Greek and Turkish - and a holiday atmosphere without the overriding commercialism of Kusadasi. White-washed houses clustered behind the busy harbour and the sea glistened around the promontory, dominated by its Crusader castle. We found a pleasant little pension up a narrow side-street: in the garden, enormous geraniums cascaded from pots and trellis-work and hens wandered freely, pecking and clucking in the shade of lime trees. It was cool and clean and perfect for a siesta.

That evening we replaced a flip-flop casualty with a new pair of mule-like plastic sandals, moulded in Japan specifically, or so it seemed, to accommodate Ashley's feet and endearingly called 'Comforts'. It was in the shower however that their design faults were revealed: the perfectly foot-shaped, concave-upwards soles, like a couple of sinking boats were soon filled with water and the hollow treads on the underside acted as suction pads, further rooting the unhappy wearer to the shower-room floor.

'Not very good, *nein, scheisse'* Ashley said, mimicking the earlier, rather blunt reply of a grinning waiter to my compliment about the kebabs we had just eaten. Every waiter in western Turkey had to know a few words of

German, just to make himself understood during the seasonal foreign occupation, but this lad was simply showing off - I failed to see why otherwise, if I were to be abused at all, it could not be done in my language or his own, instead of that of some third party who just happened to outnumber us in the restaurant!

Of course, Bodrum is not only renowned for its Japanese sandals and its German visitors. It is also the site of the ancient city of Halicarnassus and of King Mausolus' gigantic tomb, from which the word mausoleum is derived. When it was built in 353 BC the Mausoleum, according to the elder Pliny, was 140 feet tall, 411 feet in circumference, incorporated 36 columns, was crowned by a sculpture of a chariot and four, and was reckoned as one of the seven wonders of the world. By the time we arrived in Bodrum there was only his word for it: any surviving sculptures and friezes had been whisked away in the mid-nineteenth century to the British Museum, leaving nothing at the site above ground level. The revelation of such information did tend to reduce our disappointment at finding the place closed on Mondays.

We had more luck with the ancient theatre, which is open to all and sundry, including goats, and sits neglectedly halfway up the hillside above the town, luring intrepid fools to brave the battle zone of marauding children and their war-cry, 'Photo! Photo!' and to struggle with inadequate water supplies up the burning slope, amongst hot outcrops of volcanic rock. To enjoy the panorama from the theatre's upper seats alone was justification of our madness but from the caves on the hilltop we gasped again (for more than one reason) at the aerial quality of the view: Bodrum shimmered in the midday heat around its sparkling bay and romantic castle. No wonder the old theatre felt so dejected looking down at that young upstart of a fort, a mere 583 years old, hogging the limelight, after the theatre had watched its old contemporary, the Mausoleum, gradually being destroyed and while the only other survivors of Halicarnassus' subjection to invasions, sackings and natural decay were a few pieces of wall and the odd burial chamber.

Not everything in the castle was post-1402, however. Piled in the courtyards, amongst the cacti and the flowering shrubs, were scores of amphorae and other clay storage jars recovered from the seabed where they had been lying for three thousand years or more. These and a hoard of Bronze Age tools, coins and enormous copper ingots (eighteen inches long) rescued during the last fifteen years, were probably used for trade with the seafaring Phoenicians as far back as the second and third millennia BC. In those days the Phoenicians were already organising much of the commerce in and around the Mediterranean, using their 'round ships' (glorified rowing boats known in Egypt as the 'Byblos ships') to transport an ever-increasing range of goods, including their famous Tyrian purple cloth (whose dye came from the snail, *Murex)* and cedar wood from Lebanon.

In the shadow of one of the castle's round towers an archaeologist was leaning over a tank of seawater with his tape measure, studying and recording details of the sections of wood recently recovered from an 800-year-old shipwreck just offshore from Marmaris. This one had produced a myriad objects of coloured Islamic glass, now also displayed in the castle's museum. How much more sunken treasure lay awaiting discovery below those well-plied waters?

Bodrum was a dead end as far as our route was concerned - a fact which probably contributed significantly to the town's tranquillity. Certainly it attracted day-trippers from Kusadasi, provided a pleasant port of call for holiday flotillas, and was a good point from which to hop over to the Greek islands of Kos or even Rhodes; but if we aimed to continue touring Turkey by road, there was no alternative but to get back in the car and retrace our steps to Milas - which is exactly what we did.

CHAPTER 3

The people who live in the pine-forested hills between Milas and Yatagan must have found a method of breeding beehives, never mind bees. The little, painted wooden honey-factories are everywhere: there are flocks of them in the sunny fields, clusters in the shadowy clearings of the woods, stray couples nestling between the pine trees, and little families of blue and white ones hiding behind houses. It must be a navigational nightmare for the bees; and what do the locals do with all that honey? They must live on nothing else, we thought, driving through an avenue of competing roadside honey-stalls where large pots were ranged temptingly.

'I can think of worse diets,' said Ashley-the-Pooh later, spooning liberal quantities of the dark, aromatic liquid over a piece of bread. 'Wonderful stuff. Flows like engine oil.'

Before we reached Yatagan a couple of camels strolled haughtily by. Our second surprise was a vast hole in the ground, half a mile across, a deep dust bowl crawling with giant earth-moving vehicles, like a great pit for revitalised dinosaurs. We stopped to gape through the dust clouds at this massive excavation - an open-cast coal mine boasting 106 million tons of reserves (largely lignite) which, to judge by the scale and fury of the operation, were needed by the end of the week. They would be required soon if the country's ten thermal electric plants, then under construction, were to come into operation in order to help to cut Turkey's awesome energy imports - then about 70 per cent of the total national consumption. The government was intending at least to double the lignite-generated power within its five-year development plan. By 1990 lignite-fired power stations should have overtaken hydroelectric plants in total output, according to the plan - and that was not hard to believe, if the frenzied activity near Yatagan was anything to go by. Fifty feet or more of soft deposits lay between the surface and the seams to be exploited and it was the removal of this rock, and its inevitable pulverisation, which were creating the fine sandstorm. It was as though the diggers were racing against time to recover the precious fuel before the dust could settle and rebury it.

To the north the Gökbel Hills were made of sterner stuff - massive granitic gneiss eroded into strange shapes like the tors of Dartmoor. The road followed the gorge of the Cine River through this rocky wilderness until we reached the little town of Eskiçine, where the landscape became flat and calm again and so dry that crops grew only by virtue of a system of concrete irrigation channels. There were donkeys wherever we looked - pulling carts along the road, carrying packs or people through the olive groves, or simply grazing in the orchards.

From Aydin eastwards we were following the Meander River once more and the valley burgeoned with cotton, figs, pomegranates, peaches and olives. It was riddled with young highwaymen too: they squatted at the roadside with their little brothers and sisters, hiding behind large baskets of fresh figs and, at the sight of an approaching car, jumped up to stand poised with arms outstretched across the road, juicy samples dangling enticingly from their fingertips. It was a cunning ambush, confronting the motorist with an urgent choice: to plough on regardless, with a high risk of running down an 'innocent' little boy and receiving a faceful of figs through the windscreen, or to slam on the brakes and succumb to his deliciously tempting offer. Despite preferring the former option, we succeeded in arriving in Pamukkale without casualty.

It was a steep climb for the last few miles up to 1,200 feet, where the ancient ruins of Hierapolis and the present-day town of Pamukkale are found, high above Denizli on the Coruh Su (a tributary of the Meander), where hot water springs from the hillside and is directed swiftly into hotel swimming-pools. Hierapolis was founded on a religious establishment *(hieron)* which laid particular emphasis on the worship of the goddess Leto, the local Great Mother of the Gods. Pamukkale, which means Cotton Fortress, is named after the magnificent white travertine terraces which drape the hillside in tiers of curtain-like folds - the limestone deposits of the mineral-rich waters.

By six o'clock we were bathing in the warm water, reluctant to emerge into the cool evening air. We were camping amongst a collection of German and Austrian campervans at a small site attached to a motel. Suitably refreshed by our dip, we began to explore the hillside in the fading, golden light. We reached a village where two boiling-hot, iron-rich springs bubbled up and poured themselves down the rocky slope, leaving striking patterns of brown, red and green streaks, like painted waterfalls. Visiting Turks gathered round the tiny, hot puddles: plump women in long, full, floral skirts and white head-shawls plunged their chubby toes into the healing water or stooped to drink or wash their faces, and their moustachioed husbands, in sombre suit-jackets, paddled, drank or washed their socks. It was all very therapeutic. One old man, who told us that he had worked in Stuttgart for several years (Germany attracts thousands of Turkish workers), tried unsuccessfully to make us sample the reputedly healthy liquid and another, a customs officer from Istanbul, informed us in terrible English, rather unconvincingly, that he had recently spent a year in Dover.

As we watched the sun set that evening we were standing on the walls of the Cotton Fortress itself. Slippery as ice the terraces looked, but when we paddled barefoot in the warm spring-water our toes touched silk-soft, chalky white mud resting on hard limestone. We looked out, spellbound, over the magical natural staircase, its great steps hanging with icicle-like formations and descending steeply for hundreds of feet below us towards the distant valley. Against a sky of gently deepening pink, the cascades of rock gleamed pure white amongst the pools of milky blue. It was the scenery of dreams, where reality and fantasy mingle inextricably and the goals of travellers momentarily evaporate in the warmth of incidental experiences on the journey itself. One spontaneous and unexpected revelation of beauty *en route* seemed worth a dozen destinations reached.

That night, however, was less than peaceful. Throngs of persistent kittens attacked our tent continually in the hope of catching insects which, attracted by the campsite's floodlights (bright enough to keep us awake without the help of the feline population), had plastered themselves all over our shelter. It was a relief to rise early the next morning to go swimming in the pool again.

After breakfast we felt compelled to judge for

ourselves the ruins of Hierapolis, heartlessly dismissed in so many guidebooks as barely worthy of attention in comparison to the splendours of Ephesus or Pergamon. We tramped across the hillside between the topsy-turvy remains, which earthquakes set adrift centuries ago. Temple walls leaned at precarious angles, huge building blocks were perched on the brink of others, ready to topple, and winding open channels, once hot water ducts, meandered with altered gradients between crumbling foundations. We had to admit that the city lacked Ephesus' degree of preservation; but then Hierapolis, even before the earthquakes, had always been at a disadvantage - its porous, yellow-brown limestone was not as durable as much of the western city's hard, white marble, and the sheer scale of Hierapolis' buildings had never been as great as Ephesus' monuments.

On the other hand, these upland ruins had a delightful character of their own which fascinated us, despite, or perhaps because of, their dilapidation. Most intriguing of all were the outskirts of the ancient town: acres of hillside were simply littered with enormous stone tombs and sarcophagi, ransacked long ago and now lying crookedly, half-buried amongst the dry grass. Each sarcophagus was carved from a single block of stone with Greek inscriptions on the side and massive lids like solid, sloping roofs, tilted and ajar, or, having fallen, lying on the ground between the oleander bushes. This was the heart of Hierapolis for us: a jumbled graveyard of forgotten tombs, unrestored, undisturbed for years, and blending with the hillside habitat as naturally as the plants and rocks themselves.

Harmony with nature, we discovered later that morning, was something which Acigöl (the Acid Lake) distinctly lacked, as we almost passed out amidst its overwhelming stench of bad eggs, which the south-easterly wind was inconsiderately hurling across the waters in our direction. Ten miles long and four miles wide, a white salt-pan of a lake, it looked as pure and innocent as the driven snow - until the gaseous assault occurred. It seemed incredible that anyone could possibly survive working in the sodium sulphate plant on the northern shore - indeed how much of the hydrogen sulphide was a processing by-product rather than a natural (if such a revolting gas deserves the description) emanation was open to question. We certainly had no intention of hanging around to find out. Instead we fled to the purer atmosphere of a nearby village to buy some food for lunch. There, sunflowers lay drying on the flat roofs, strings of red peppers hung from walls and outside the tiny restaurant stood a cupboard full of bread for sale - but there was no obvious sign of a cheese-merchant.

'Peynir?' I questioned the bread-man, sending him diving back through the dark room, which was packed with ravenous men, devouring with wolf-like vigour great bowls of spicy soup and hunks of bread. I smiled and nodded alternately at an old man outside who, despite my understanding not a word he said, continued to chat away quite happily to me in Turkish, until his friend re-emerged with a deformed lump of goats' cheese resembling metamorphic rock, which, in the absence of either good sense or edible alternatives, I bought.

'Turks,' Ashley commented, above a chorus of parting 'hellos' from multitudes of waving boys, 'will sell you anything.'

The land was as dry as the old cheese. The wheat had been harvested and dust devils, like mini-tornadoes, whirled up into the sky from the bare, yellow fields. South of Dinar the barren scene was interrupted by a shady avenue of willows and poplars where we stopped for lunch by a convenient water-tap. No sooner had we put chisel to cheese than two painted horse-drawn carts drew up next to us and fifteen people, two hens and a large Alsatian dog climbed, flapped and bounded down. A cacophony of shouts and squawks then accompanied a frenzy of activity around us, as clothes were washed, water-bottles filled, squealing children scrubbed and the two horses fed and watered. Finally two young lads, deciding that the dog deserved a bath, pushed him onto his back, grabbed a couple of legs each and dunked him swiftly in the nearest irrigation channel before he struggled free and yelped to safety. Then, in no time at all, the entire band had remounted and the caravan was on its way again, leaving the oasis free for the next passers-by - an old couple with a donkey, followed by two men on a tractor and a couple of lads with baskets of unripe peaches which they washed and offered to share with us.

To the south, the shores of blue Lake Burdur, in contrast to Acigöl's, were green, fertile and abounding in lush vineyards and orchards. We bought another juicy, giant melon for next to nothing from a woman sitting beside a mound of them at the roadside. She lifted up her long, voluminous skirts to look down her bright socks, which were stuffed with bank notes (coins being uncommon since ten lira notes, worth a little over a penny, were in circulation), but she eventually found the correct change in her apron pocket.

Ahead, between Burdur and the Mediterranean, lay an upland belt, the western end of the Taurus mountains, and we were soon climbing from the lake amongst soft, white, salty slopes, newly planted with terraces of pines, and into limestone hills where multitudes of black goats grazed on dry grass. At 4,018 feet we reached an unpronounceable pass, the Çeltikçi Geçidi, and entered a beautiful region of rich farmland. Apples, melons, maize and tobacco, far lusher than any crop we had seen elsewhere in Turkey, grew in the kind of profusion generally reserved for weeds. Mountains of harvested melons greeted us in every village and trundled by on carts loaded so high that green avalanches seemed imminent.

Soon we were coasting down to Antalya.

It was good to be by the sea again, we agreed, from our balcony's Formica-topped breakfast table, looking out at the hazy blueness beyond the ruins of ancient Side. Everything looked so much rosier in the morning.

'Let's stay here for a couple of nights. Yesterday's journey from Pamukkale was a killer and we could do with a rest.'

The previous day had certainly been a long one. It was eight o'clock when we finally reached Side (little more than a village), where luminous forests of 'Pansiyon' and 'Otel' signs loomed out of the darkness in wild, misleading welcome. It took us some time to discover that a 'No vacancy' sign had yet to be introduced to Side. The pension room, which we took by default, was home to myriads of emphatically nocturnal mice and mosquitoes, which, after several hours of scampering and buzzing respectively, considerately went to sleep at dawn, allowing us full appreciation of the muezzin's call to prayer and of the chorus of local cockerels. Under the circumstances, any breakfast would have been a delightful relief, even without fresh melon and a private balcony facing the sea.

Like most of the ancient cities in western and southern Turkey, Side was founded by Greeks, taken over by Romans, then Byzantines, and has the remains of a splendid theatre. Side's is unusual, in that its colossal structure is free-standing, built on huge arches instead of relying on a hillside for support. Beside it, the remainder

of the ruined city, once the most important in Pamphylia
and, for a time, renowned as the chief slave market of the
Cilician pirates, pales into significance. On the pebbly
beach by the harbour fragments of limestone pillars,
broken arches and pieces of pottery, ground together and
worn smooth by centuries of waves, prepare to be
incorporated, like fossils, in a new generation of
sedimentary rocks.

We followed the example of the majority of Side's
visitors - gave the museum a quick once-over, headed for
one of the beautiful, sandy beaches and collapsed. We
joined the ranks of people who, tormented nightly by
mosquitoes and mice, lay snoring in the warm sun.

Turkey has adopted the thoughtful practice of adding
population statistics (and sometimes altitude too) to
road-signs announcing towns, presumably in order to
allow those tourists who tremble at the very thought if
being outnumbered by more than, say, 25,000 to one by
Turks to turn back before entering the larger towns.
Alanya, for example, at whatever date the notice was
erected, had a population of 22,200 - well within our
limits of acceptability - and so we ventured in the
following day. Leaving the car by the harbour in the
congenial company of an ancient, green 2CV whose
speedometer scale reached an outrageously optimistic
maximum of 200 kph, we set off up the hill which rises
steeply on a rocky promontory above the town. The
hillsides were cocooned in walls constructed by the
Seljuks in the thirteenth century to defend the fortress
rock and said to be a total of eight miles long. We passed
the great octagonal red tower, Kizil Kule, built to guard
the harbour and the Seljuk shipyards, and scrambled up a
maze of little rocky paths and alleys between tumble-
down houses where vagrant hens strutted under
precarious-looking wooden balconies. Flagging from the

heat, we finally met the real path, halfway up, and panted to the summit at nearly eight hundred feet above the sea.

The view from the Seljuk fortress was rewardingly magnificent: a panorama of mountains, beaches and deep blue sea, a blend so beautiful that to mention its constituents can only hint at the power and inspiration of the whole. It made me want to sing. Only the prospect of thirty German tourists suing me for damages to their eardrums deterred me.

A notice at the fortress informed us that Alanya was inhabited as early as 1820 BC, 'kept changing hands and has lived the ages of Isaurans, Lydians, Persions, Macedonians, Hellenistic, Roman, Byzantine, Seljukian and Ottomans,' adding, on a reassuringly patriotic note, that 'the uppeared monumenst are copletely Turkish except for two churches.'

Apparently, 'Turk captured Alanya in 1220-21 by Seljuk Sultan Alaaddin Keykubat I and Ottomans ruled 1472 till republic. Alanya had form different names during the ages. Roman time, Korekesyon (jackdaw), this bird still lives in Alanya. Byzantine time, Kalanoros (the nice mountain). Seljuk time, Alaiye. Republic time, Alanya (by the order of Atatürk).'

Now it had expanded well beyond the fortified promontory; hotels, each allocated a private strip of sandy beach, sprawled along the coast for miles. Understandably, it was a popular holiday destination.

On our way down the hill a Turkish family, whose younger members were halfway up an acacia-like tree, called us over to join them, offering us handfuls of the dry, dark brown pods which they had gathered and were now gnawing avidly. Hard and unappetising though the wild snack looked, we smiled, followed their example gratefully and found, to our surprise, that there were

House in Alanya

certain chewy portions of the pods which tasted sweet and rather like tough dates. It was only later that we learned that we had been eating the fruits of the locust or carob tree. At a little tea-shop further down we stopped for a few glasses of sweet, black tea, sitting outside at a shady terrace table beneath a canopy of gourds, while the old lady showed us her hand-woven silk scarves, and demonstrated the drawing and twisting of the fine thread from silkworm cocoons. (Silk weaving was a thriving cottage industry in Alanya - we only had to look through an open window to see women of all ages busy at their little looms.) Her ageing husband, who arrived in a state of near exhaustion having climbed halfway up the hill with what looked like a month's supply of shopping, sat down to regain his breath and then proudly showed us his cacti, which he had bought while working in Germany and which grew in a motley collection of old cans and tubs along his wall.

Just a few miles to the south-east of Alanya the beach where we stopped to bathe was well clear of the hotel zone and almost deserted. Some local boys were kicking a football about a hundred yards away and a lorry drove onto the beach, was filled with sand by three men in baggy, black trousers and bobble hats and then refused, predictably, to budge. Otherwise, we had the place to ourselves.

Unexpectedly, it was bananas which dominated our lives for the next day and a half. I had not imagined that they would thrive on these Turkish shores, as far from the Equator as Gibraltar or Tokyo, but, as we followed the coast road to Anamur, twisting and plunging on the brink of the Taurus mountains, there were palms at every turn. Vivid green terraces striped the steep slopes; triangular plains at river mouths were lush with the tropical plantations; boys hurled themselves in front of the car, wielding large, unripe hands of the fruit; flat rooftops were shaded with canopies of dried banana leaves; and we even dreamed of the things at night. Unlike the Turks, however, we did not sleep on flat roofs, day or night, to keep cool. Theirs was a habit of disastrous consequences, according to an Istanbul newspaper, which reported that the country's hospitals were seriously overcrowded in summer with injured people whose bodies, now jointed in unnecessary places, had been gathered from the ground in varying degrees of consciousness after simply rolling out of bed.

Dicing with death seemed to be a popular sport in this banana-prone region - and one not restricted to the human species. We had just stopped to lift a suicidal tortoise from the middle of the road into the safety of a plantation, when a motor-bike with no less than four men on board roared past, lurched round the bend and was followed by a second, bearing two men and a moped, strapped across the back. Children, with no concept of the dangers of a main road, would wave to us quite happily from the middle of it as we swerved to avoid their straying protegés - kids and calves with still less sense. Fear appeared to be an undeveloped emotion amongst these cheerful souls.

We had been warned at Gazipasa, by a German bus-passenger who had taken seven hours to travel the 140 miles from Silifke and who was wondering if he would reach Side before Christmas, of the road conditions on this coastal route. Even so, it exceeded expectations - designed primarily as a series of helter-skelters, the road appeared to have been compressed into a concertina of tight folds so that, on the map, it looked like a long, wiggly extrusion of red toothpaste, and in three-dimensional reality was infinitely worse. Some way from Gazipasa the asphalt gave up completely and the car virtually disintegrated amidst boulder-induced rattles and tremors which, on the Richter scale, would have registered somewhere between eight (the category including 'Steering of motor-cars affected') and nine ('General panic. Weak masonry destroyed'). By the time we reached Anamur I was feeling decidedly peculiar. We stopped for a recuperative visit to the splendid thirteenth-century castle and, just as my body was beginning to feel all the more composed for a glass of tea with the caretaker and a short stroll, I almost toppled into the sea down a deep, unguarded shaft which had once served as a waste disposal unit for unwanted prisoners.

After that things could only look up. The road improved, bananas gave way to small fields ploughed by men and boys with donkeys, colourful circles of women sat at wooden looms in the open air, weaving rugs in bright wool, and we found a beautiful sandy bay half a mile long where we bathed in the wind-tossed sea, doubling the number of visitors.

We took our last dips in the Mediterranean at Kizkalesi, where the sand sloped gently into the sea, making the miniature tide just noticeable and the shallow water beautifully warm. Unlike the 'package' resorts of the Aegean coast, this little town was most popular with the Turks themselves. Some were camping on the beach with their enormous, thick canvas tents, their tables and chairs and such a quantity of pots and pans that we imagined they intended to survive a week without recourse to washing-up. Others could be found lying face downward in the sand, using their arms to bury themselves, like giant turtles scooping out holes with their paddle-shaped limbs prior to egg-laying. In the evenings families roamed about the town, nibbling freshly roasted nuts and barbecued maize, or drank *çay* in open-air cafes while transfixed by noisy American films on distant televisions. It was a small, friendly place where the sand and the visitors drifted up between the souvenir shops on narrow streets which ran down from the main road and ended on the beach.

A few hundred yards offshore, on a tiny island, lay one of the two Rubenid castles - dating from the twelfth century and rebuilt by the Turks in the fifteenth - after which the town is named. Now visited by rowing-boats and energetic swimmers, it was once connected by a causeway to the second castle, on the rocky shore to the north of the present town. There we scrambled amongst thistles, thorny bushes and bay trees to see the old fortress walls - patchworks of second-hand, rectangular and circular-sectioned blocks which were slices of columns from even older ruins of the Greek city, Corycos. Clambering inland over the rocky terrain, towards the remains of an ancient temple, we became entangled in a grove of hostile lemon trees which attacked us mercilessly with sharp thorns. The temple looked as though the Christians had made a few changes before the Turks started dismantling it. Rectangular windows had been infilled with decorated arches, domes added and crosses carved into the walls, which were now the playgrounds of darting lizards. Rock tombs and weathered sarcophagi, reminiscent of Hierapolis, were fashioned from the solid rock with only their lids above the ground, their grey, forgotten limestone engraved with Christian crosses.

From Kizkalesi to Mersin, a port on the western edge of the Cilician Plain, citrus groves lined the coastal road, giving way only to patches of commercial greenhouses whose wooden frames were glassless but hung with fluttering shreds of dusty polythene. New or incomplete apartment blocks and holiday hotels straggled along Mersin's south-western fringe; to the north-east, heavy industry had consolidated the dockland area; and, in the middle, nearly a quarter of a million people were dashing about their daily business in a city seething with cars, buses, horses and carts. We halted at some traffic lights and a boy, deftly balancing a tray full of tea-glasses on one hand, darted across the road, weaving between the lines of traffic. Men carrying trays of sesame buns on their heads or pushing pram-wheel trolleys of fruit and vegetables patrolled the busy pavements.

Beyond the docks, where the fertile plain began to open out, great armies of people moved across the fields harvesting acres of ripe cotton; but at Tarsus, the birthplace of Saint Paul, we turned northwards, leaving the Mediterranean to climb up into the Taurus mountains. At the roadside baskets of grapes, fresh from little vineyards which nestled amongst the rocks, were offered to motorists; and in the distance, glossy black goats dotted the hillside like a plateful of shiny olives. Just below the mountain pass known as the Cilician Gates, or Gülek Bogazi, through which Alexander the Great marched unopposed in 333 BC, a donkey foal lay obstinately on the steep road, ignored by its relatives on the verge, forcing convoys of fuel-tankers to swerve dangerously. Up here the houses had sloping roofs of corrugated iron and it was pleasantly cool amongst the pine forests at three thousand feet, with mountains of two or three times that height to east and west. The pass of the Cilician Gates, however, was not the highest point we reached. We crossed Caykavak Geçidi, another pass, at an altitude of 5,080 feet and then began our descent into southern Cappadocia, a bare and dusty tableland dotted with old volcanic craters; even its arable expanses, now harvested, had a barren appearance.

Soon we were stooping in a dark, narrow passage, seven storeys below ground, wondering, in our eagerness to resurface, where the lift was. Of course it was a vain hope - the only shafts in the vicinity were sunk thirteen hundred years ago for ventilation purposes or water (some of the wells being as much as 400 feet deep). We were in the underground city of Derinkuyu, groping our torch-lit way along the soft-rock tunnels, in and out of little chambers and up and down tiny stairways; exploring a strange world largely excavated in the seventh century by Byzantine Christians escaping from Moslem persecutors, although it is said that the Hittites were at work there long before. Underground passages connected Derinkuyu to another sunken city six miles away, Kaymakli, which was similar but currently had only three of its seven levels re-excavated for visitors.

The temperature dropped markedly as we descended - a significant advantage for the city-dwellers, who could store supplies of food for months on end. They even had a wine press in the form of a shallow pit which drained into a storage urn below and, after boiling some of the juice for syrup, they would ferment the rest - presumably in an effort to keep themselves warm. The heavy, six-foot wheel-doors, which they rolled across the entrances in times of trouble, now rested against the cave

Wheel-door, Derinkuyu

walls like disused millstones with holes where wooden handles once fitted. It was hard to believe, as we peeped into cubby-holes and groped from room to room via sandy passages, that we were in a city built for humans and not delving through the fairytale burrows of Bilbo Baggins and his friends.

It was even colder that night on the surface than it had felt fifty feet or so underground at Derinkuyu. We camped near Nevsehir, at a motel with a neglected swimming-pool and an out-of-season air, shivering in our sleeping bags on this Cappadocian plateau at a height which was, after all, something between the summits of Snowdon and Ben Nevis. We thawed under blissful hot showers, envying, for once, the party of German 'campers' with their two monstrous luxury coaches and trailers equipped with warm, blanketed bunks, hot kitchens and wardrobes of thick clothing.

We spent the next day visiting the rock churches and caves of the Göreme Valley, which is now an open-air museum, and the surrounding area. The scenery was some of the most spectacular we had seen in Turkey - a wide plateau of pale, volcanic rock displaying bands of different pastel shades, where valleys, slicing through the soft material, were peopled with tall rock pinnacles eroded into strange shapes. Some were giant toadstools with their caps of harder rock, others stalagmites, carved pillars of towering chimneys. The key to the region was the softness of the rock - horizontal layers of wind-blown, volcanic material ejected by what is now a 12,848 feet mountain crater, Erciyas Dagi, to the east. Ever since the Hittites discovered that the rock was easily worked people have continually been carving, excavating and tunnelling in these weird cones and steep valley walls. The landscape is riddled with pigeon-holes (apparently the first in the world), with caves, footholes, hollows and passages, like a vast timber store bedevilled with generations of woodworm. Naturally, the most concentrated area of beautiful caves and churches, the Göreme Valley, is also the most visited. Thousands of pairs of erosive feet and hands are constantly rubbing away at the friable rock, unintentionally accelerating the weathering processes of wind and rain and leading to the ultimate destruction of the fragile formations. The little cave-churches, with frescoes which were painted by Christians in simple ochre patterns as early as the seventh century and elaborated in the eleventh and twelfth centuries, have pretty names, such as the Slipper Church and the Apple Church - the latter so called because of its view of former orchards in the valley below. There are monasteries where refectory tables and benches were carved from the cave-floor and there are tombs, fonts, altars and passages. As at Derinkuyu and Kaymakli, communities of Christians hid in these valleys, fleeing from persecution.

Before long we also fled. There is a limit to the number of people who can crowd into a cave-church with the volume of a six-foot cube and yet come out alive, and, having been trapped inside a few of these hollows

Goreme rocks and cart

by the influx of several coach-loads of Austrians, Germans, Italians and Americans, we had come dangerously close to discovering what that figure is. It was far more peaceful as we drove northwards and stopped to walk up a hillside path, past a dusty vineyard where black raisin-destined grapes were spread between the rows and a tethered donkey nibbled at the yellow grass. Our feet sank into the soft dust of warm gullies; we climbed strangely-sculptured rock towers to discover beautiful panoramas of the plateau and banded, scarp-faced hills, like views from a crow's nest over sea and cliffs.

Avoiding the carpet and alabaster-ware gift shops which alternated along the main street in Avanos, we stopped long enough to pick up some food before escaping on the eastward trail to Sarihan, the ruin of a splendid caravanserai. It was built in 1249 by the Seljuk Turks as one of their many trade-route 'motels' for travellers and their caravans of camels and horses.

An old man in a flat cap with a bundle of tickets in his hand, and an attractive little dark-eyed girl with plaited hair (presumably his granddaughter) were sitting at the entrance, waiting for a visitor. Our arrival prompted an immediate tea-party and a stove was set up on the wall outside while we communicated with some difficulty with our baggy-trousered host. We admired his ancient, Russian-engined Turkish motorcycle and smiled at the silent little girl who sat coyly by the teapot in her voluminous floral trousers, brightening the wall like cascading rockery plants in bloom. Her grandfather threw a fistful of *çay* into the pot, added the boiling water and seasoned the brew with half a bagful of sugar. In the heat of the early afternoon the little glasses of strong, sweet liquid were remarkably refreshing.

When the party was over we thanked them profusely, bought two tickets and walked through the ornate entrance to find ourselves in a central court with large, cool rooms on all sides. Most of the walls, which were faced with tuff from Kayseri, were crumbling, but many of the decorated doorways and arches were still intact. In these, carved blocks of volcanic rock with intricate curves were keyed together, like pieces of a jigsaw in pink, yellow, cream and buff.

'Thousands? But... How much? How many lira you pay? Write it ... here,' passing a scrap of dirty paper across the table.

'Oh, about 6,000 TL,' we wrote, after a quick calculation.

'OK, I give you 3,000 lira,' the man replied without hesitation, clutching the torch possessively to his chest.

'No, no! It's not for sale! We need it ... badly!' It was not the sort of thing which we could expect to replace in eastern Turkey, where there were people who had yet to experience electricity, let alone fluorescent tubes, and where darkness was generally left to the wolves, jackals and ferocious, half-wild sheep-dogs with two-inch barbs protruding from their necks.

'4,000 lira,' came the next bid.

'NO! NO!' We shook our heads frantically and reached for our treasured possession. 'NOT FOR SALE!'

'5,000!'

'NO! Please give it back!' Ashley grabbed it forcefully. Finally accepting defeat, the two disgruntled men rose, grumbling and growling to one another, and moved out in disgust to some stools on the pavement from where they continued to mutter obscenities in our direction, much to the amusement of the three lads. We drank our tea, swore never to put the wretched torch on public display again, and went back to camp.

CHAPTER 4

Urgüp and the Göreme Valley lie within easy striking distance of the capital, Ankara, and are about as far from the Aegean coast as the majority of Turkey's visitors wish to venture. Yet beyond, to the east, lies the other half of the country, where the plateau becomes wilder and more rugged, relief maps turn to darker shades of brown, and an almost entirely mountainous and once volcanic region, eastern Anatolia, with an average elevation of 6,000 feet and peaks of over 11,000 feet, heralds the frontiers with Georgia, Armenia and Iran. It was for this higher, more remote area that we were now heading.

We paused briefly in Kayseri (Roman Caesarea), to see some of its wealth of Seljuk monuments and walk through the *bedesten* or covered bazaar, renowned, according to a university student who latched onto us in order to practise his English, for its dried meat and carpets. The bazaar lies in the old part of the city, mixed up with the mosques, *medreses,* tombs and the citadel, and encircled by the modern quarters of Kayseri where most of its 300,000 people live and go to work in the textile factories, sugar refineries and cement works of the industrial zone. Whole areas of the bazaar were packed

Winding road near Pülümür, Turkey

with sheepskins and sacks of wool for carpet-making, while other streets were monopolised by butchers' shops where almost every conceivable part of a sheep's anatomy was hanging up for sale or staring at us below rows of exotic sausages - presumably the fate of the remainder of the animal. In fact, if there was anything a sheep could offer, from cheese to trotters, or rugs to slippers, Kayseri bazaar was the place to find it.

East of Kayseri, we crossed a dry, treeless, hedgeless and unfenced prairieland where tractors, enveloped in their own dust clouds, ploughed the stubble plains and where distant villages, apparently of thatched, stone dwellings, revealed at closer range flat-roofed houses crowned with giant haystacks. Our eyes thirsted for the rare interruptions to the brown scene - wind-breaks of poplars, shade-giving olive groves and orchards in small alleys, or the turquoise flash of a sleek roller bird landing on a telegraph pole.

Soon we were climbing into the Tahtali Daglar, a range of craggy mountains as desolate as the Scottish highlands but drier, higher and more barren. We picnicked at about 6,000 feet, watching a dozen Griffon vultures soaring high above and then congregating on the ground a few hundred yards away, white-dog-collared, like a conference of clergy.

The descent towards Malatya was slow and hilly: the second gear was in constant use and it was difficult to believe that our net movement was downwards. Steep escarpments alternated with narrow, green valleys where cattle and sheep grazed on strips of pasture. Herdsmen, tractor drivers and busloads of people from Gürün and Darende waved and smiled at us encouragingly, but it was after dark and seven hours of driving that day that we reached the sprawling town and prised our stiffened bodies from the seats.

We arrived at a small hotel and, as is the custom, deposited our passports with the receptionist. Two minutes later he was knocking at our door, demanding money and, as far as we could tell, claiming that our identities were false. Tourists may be rare in Malatya, we thought, but surely he could recognise a genuine British passport when he saw one.

'What country you come? Who are you? Nationality? Where you come?' he jabbered feverishly. 'What is this nationality?' he added, pointing anxiously at one page.

'British,' we replied, 'English. We come from England.' It was to no avail.

'No, no. See. What is this nationality - you Jee-orfiss-it? Where is this?' and as he showed us the line, we understood his dilemma. It took us five minutes to explain to him that Geophysicist was an occupation and not a national identity, and even then his suspicion was undiminished and his anxiety only quelled by our agreeing to pay for the room in advance and take back our 'fraudulent' documents without delay.

Suppressing our laughter until we were well away, we went out to a small restaurant where we erupted, while ostensibly watching the television news, thereby upsetting an increasingly suspicious restaurateur who probed Ashley with searching questions about our politics before allowing us our post-prandial *çay.*

'It's a funny old town,' I said, as we strolled back to the hotel past indefinable stores, each selling strange combinations of goods such as motorcycles, televisions, sewing-machines and baths.

'Nice cabbages though,' said Ashley, indicating some giant specimens, fifteen to eighteen inches across, stacked unexpectedly between miscellaneous electrical items.

At 6a.m., woken by the orchestral sounds of the hotel's plumbing and the raucous shrieks of boys selling sesame-buns in the street below, we were already too late to wash. The cold taps, to judge by the previous evening, never worked anyway, but even the hot taps, this morning, after a token dribble of cold water, renounced all interest in life. Fortunately we had a full water-bottle to make some coffee for breakfast.

The road to Elazig struggled, as did the waving shepherds and their flocks of fat-tailed sheep, up and down the northern flanks of the Malatya mountains, until it reached the valley of the Euphrates (Firat, to the Turks). Here the great river still had almost 2,000 miles to run before it reached the Arabian Gulf, but it was already about a hundred yards wide and looked remarkably deep considering that this was the season of its lowest level. The Euphrates begins life on the Armenian plateau as two principal tributaries which converge a little way north of Elazig; one, the Kara Su ('muddy water'), rises near Erzurum and the other, the Murat Su ('clear water'), to the north of Lake Van. Below us the broad river flowed smoothly as we crossed a bumpy old bridge and glanced upstream at the incomplete new one, soon to replace it. On the eastern side the hills were scored with dry little valleys and gullies, where trees clung with grim determination.

Then the road levelled out and simultaneously a strong wind began to hurl itself against us from the direction of the lake. It is an artificial one which was created by the building of the Keban Dam and on whose shores the nineteenth-century town of Elazig lies. In the fertile plains around the lake, at the foot of barren mountains to north and south, sheep, cattle and water-buffaloes grazed, while families of casual labourers who had pitched their tents in the fields picked cotton and harvested sugar-beet for the local refinery. The wind ruffled the lake's surface and whistled through two deserted storks' nests, balanced precariously on telegraph poles and abandoned by their builders, probably fleeing for their annual East African safari.

North of the lake, where beautiful bands of green, brown and cream rocks dipped away into the mountains like tilted blocks of Neapolitan ice-cream, a 'Ferrokrom' plant was processing locally mined chromite, one of Turkey's most important natural resources.

Apart from a minor dent, contributed in Istanbul by a careless parker, the car had suffered little damage until that morning when, to our dismay, we found a large nail lodged in the right-hand rear tyre. In an effort to preserve the inner tubes for future, direr circumstances, we decided to test the vulcanising skills of an 'Otolastik', one of the many establishments which lurk behind piles of bald tyres along every major road in Turkey. We found one in a small village on the road to Tunceli and parked beside an equally familiar, brightly-painted lorry, lavishly decorated with romantic scenes of lakes, swans and blue-green trees. Immediately a crowd of men and boys swarmed around the strange white car, and a hen, with bound legs, squawked at me through the window from the arms of the nearest onlooker. Interest in the spectacle increased as we unloaded half the contents of the boot to reach the buried jack, keeping at bay the willing pairs of helping hands which appeared in wild profusion, while the wind swept dust and feathers into everything.

The 'Otolastik' operation itself, which cost no more than fifty pence but took two or three men almost an hour to perform, was a vicious affair. They levered the tyre from its rim, using, to our horror, something resembling a pick-axe, yanked out the offending three-inch nail and plastered the gaping wound with a filthy rubber patch.

Meanwhile, one of the other lads alarmingly whipped out his sheath-knife and plunged it - not in the tyre, thank goodness but into a large water-melon which he had just fetched from the village stores and which he proceeded to segment skilfully. We all partook thirstily - slurping the juicy, pink flesh and spitting the pips all over the dusty forecourt, as was the Tuncelian custom.

With a burst of new confidence, the car bounced northwards up the pot-holed road, following for a while a tributary of the Firat in a wild and beautiful gorge surrounded by wooded hills. Beyond Tunceli the steep layers of volcanic rocks were overlain by great mounds of bright red puddingstone and, as we climbed up through another spectacular deep gorge, the scarlet conglomerate towered up a thousand feet on either side. Below us the river was difficult to cross, even in September after the summer drought, and at intervals we saw buckets and windings used for hauling goods across. At a wider part of the gorge a lorry had run down a rough track into the water where the driver, using a broom and bucket, was cleaning it lovingly, like a zookeeper washing his favourite elephant.

Rattling over the increasingly rough surface, we passed

through a number of short, narrow tunnels in the gorge wall and up into a sequence of schists and slates, contorted into spectacular, swirling folds. For some time the splendid scenery helped to divert our attention from the appalling road conditions; but then the deterioration reached a state where pot-holes predominated over asphalt until finally entire sections of the road had slipped into the river and we had to squeeze our way past to avoid lurching overboard and dropping fifty feet or more into the chilly water. When we eventually jolted up the last hill to Pülümür that evening we were praying for a warm place to stay with a firm bed and preferably no earth tremors. One rattle more and our battered bodies would have disintegrated into irreparable heaps of Humpty Dumpty-like rubble.

We might have looked like Humpty Dumpties too, the way two dozen boys raced up and amassed themselves around the car as we ground to a halt on the steep street opposite Pülümür's only hotel. I fought my way through their midst, to a clamour of, 'Hello! Hello! What is your name? What is your name? Hello, Inglish!' only to find that the hotel entrance was locked. Then a young man emerged from the *çay*-house next door (from which the entirely male clientele was now staring at the new arrivals) and showed me a draughty room. At over 6,000 feet, with the wind howling through the little town, and particularly through the cracks in the bedroom window, a drop of hot water would not have gone amiss, but it was sadly absent and, as there was no alternative, we took the bare, concrete room with its iron bedsteads and rapidly donned three extra layers of clothing.

In search of warmth and food, we hurried up the dark street and located the one and only restaurant - a dingy little room where half a dozen moustachioed men were ranged around the television, drinking soup. Our entry caused some disruption, the lads nearest the set (or practically underneath it) being ousted from their table in order that the two foreigners, protesting mildly, should occupy the 'best' seats. We then felt obliged to strain our eyes upward and watch, with feigned enjoyment, the gruesome exploits of Sylvester Stallone in his Rambo guise - a blood-thirsty piece of entertainment which any right-minded person would have switched off until dinner was over. A more beneficial consequence of sitting by the television was its proximity to the heat of the kitchen which was definitely preferable to the draughts on the back row. On offer for dinner were *çorba* (soup) or *pilav* (rice) to both of which we eagerly said, 'Yes, please.' Bowls of hot, spicy *çorba* served with slices of lemon and accompanied by hunks of white *ekmek* (bread) followed swiftly and soon disappeared - even Rambo had failed to annihilate our mammoth appetites, exacerbated by the cold and windy night.

'That was good for starters,' said Ashley. 'Now bring on the real food.' Unfortunately the 'real food' was not forthcoming. Instead a boy armed with a tea tray flew in through the door with a gust of icy wind and deposited in front of us a couple of hot little glasses, along with more sugar lumps than such a quantity of tea could possibly dissolve. We shouted thanks to him, above the racket of machine-gun fire, and he flew out again with a wild look of terror, as though the fast-approaching helicopter would crash-land in the restaurant at any moment. When the climactic violence had abated, we broached the subject *of pilav* with the waiter, who seemed not to understand but brought us another round of *çorba* anyway. When this was followed by a second flying visit of the tea-boy, and since no one else in the room seemed to be eating anything other than *çorba, ekmek* and vast quantities of sugar soaked in tea, we decided that the *pilav* had probably either been ground up in the soup or simply added to the menu to give the illusion of choice.

After the steamy Vietnamese jungles, the streets of Pülümür felt so distinctly chilly that the aroma of the bakery seemed heaven-sent. Our noses led us easily to the cosiest place in town where sensible Pülümür men, with little interest in either Rambo or card-games in the tea-house next to the hotel, were keeping warm around the baker's oven. Having bought a hot loaf and developed a suitable glow, we reluctantly trudged back to our cold dormitory and pinched some blankets from the empty next-door room. Ashley was beginning to feel decidedly 'flu-ridden and shivery and the knock at our door, half an hour after we had gone to bed, was not received with pleasure. It was so insistent, however, that we were forced to open the door. There was the hotel manager, or whoever it was who had opened up the hotel for us, demanding our blankets on behalf of two of his guests who seemed to have materialised unexpectedly in the adjacent room. Unwillingly we surrendered the bedclothes and shivered back to bed, only to be disturbed again soon afterwards by the landlord's return, this time offering armfuls of different blankets. Our gratitude was tinged only by a minor puzzle: why had he not given these to our new neighbours in the first place and left us in peace? Clearly at work was some secret Pülümür logic which our western minds were incapable of deciphering.

In the morning I felt terrible and Ashley looked even worse. Doubling our altitude, from Malatya one night to Pülümür the next, seemed to have taken its toll. Adhering to the 'feed a cold' principle, I administered to my bed-ridden patient a large, therapeutic breakfast of boiled eggs, bread, honey, grapes and coffee, which went some way, he said, towards filling the gaps left by the çorba. Then, heartened by our healthy appetites, we set off for the 'E80' - the major trans-Turkey route from Bulgaria to Iran.

It took us one hour to do the sixteen miles from Pülümür to the E80 - which, even for a 2CV, was painfully slow. On the other hand, it could hardly be called a road on which we travelled and it certainly wasn't surfaced - it was dusty, boulder-strewn and riddled with hairpins. We were crossing the Munzur Daglari, a rugged range of mountains whose highest peak less than thirty miles to our west, is 11,316 feet high. The sky was a cloudless blue and the air so clear that we could pick out the summit beyond the intervening ridges and, as we came over a pass at 6,234 feet, before us lay an apparently infinite trail of loops, tumbling down the mountains to the Kara Valley like an unravelled ball of string. There was no one in sight - not even a fat-tailed sheep. Only the bedraggled thistles at the roadside waved as we passed and on the dry scree-littered slopes there were no flocks, just patches of small trees. Followed by a wake of chalky dust we trundled down the rocky track - a winding descent of almost 2,000 feet - to the foot of the beautiful, silent mountains.

By the T-junction with the E80 a lorry with a high load had become inextricably wedged beneath the railway bridge but there was just room for us to pass before we turned right for Erzurum. The asphalt surface felt as luxurious as a bed of roses after one of nails: we sailed along smoothly between the mountains, following the Kara Su eastwards along the ancient highway. Further upstream a low pass, defended by the old stronghold of Erzurum, connects the Kara with the Aras Valley, forming an east-west route across the Armenian Plateau - one long-used for commercial and military purposes. Now, while sheep and cattle grazed quietly by the river and groups of people worked in the sunny fields pulling sugar-beet and cutting the tops off, we were engulfed in thick, black fumes from the heavy lorries which rumbled towards Iran, belching all the way. It was only when we turned off the main road, escaped from the pollution and stopped for lunch that we became aware once more of our deteriorating health. The predominant symptoms were simply tiredness and aching heads -nothing more than a bad day at the office might have induced - but Ashley had 'flu-like complaints too and was in no mood to do anything but find a warm bed and hibernate.

It was not far to Erzurum and we soon found a central hotel room with luxurious facilities, such as curtains, towels, a private shower-room with hot water (hot in the evenings anyway), linoleum floors and a telephone (admittedly inoperative), all for about £3 per night - which seemed too good to be true and, on our departure, turned out to be just that. The stubble-chinned old crook at reception then announced that he had mistakenly quoted us a cheap rate and that the real charge would be roughly twice as much. Nevertheless, it was worth it for a hot shower and adequate supplies of blankets, whose mothballs incidentally provided a suitably intoxicating atmosphere for eleven hours of sleep.

Historically, Erzurum has been of strategic military importance - latterly in the defence of eastern Turkey against Russian armies who were repelled in 1877 but who captured the fortress in 1916 and held Erzurum until the Bolshevik Revolution of 1917. As early as the fifth century the Byzantine Emperor Theodosius the Younger built the citadel of Theodosiopolis and only under the sultans of Rum, after numerous wars and disputes over its possession, did the fortress become known as Arz-ar-Rum ('frontier of Greece') - hence its present name.

The citadel had a forlorn air now. The only witness to

Russian gun, Erzurum

its hard-fought battles was a small collection of cannons in the bare courtyard - two great Russian guns built in 1892 and 1898, and a row of bronze Turkish front-loaders resting on crumbling stone supports. 'Come, see, mister, madame! Boum! Boum!' called the crowd of boys who were congregating within the tall, grey walls for a dusty game of football. They were a tough-looking, dark-skinned bunch of assorted ages, cheerful in their ill-fitting clothes. Yet the combination of their uniformly short hair (crew-cuts being a common lice-prevention measure for Turkish boys) and the forbidding surroundings gave them the air of young prisoners, let out into their compound for the daily ration of fresh air and exercise.

Here, at 6,400 feet up on the Armenian Plateau, where winter temperatures reach -24°F, accompanied by blizzards, in a town prone to an alternation of invading armies and devastating earthquakes (such as the one in 1859 which destroyed 4,500 houses and 9 minarets), the inhabitants have to be tough to survive. Only in the 1960s did the population of the *il* (county) of Erzurum recover to its estimated 1914 level after the last disaster - the mass deportation of Armenians in 1915 by the Turkish government - wiped out almost half the local inhabitants, many of whom died or were massacred *en route* to Syria. Politically, Armenia now survives only beyond the eastern Turkish boundary. Erzurum, part of the 57,000 square miles stranded on the western side, has been severed from its ancient roots and from the former glory of the Armenian state, which was once - under Tigranes the Great in the first century BC - said to be the mightiest monarchy in Asia.

Outside on the paved streets beneath the blank, grey citadel walls, thirty feet in height, children played 'tag' amongst lines of washing strung between stone buttresses. On the way up to the Seljuk Türbesi (tower-like tombs for sultans), and in the shadow of one of Erzurum's more ramshackle minarets of corrugated iron, another street game was in progress: it looked like a variation on the bowls theme but each participating boy, instead of rolling a ball, was throwing his personal piece of sheep's bone (a vertebra, to be precise) towards a stone which was the jack. The rules were obscure and clearly subject to conflicting interpretations amongst those who thought they knew them, for there was much shouting, chasing and tussling between the young players, as well as amongst the cheering crowd of disruptive 'referees' who greatly outnumbered them and periodically rode bicycles through their midst. Attention was diverted briefly to the two passing foreigners. Cries of 'Alleman, Alleman! Inglish, Inglish! What is your name?' accompanied a good deal of jostling for positions, in anticipation of the unlikely event that sweets or crayons might be forthcoming. We sought refuge in a nearby shop which, remarkably, amongst its varied stock of books, sweets, boot polish, tea and other provisions, yielded a bottle of the normally elusive *ispirito* for our stove.

The modern shops and restaurants were restricted to the busy main boulevard where cars streamed past tall buildings, pedlars dispensed buns and roast melon seeds, and shoe-shine boys sat at intervals along the pavements waiting to trip up their next customers. A stone's throw away was the tranquillity of the thirteenth-century Yakutiye Medrese (theological college), with its beautifully carved stone portal hanging with stalactite vaults and its richly patterned minaret of blue and brick-red tiles, so delicately set that they resembled the stitchwork of an intricate embroidery. Beyond the Medrese's neglected grey walls, from whose tops wisps of dry grass sprouted like the tufts of hair on the back of a baby elephant, we came to a quiet little square where horses with parked carts were dipping contentedly into nose-bags. Their owners had gone down to the old bazaar or the adjacent shops where traders dealt exclusively in goods such as honey, cheese, sheepskins or leather and where bewildering varieties of paraffin stoves and heaters could be bought, sold or mended. We confined our purchases to the honey-shop but in the evening, as we were donning thick sweaters and scarves as rapidly as the temperature dropped, we did wonder whether a paraffin heater might have been more appropriate.

Just to the east of Erzurum the straight, poplar-lined main road was about to be widened and resurfaced - ideal conditions for us to begin the car's 10,000 miles service, for there was a conveniently wide verge of coarse gravel away from the passing traffic. Above us the dry September leaves rattled in the wind, like strings of milk bottle tops, while the lorries droned by towards Iran. Cereal land, now bristling with stubble like acres of dusty door mats, stretched from the road to the foot of the barren, brown mountains, a few miles to the north and south. Back on our eastward trail we joined the Aras

Valley and were running alongside an old, black steam engine, puffing along at twenty miles an hour with two or three carriages, which we had the satisfaction of overtaking.

At Horasan we turned left for Kars, sticking faithfully to the Aras for a few miles and abandoning the Iran-bound route and all its traffic. Now bullock-carts and a number of trucks collecting gravel from the meandering river's banks were all the vehicles we saw. Below the clear blue sky there was no greenery - only yellow-brown mountains, earth-coloured houses with honey-brown haystacks and mounds of chocolate-brown *tezek* (pieces of animal dung stacked for winter fuel). Even the sheep were brown.

Then we entered a gorge of volcanic rocks the colour of carnations. Beautiful bands of pink and white tuff were weathered into Göreme-like formations below steep escarpments, pouring with scree and capped by thick crags of dark, rust-coloured lava. Where the pale tuff vanished, the scenery was reminiscent of Iceland - sparse vegetation in a land of dark volcanic outpourings where banks of basalt, as though beautifully carved, displayed natural flow structures and columnar jointing. Suddenly, as the car struggled up round a bend away from the river, we were dazzled by mounds of roadside rubble - spoil-heaps glistening with pieces of shiny obsidian, the black glass which forms when lava cools under water so quickly that it has no time to crystallise into rock. It was too good to miss.

'Stop!' yelled Ashley, unexpectedly for he had already suffered a few of my hammer-wielding excursions that morning.

'Don't worry, I was going to anyway,' I said, surprised, but already leaping out to examine the beautiful specimens.

'No, you can't go on like this. You're driving like a short-sighted geriatric with a punctured tyre. It's all very well appreciating the geology, but trying to steer the car between pot-holes at the same time is simply not on.' By this time I was up to the ankles in obsidian, hotly pursued by an angry husband with frayed nerves. I tried the calming approach.

'But just look at this gleaming glass; here, feel it. Isn't it smooth? Wouldn't that make a lovely paperweight?

'No, and before you ask, no, we can't carry great lumps of rock home with us,' said Ashley.

Under normal circumstances I might have conceded at the outset, 'OK. You drive. I'll look at the scenery,' but today the passenger was coughing and sneezing to the extent that he had expressed the rare preference for me to take the helm. In the end we reached a truce. I negotiated a small place in the car to install a souvenir lump of obsidian by promising that I would keep my eyes firmly on the road from now on.

We began climbing into pine-forested mountains of Alpine beauty, where buzzards soared and herds of brown cows grazed in the grassy valleys between escarpments of lava and outcrops of powdery, white, snow-like tuff. The sight of so many trees was unbelievable in eastern Turkey, whose mountain slopes, once densely wooded, have been ruthlessly denuded over the centuries with little attempt, until recently, at reafforestation.

Shortly, however, we emerged onto a dry plateau to be confronted by a number of soldiers manning a military barricade. One of the men came over to the car, pointed to the large lay-by on our right and, tapping his watch, indicated the passing of an hour. Neither our Turkish nor his English was up to further explanations, so we waited helplessly in the lay-by, eating lunch, while two or three lorries arrived to a similar welcome. After only twenty minutes we were allowed to move on and found ourselves in the midst of an exercise of the Turkish army, whose hostilities, feigned or otherwise, we hoped were over. Warlike arrays of tanks, jeeps and guns crawled all over the plains, there were trucks hidden beneath camouflage netting and soldiers popping up from bunkers wherever we looked.

'Hello, we'd better wake this one up!' said Ashley, pointing to a lad who was taking a surreptitious nap in his little dug-out a few yards from the road.

Before long we were in Sarikamis, a small town dominated by a large military station whose soldiers paraded the streets with disconcertingly big guns. We were still sixty miles from the border but already it felt like a war zone. Just as we were wondering whether it was safe to go any further towards the frontier and to Kars in particular, we reached the centre of town and the tarmac disappeared abruptly, along with all trace of road signs.

'Maybe we're not allowed to proceed, anyway,' I said. In the early 1970s, I had read, even Erzurum was in a protected military area which foreigners could enter only with official permits. 'Well, there's one way to find out...

'Kars?' I shouted to the nearest soldier, who happened to be standing at a fork in the road.

He pointed left and we went bouncing up an increasingly irregular track, generating enormous quantities of dust but making little progress. A crowd of men and women in a claypit looked up from their brickmaking in disbelief as we passed, shook their heads and resumed work amongst their red stacks.

'It's no good, we're on the wrong road - I can feel it in my bones,' said Ashley, between jolts, somewhat understating our state of osteal disintegration. 'For one thing we're heading west, and for another, there's supposed to be tarmac all the way to Kars.'

We ground to a halt and the dust settled to reveal a man from the brickworks who kindly directed us back to Sarikamis. There a surfaced road, heading in a suitable direction, appeared before we reached the centre, thus saving the soldier from certain death.

'I should have strangled that man for sending us off on a wild goose chase into the Alla ... Alla-whatsit mountains like that.'

'Allahüekber,' corrected Ashley, with the advantage of a map.

'Yes, Alla-hew ... Alla-phew-hek-berrr ... Well, anyway, I bet he's laughing his head off now.'

'Your just dessert for all those Americans you sent beetling up the Edgware Road to find the Tower of Lond ... AAH ... TISHOO!'

As it turned out, it was a good straight run to Kars across the rolling plains. Admittedly there were plenty of ups and downs but the downs predominated as we dropped from 7,800 feet at Sarikamis to 5,740 at Kars. Like boats in a sea swell, villages seemed to float in the brown landscape, some hidden by the undulations, showing only their minarets protruding like masts above the waves, and others as bold as bright-sailed yachts with their blue-painted houses and big yellow haystacks.

Kars looked relatively drab. The main street was riddled with puddles and rather seedy-looking hotels where, evidently, hot water was too much to ask for. We chose a place where the hotelier did at least speak a little German and where, for 1500 TL (£2) a night, we could see the castle from our window and park in the street below. The bad news was our discovery that the life of the 'Otolastik's' repair was three days only - now the nail-hole was no longer plugged and we had a rapidly deflating tyre. There was nothing for it but to insert an inner tube.

Anyone who has attempted this operation will know that it is difficult at the best of times, even with the aid of half a dozen tyre levers and a tube of 'Beadlube'; but when it is performed in the fading light near the Armenian border, with a growing crowd of male spectators constantly pushing and elbowing each other, fingering every available tool, peering in through the car windows and spitting half-chewed sunflower seeds in your general direction, the thing becomes more than a trial of patience. An old man kindly insisted on lending a hand but, although we had not the heart to refuse it, his 'help' was an unnecessary hindrance. Several younger men competed for a turn at the foot-pump as though it was a feat of great strength, and for ten minutes the successive high-heels of their platform shoes tapped up and down on the pavement until the tyre was almost at bursting point - which was all very helpful until, in our attempts to 'pop' the tyre on to the rim, one of the team tried attacking it with my geological hammer. Ashley grabbed it from him before he could inflict any serious damage but this precipitated an outbreak of presumably Armenian battle cries and wild skirmishing among the boys, leaving bodies plastered over the bonnet and sprawled across the pavement and reducing British nerves to tatters. Only rarely can it be said that our initial impression of a place was impaired by the friendliness of its people, but Kars was a case in point.

We revived ourselves from the cold and tribulations in a nearby restaurant, where we chose from the pots in the kitchen some spicy, hot soup (which Ashley, on account of his cold, was unable to taste), followed by stuffed (and subsequently squashed) tomatoes, beans and, of course, generous hunks of bread, which forms the bulk of the Turkish diet. Contemplation of the all-too-familiar standards of culinary hygiene was fortunately prevented by the omnipresent television - tonight our fellow-diners were stuffing bread into their mouths with one hand and with the other were thumping the table in delight at a slapstick comedy, the Turkish answer to *On the Buses*. It was the sort of pantomime in which you know that the bucket of chicken feed is going to fall off the luggage-rack, tipping its contents all over the unsuspecting passenger, at least ten minutes before it actually does so.

CHAPTER 5

It never ceases to amaze me how places can be transformed overnight, how you can go to sleep wondering why you bothered to come to such a one-horse frontier town in the first place and yet wake up in fine spirits, raring to be out in the sunshine and seeing the local sights. Of course, by no means everyone is so affected by the dawning of a new day, and at 6 a.m., when the clip-clop of horses' hooves on the street below had inspired me to jump out of bed, I could hear groans of: 'Whattimeisit?Ifeelterrible,' which I interpreted as Monday morning symptoms. Soon, however, the town was bustling with traffic and people and even Ashley could not remain inactive. Nearly 59,000 people live in Kars and every one of them was on the streets by half-past six, not to mention half the farming communities of the *il,* bringing their goods to market. The streets were lined with stalls of fruit and vegetables, horses and carts rattled wildly by, flocks of sheep were driven along the pavements, complaining turkeys were unloaded from tractor trailers and women tottered home with yokes and pails of water (crude affairs - straight poles balanced uncomfortably on one shoulder -which the more liberated females had abandoned in favour of plastic jerry cans).

Sixty-five years before, on the same spot, we would have been in Russia. Now we were forty miles or so west of the border in a town of peculiarly confused identity. During the ninth and tenth centuries it was the seat of an independent Armenian principality; in the eleventh, the Seljuk Turks captured it, only to lose it in the thirteenth to the Mongols, who held it until 1387 when Tamerlane marched in ... and so on until, after the 1877-8 war with Russia Kars was ceded to the Russians by the Treaty of Berlin and was finally returned to Turkey in 1921.

We met Kars' two other tourists on the way up to the citadel that morning. An unlikely pair and sole residents of the Turist Otel (which, had we located it earlier, would have provided us with hot water, at certain hours), they had become friends over breakfast. The tall teacher from New Zealand was fascinated by antique *kilims* (the Turkish woven rugs, as opposed to the more familiar knotted carpets); his small Japanese companion, adorned with cameras, had been working in Germany and was attempting the world record in photographs per minute without the aid of a motor-drive. We chatted about our travels. The Turkish bus system was so good, they assured us, why did we bother with a car? Why indeed, we began to wonder, thinking of the little monkeys fiddling with the door handles and wing mirrors as we had left the hotel.

'Photo! Photo!' taunted more children, 'dancing around our Asian friend.

'What is your name, sir? What is your name? What country? Alleman? Inglish? Alleman?'

'*Ja, Ja.!*' he joked, 'What you think? I look like Alleman?!' pausing between close-up shots to point to his eyes. We all joined in the laughter and the kids, disconcerted at finding themselves, for once, the objects of derision, not the perpetrators, scampered away to the shelter of a baker's shop.

Leaving the rectangular layout of the town centre, we climbed the steep path to the top of the basalt hill, from which the sombre, grey citadel, below a blue sky, overlooked the River Kars and the clusters of flat-roofed, part white-washed, stone dwellings which littered the slopes like discarded shoe-boxes. There was no hope of growing anything on the rocky hillside, although the odd tuft of withered grass struggled from a rooftop. In a brave attempt to add colour to the scene, someone had painted his house in a dreary shade of pink.

'How old is this castle, anyway?' I asked, ignorantly, as we wandered along the lower battlements.

'Twelfth century. Built by the Seljuk Turks,' Ashley read from the tourist leaflet.

'No, it's not, mate,' objected the New Zealander. 'My book says it was put up by Sultan Murad III in the sixteenth, to keep out the Persians.'

'Where's our third opinion?' As he was hanging precariously over a wall, with a large telescopic lens, we thought it safer to leave the matter unresolved. In any case he didn't have a guidebook.

Just then two armed soldiers appeared from behind us, explained politely that the *kaleyi* was closed for 'two day' (or was it 'today'?) and escorted us all swiftly out through the entrance.

'*Tamam, tamam,* OK,' said the teacher. 'Just tell us how old the *kaleyi* is, will you?'

'Yes. Kars *kaleyi* very, very old,' said the two soldiers helpfully.

We visited a tenth-century (we all agreed on this one) Byzantine building on the way down the hill. We had read that it housed the museum, but there was nothing inside except the inevitable consequences of two dozen pigeons' having taken up permanent residence. Solidly stone-built a thousand years ago as a Christian church, it was later used as a mosque by the Seljuk Turks and again by the Russians after 1878. We were sad to see it now in such a sorry state, and yet Mr 'Nikon-Pentax' found it surprisingly photogenic.

'You should take a look at some of the *kilims,* you know,' said his friend, while we waited for the seventeenth colour film to run out. 'Some of the antique ones are as good as new. Unlike the well-worn carpets, they were kept for special occasions and only used for covering saddles or hanging in the tents. The designs are far more beautiful too. And when you think of the work involved in all the colour changes, the mind just boggles. It's much easier to put different knots in a carpet than make patterns in a woven rug. You can't beat the craftsmanship and the quality of an old Turkish *kilim* - I've got quite a collection back home...'

'OK, OK.' It was Nikon-Pentax, returned. 'We go now. *Hhai. Hhai.*'

'*Hhai. Hhai,*' we echoed in agreement.

'Super' was unheard of in Kars but we dosed the car with 'Normal' instead, topped Ashley up with cough medicine, and bundled off in the direction of Mount Ararat. Even outside the town's limits, livestock was a hazard: first we nearly ran into a mare, calmly suckling her foal in the middle of the road, and then a herd of migrant cattle decided to cross. Beyond the pastures, newly ploughed fields revealed rich volcanic soil, as dark as peat, forming a patchwork with yellow stubble, dotted with piles of cleared stones. Then we were climbing up to the Pasli Geçidi, a pass at 6,600 feet, before plunging down an unsurfaced road between brown, scree-coated mountains of 9,000 or 10,000 feet. One solitary little village, nestling in an isolated, green gully, shaded by poplars, survived in that inhospitable environment - quite inaccessible to all forms of transport save donkeys, mules and flying carpets.

Appalling though the road was, as we approached the Aras Valley the scenery more than compensated. A gorge of brilliant red shales and massive pink porphyry in which little springs bubbled up at the roadside opened out into a broader valley where underground water surfaced on the hillside and trickled down the rockface, depositing salt formations like miniature Pamukkales. To the south, near Lötek, soft volcanic hills - brilliant bands of red, green, brown and cream - formed a warm backdrop to a verdant, tree-filled valley which joined the Aras near Kagizman. There, having reached the good road to Igdir, we began to follow the great river as it meandered along a broad valley towards the border, ultimately to pour itself into the Caspian Sea, not far from Baku.

High up, only streaks of white, the trails of springwater, striped the barren, banded mountains; but at lower levels there were cultivated terraces of vivid green near villages whose haystacks outnumbered houses. There were haystacks on the road too, rumbling along on bullock-carts so overloaded that it was difficult to see beast or boy-driver beneath the mounds, and even harder to imagine how they knew where they were going. People were bathing and doing their laundry in the shallowest water beneath the clear blue sky, while their flocks of deep-brown sheep grazed where the banks were grassy.

We drove down to the water's edge too, not to bathe, but to continue the 10,000 miles service on a grassy terrace above the gravel banks. To be precise, Ashley carried out the technical bits while I cleaned out the front of the car's interior, involuntarily contributing to the silting-up of the Caspian Sea by washing the dust-caked floor mats in the all-purpose river.

It was not long before a tractor came bouncing down

the track towards us and a stern-faced farmer and two young acolytes jumped down from the cab and marched threateningly towards us. Uncertain of the trespassing laws pertaining to the Aras Valley, we were preparing to plead ignorance and hoping for a light sentence. But our visitors revealed themselves, not as irate landowners at all, but as friendly neighbours offering their help - or at least their sympathy in our hour of need. For they said nothing but hovered, wide-eyed, around the engine as Ashley worked, giving him pitying glances as he struggled in vain to remove the fan and pulley, which in a 2CV inconveniently isolate the points from the outside world - all of which is not easy to explain in Turkish. When they departed it was with sighs of commiseration for the frustrated mechanic, who finally admitted that he lacked the necessary tool to reach the parts that socket spanners fail to reach.

Somewhere between Tuzluça and Igdir and only six or seven miles from the frontier we had our first glimpse of the snow-capped peak of Agri-dagi (try Aroo-dah-yoo or simply Mount Ararat), 16,945 feet and Turkey's highest mountain. It was only south of Igdir, however, after emerging unscathed from another mock battle-zone of the Turkish army, that we saw the full glory of the great summit (or rather, twin summits, for Little Ararat sits beside the Great one), where Noah's Ark lurks as elusively as the monster in Loch Ness. The evening sun was like a floodlight on the western slopes of the old volcanic cone: and the summit, towering 11,000 feet above the plain, was beautiful in its isolation, for there are no nearby peaks to detract from its majesty. This was the 'Mother of the World', so sacred to the Armenian people who believed that God forbade anyone from reaching the summit and viewing the remains of the Ark; here were the ancient kingdom of Urartu and Genesis' 'mountains of

Mount Ararat

Ararat'; here ...

Suddenly, my reveries were curtailed by an ambush of boys who sprang from the shadows of the Bayazid plain. No sooner had Ashley slithered down the road embankment to take some photographs than I was surrounded by half a dozen hostile faces, gathering like vultures around a carcass. Before I could close the windows a number of crew-cut heads and dirty little arms were poking their way into the car, rooting about for cigarettes, crayons, shirts and anything else which might be available, while their friends made unsuccessful attempts at extracting the exterior lights with their bare hands. When my angry shouts were obviously misinterpreted as signs of approval, I felt, to put it mildly, alarmingly defenceless and was on the point of driving away with all the acceleration the car could muster (in the unrealistic hope that this would dislodge the parasites), when, to my relief, Ashley reappeared and the scoundrels, sensing danger, dispersed to the roadsides. There they picked up loose stones and threatened to launch them in our direction, but for some unknown reason refrained from doing so.

At 6 p.m. we arrived at Dogubayazit and rolled into a welter of roadworks, soldiers and milling civilians who wandered unsmilingly and aimlessly everywhere, it seemed, except on the pavements. Fording a river of wet tar, I went to vet a couple of hotels, the second of which was bearable, although the toilet lacked water and the sheets had certainly not seen any for several months. Once inside it took us several attempts to make a cup of tea, for which we were dying. Each time we set up the stove on the concrete floor we had to hide it again because there was someone knocking at the door - once the hotelier came to warn us that the steam roller and tar-sprayer were heading for our car, which we rescued in the nick of time; another caller was the previous occupant of our room who had left his newspapers on one of the beds.

Like Kars, Dogubayazit is a small frontier town with an ancient history, but there the similarity ends. Destroyed during the nineteenth-century campaigns with Russia and in the First World War, Dogubayazit has been restored by the Turks into a busy trading centre for animal products and has a character quite different from that of Kars. Where Kars had the rural charm of a market town, Dogubayazit was about as enchanting as a motorway service station. The route to Iran was a great deal busier than the road through Kars to the Armenian border: and the carpark of Dogubayazit's upmarket Hotel Ararat was packed with Teheran-registered Mercedes fleeing from or to Europe with everything but the kitchen sink. The very presence of this transitory population was as unsettling as the ubiquitous patrols of armed soldiers emanating from the town's military camp.

Perhaps we were unlucky, but everything about the place seemed to be conspiring against our comfort and peace of mind. With shoes plastered in tar we settled in a popular restaurant and ordered soup and some indeterminate concoction based on aubergines. The unavoidable television subjected us to a terrible Turkish film - a tragedy of monumental proportions in which two murders and a suicide had occurred before we had even finished our soup let alone started the main course. Then a platoon of soldiers marched in, civilians were politely uprooted from the seats nearest to the set and the privileged guests were given pride of place at a group of tables, hurriedly aggregated for their party. There was no doubt who was boss in Dogubayazit - fear of the uniform was only too evident. The waiter, who had been slouching against a table watching the sequence of televised disasters, now flitted nervously from table to table, emptying half-full water-glasses over the concrete floor and sweeping off breadcrumbs with his dirty cloth which he then used to polish the glasses ready for the next customers. Dogubayazit was, incidentally, one of the few places in Turkey where we regarded water-purifying tablets as a necessity - not on account of the restaurant's standards, which were no worse than elsewhere, but because, in the hotel, water was not tapped from a main supply but from a tank filled daily from an unknown, and therefore dubious source.

In the morning, contrary to Kars-generated expectations, things did not improve. We awoke at 6 a.m. to a dawn chorus of shop-keepers rattling open their metal shutters, cars hooting, discordant radio music blaring and men spitting in the bathroom next-door. After boiling some eggs for breakfast we fled from the Otel, whose insanitary smells were becoming intolerable, only to find that the car had been suffering during the night too. The leather bonnet strap had been cut and removed and there were signs of tampering under the bonnet, although fortunately no other loss nor serious damage. Any doubts we may have had about Dogubayazit's old

Ishak Pasha Palace, Turkey

reputation as a base for Kurdish robbers now lay buried in the snows of Agri-dagi, along with Noah's Ark.

'Let's get out of this dismal place before anything else happens,' I said, but Ashley, sitting at the wheel like harassment personified, was refusing to budge. It was understandable. Two dozen young onlookers, the closest of whom had their faces pressed against the windows, had been watching us in disbelief while we packed the car and fastened our seat belts. Now they still stared.

'Yes, we are genuine human beings,' Ashley was saying to them. 'We may have "GB" stuck on our rear end but that doesn't mean we're from outer space.' Naturally, his words were wasted on the unhearing crowd but as an outlet for his annoyance they offered certain therapeutic benefits.

'*Tamam.* OK,' he said, beginning to see the funny side. I'm not moving until they do. Let's try to stare them out,' and each of us fixed an unblinking gaze on the nearest pair of eyes until the reversal of attention made them, like the children at Kars, melt away in evident unease.

Sensing the freedom of previously caged animals

liberated, we bounded up the steep hillside above the town for three or four miles of winding road to the ruined Palace of Ishak Pasha. This must be one of the most beautiful buildings in Turkey. Long after the 'anything looks wonderful after Dogubayazit' sentiment had faded from my mind I could think of few of the country's sights which could compete with this one both in splendour and in setting. For me, the Palace of Ishak Pasha is a prime example of the essential interplay of a building and its surroundings. Designed in the late seventeenth century for the governor of the province, Ishak Pasha, by a Persian architect, it is a beautiful construction in its own right but owes its outstanding character to the magnificent hilltop site. As though caught on a cloud between earth and heaven, it hovers in isolation above the hazy plain and yet looks up in awe at the great 'Mother of the World'. Its smooth, honey-coloured stonework glows warmly in the mountain air against the jagged hillside, the curves of its arches and domes contrasting starkly with the natural rock. The complex (it is more than a palace) has fortress walls enclosing a series of courtyards leading to the banquet room, the council chamber, the guards' room, the living quarters, and so on. The harem, for example, consists of about a dozen identical ladies' rooms, each with its own little fireplace, while the mosque, whose interior features include a beautifully painted, domed ceiling, has a tall, rocket-like minaret, striped with alternating courses of contrasting stone. Many of the carved decorations throughout the palace - on the walls, round the window arches, on the stalactite vaults of the portals - are still as clear cut as freshly moulded cornices of plaster, and their floral and geometric designs as imaginative as the illuminations of ancient manuscripts.

Alone at first, we were captivated by the fabulous quality of our surroundings - the same feeling which I imagine would overcome me at Machu Picchu, high up in the Andes, haunted me in this dream-like world: it seemed incredible that people had actually lived in such a magnificent and far-flung portion of the earth. Merely to taste the magic of Agri-dagi and the Palace of Ishak Pasha, if for no other reason, it was worth driving two and a half thousand miles across Turkey in our 2CV.

CHAPTER 6

As the crow flies, it is 80 miles from Dogubayazit to Van, but by road it is 200 miles and by 2CV about five and a half hours. The great obstacle is a range of mountains called Ala-daglari, which rise to peaks of 11,000 feet or more and force the traveller in a westward arc, along the upper reaches of the Murat Nehri ('clear river', which joins the 'muddy' one to form the Euphrates) and then around the north-eastern shores of Lake Van.

The Murat meanders westwards as far as Agri, providing pastures for cattle and sheep beside its blue waters, but then it turns sharply to the south and the valley changes dramatically. Between the little riverside towns of Hamur and Tutak we found the most breathtaking scenery of the day's journey: steep hills beset with dark crags and basaltic columns swept down to the valley floor, squeezing it into narrow gorges and then freeing it into broader reaches like the closing and opening of a vice. A man up to his waist in water was casting a large net into the sparkling current; his partner, a small boy, held up a string of twenty large, shining fish at the roadside as we passed. We rounded a bend and there, standing motionless at the water's edge, were three fine herons, doubtless wondering where all the fish had gone. Pockets of simple stone and mud-built dwellings, barely villages, were tucked into the available spaces on the wider bends and the communal laundry was a broad, shallow, colourful sweep of the river. Whole families were doing their washing there - not only clothes and bodies but anything from carpets to tractors. Clean items were laid to dry on the gravel banks where children skipped about in various states of undress between patches of bright clothing, like butterflies amongst beds of garden flowers.

As though bidding farewell to summer and encountering autumn, we climbed from the valley to the windswept plateau. A multitude of dust devils spiralled upwards, like smoke from twisted chimneys, and donkeys grazed near nomads' tents of dark goat-hair or woollen cloth, flapping in the wind. What we took to be the local bus - a tractor towing a couple of trailers and twenty people - went bouncing across the land towards a village where the haystacks were part-plastered in mud to keep out the wind and rain. It was, however, the *tezek* which stole the show as usual.

Admittedly, manure doesn't normally spring to mind as the inspiration for great artistic creativity, but throughout eastern Turkey the storage of this dried animal dung had become a veritable art form. Just as the Scandinavians, for example, take pride in their neat stacks of perfectly cylindrical logs, in Turkey, where the forests have largely been destroyed, beautifully sculptured mounds of dung-fuel graced every village. The building-blocks, like firm cow-pats the size of dinner plates, were shaped by hand and left to dry on walls and roof tops before the construction work began. The variety of the resulting designs was enough to put the housing architects to shame: there were conical stacks decorated with extra pats, like giant chocolate drops on a children's birthday cake; there were low beehive mounds and tall towers; some stacks had square bases and domed tops; others were truncated pyramids with zigzag patterns, each alternate course of pats inclined in a different direction - every one a work of individual craftsmanship. If there were an Anatolian equivalent of a 'Britain in Bloom' contest, it is not hard to imagine what might be judged in lieu of flowers.

Outside the small Greek-sounding town of Patnos, which was dominated by another army camp, the copper telegraph wires glinted rosily in the sunshine against a blue sky. In the distance, we could see the snows of Süphan Dagi, an extinct volcano of 14,544 feet looming above the northern shores of Lake Van; soon we were driving around that brilliant blue expanse of salt water which covers an area seven times that of Lake Geneva. Pebble beaches alternated with strips of pasture where cattle and sheep grazed near the water's edge, but in places the hills sloped more closely to the shore and we had to struggle up and over. It seemed surprising that the bitter and undrinkable lakewater, thick with such unappetising salts as sodium carbonate and borax, could yield grass which was palatable to the local livestock. Either their tastebuds are specially adapted, as are the *darekh* (freshwater fish capable of living in these saline conditions) which are caught in Van's shallow lagoons during spring and autumn, or the grass thrives only where good fresh water wells up from the coastal springs.

Cockroaches, I discovered in Van, are only tolerable if they keep to the floor in limited numbers, but as soon as they appear in quantity, I am driven towards a nervous breakdown. Our hotel room was evidently a breeding-ground for the little hard-shelled pests and in the evenings they came out in force: armies of them went marching up the walls, trotting over the beds, burrowing into our clothes and popping out of light switches, curtain rails and plug-holes. On the first night, we waged a brutal war, slaughtering them with shoes and Shell-tox until we had to sweep away the bodies like a carpet of dead leaves.

Whether the cause of Ashley's subsequent predicament was the sight of two or three dozen of these insects or the dubious *ayran* which we drank with our evening meal I shall never be sure, but the results were all too clear. He was rushing between bed and bath-room for the next day and a half, sustaining his feverish body on alternate doses of Diarolyte and black tea. He slept fitfully between my frequent horrified gasps, such as when I opened a paperback to find a cockroach lurking between the pages or, on leaving the room in search of a chemist's had my bottom pinched by the randy young hotel cleaner. The constant hum of people in the narrow street below our window and the periodic drone of praying Moslems on the landing were relatively soothing.

I knew that the patient was improving as soon as I found him leaning out of the bedroom window, pouring water over a number of boys who were tampering with the car, strategically parked below our room.

'Gotcha, you little brat!' he yelled with renewed spirit as another one jumped off the bumper and scampered away down the street.

'Let's go and see the castle,' I suggested, tired of being incarcerated with cockroaches.

We drove out to the long ridge of rock which points, like a great bony finger, from the lake-shore towards the town, and which is crowned by the ruins of an ancient fortress. It was built in 825 BC when Van, then known as Tushpa, was the capital of the kingdom of Urartu, and there are still some cuneiform inscriptions in the rock wall, engraved by order of the Persian monarch Xerxes in the fifth century BC. Modesty appears not to have been Xerxes' strong point:

the greatest of gods, who has created this earth, who has created that heaven, who has created mankind... has made Xerxes king, sole king of many kings, sole lord of many. I am Xerxes the great king, the king of kings, the king of the provinces with many languages, the king of this great earth far and near, son of king Darius the Achaemenian. Says Xerxes the king: Darius the king, my father, did many works on this hill... yet an inscription he did not make. I ordered this inscription to be written. May all the gods protect me and my kingdom and my work.

Steps, carved in the rock, led us to the top from which we could see the old city laid out at the foot of the ridge. It was a hummocky area of ruined walls and Seljuk mosques which were crumbling between grassy mounds where more of the past lay buried. Of the fortress still less remained, but the Seljuks and Ottomans have used the site too, leaving, amongst other ruins, a tall minaret. We could hear the 'slap-slap' beating of clothes on stones as women did the washing in a stream amongst the trees below us. On the north side of the ridge local families picnicked and paid visits to the little cemetery, while cattle grazed around them. We returned to the car past a tiny *çay*-house where bottles of orangeade were cooling in the stream amongst the ducks. Three little boys sat on stools made from wood and strips of old tyres and fan-belts, while their friends ran about in the mud nearby having kindly left their footprints all over the car's bonnet. Ashley popped into, and almost instantly fled from the Gents' hut, on discovery of a ceilingful of malarial mosquitoes. The playful boys crowded around the car as we left and hurled the odd stone half-heartedly in our

Girls at Van, Turkey

direction. One of their number jumped on the back bumper for a ride which was soon curtailed by a deliberately violent emergency stop.

Their sisters were waiting for us on the other side of the ridge on the marshy ground around the old city. One of them ran up to shake my land with her thumbless one, a silent invitation to benevolence. Then, voluntarily, they posed for photographs - a strange, unsmiling group in predominantly blood-red clothes. Three wore long, full skirts, woollen tops and simple jewellery - rings and bangles: the fourth, a barefooted toddler in the arms of the eldest, who must have been sixteen or so, was swamped in a pink sweater two years too big for him and a pair of bright pyjama trousers. They were pitiable souls, not for any outward signs of poverty - for they were neither mal-nourished nor inadequately clothed - but for their apparent lack of *joie de vivre*. While their brothers were romping through puddles and jumping on tourists' cars, these sullen girls were performing their routine drudgery of begging from foreigners. With the current dearth of tourists in Van (we saw no more than three or four), it was possible that these girls were simply bored: but, sadly, they left us with the ungenerous view that it was all a front, part of their sympathy-provoking act. It was cheering to believe, at any rate, that when we had gone they would switch off the misery and play as happily as the boys.

'Scuse me. You like Van? You like the people here?' inquired a smart young stranger in a three-piece suit as we were buying apples in the colourful market that afternoon.

'Yes, yes, very much, thank you,' we answered diplomatically, putting aside all thoughts of cockroaches, Diarolyte and hotel-cleaners, and remembering the avenues of poplars, the deep blue lake, the ancient remains of Tushpa and the mountain views. Yes, it really was quite an attractive place when you thought about it reasonably. It was not a large town - big enough to have one or two carpet stores, with rugs laid out on the pavement to improve their 'worn' qualities and so increase their value; and yet small enough for the majority of the people to have the time and inclination to be helpful and obliging. We had spent a good part of the afternoon in hardware shops with sympathetic owners trying desperately to find a suitable implement for our requirements, namely to reach the bolt which secured the car's fan and pulley. Passed from one friend to another by a series of recommendations, we finally ended up with an appropriate tool from the sixth establishment, and a bag of apples from one of the earlier ironmongers, who was so distressed by his failure to serve, that he had refused to let us go empty-handed.

'And the people are very nice, too,' we added sincerely to the well-dressed man, expecting him to smile with satisfaction at the answers he had wished to hear.

'Oh,' he said glumly, I can't wait to go back to

Istanbul. I've been working here as an engineer for the government for three long years and Van is not the place for me. Eastern Turkey and its people are just not ... well ... how shall I say? ... not the same as western Turkey.' He spoke with the distaste of archetypal British southerners, venturing for the first time north of Watford Gap, and I felt rather sorry for him. We tried to cheer him up by talking of our trip, but he was too enwrapped in his own sorrow so we left him to his shopping.

The following morning we rushed down to the ferry terminal, hoping to cross the lake to Tatvan on the western shores. There was a departure daily, between 9 a.m. and 10.30 a.m., the Tourist Office had informed us at 10.25, and an afternoon one generally between 2 and 7. Our hopes of catching the morning ferry (surely delays were guaranteed, we thought) were soon shattered: there was no sign of any boat at the landing-stage, nor was there anyone on hand to ask about it. I banged on the door of a wooden hut on the jetty and, receiving no response, was turning to walk away in despair when a groan emanated from within and an old man appeared, rubbing the sleep from his eyes.

There was a 'ferri-bot' due at 1 p.m. for a 2 p.m. departure, he told me. It was 1,000 lira for us and 800 for the 'oto'. While we waited he asked us in for *çay* - actually *çay-citron,* a refreshing version like hot lemon squash - and we chatted amicably about our journey and his eleven children.

A colleague arrived, the introduction routines of handshakes, 'Allemand?' 'No, English,' were repeated, and then he informed us that the ferry was really due in at two and would leave at three. There followed much deliberation between the two friends about the appropriate fare for the car: there was some inexplicable difficulty over whether it fell in the category *of taksi* or minibus, rather than simply 'oto'. Then a third man arrived and after rather laboured communications we found that the ferry was arriving at three for a four o'clock departure and would reach Tatvan at eight.

'At this rate, we'll still be here tomorrow!' said Ashley and went to check the points. In the middle of the pier, far from the nearest interfering child, it was ideally peaceful for servicing the car and all went well . . . until the 'phone rang. Minutes later the old man came out of the hut, announcing: 'Tatvan telefon, ferri-bot Tatvan. Ferri-bot Van nine *saat*, at which our hearts sank. Further questions confirmed that the boat was still sixty miles away at the other side of the lake and wouldn't arrive until nine that evening. It was at this point that our long-held intentions of 'taking things as they come' and remaining calm and patient in the face of all incidental and inevitable delays disintegrated. We took to the road, much to the annoyance of the ferry-men who made last-minute and rather bad-tempered demands for cigarettes and car-tools, to no avail.

'After all,' said Ashley, justifying our impatience as we sped through Gevas on the southern shores, 'we could have been stuck there for weeks with nothing but lemon tea.'

Soon we were climbing from the lake into steep hills. It was cloudy and the scenery had a certain Scottish air - of lochs and mountains, glens and wild moorland. Then the sun returned, a boy jumped out with a handful of walnuts for sale and a second signal of autumn flashed to us from a cluster of brilliant red and golden poplars glinting halfway up the mountain-side. There were haystacks on the slopes too and small fields of tobacco in the steep, sheltered valleys.

Over the Kusgunkiran Pass we went (7,333 feet) and down a winding road along valleys thickly wooded with poplars and willows, between dry, grassy mountain slopes. Children, minding cattle, sheep and goats, roamed between nomads' camps and villages of neat little box-like houses of poplar trunks and stone, roofed with thick stacks of poplar branches coated in mud. At the roadside a small boy held aloft an enormous hen by its feet in a brave attempt to sell the old bird to us

Then the road seemed to tumble down the steep mountainside to the dazzling sunlit lake, which lay before us like a sheet of wrinkled silver foil. We followed the lakeside for a short distance, trapped between the salt-white pebble beaches and the slopes, densely wooded with tiny oaks. As we climbed away once more we passed buffalo-carts whose wheels were solid, spokeless, wooden discs and entered a fertile narrow valley where a river meandered between nomads' camps and flocks of grazing sheep. Little boys, seeing the car, rushed to the road to beg theatrically for cigarettes, using exaggerated mimes of smoking, while their disdainful elders walked stiffly by in what looked like sandwich-boards - those thick and highly practical, but ludicrous-looking, wide-shouldered shepherds' cloaks, the *kepenek.*

Swerving to avoid an assortment of Tatvan's domestic animals, which were ambling or running across the road, we entered the bustling lakeside town and wove our way across its crowded centre between errant street-vendors and men in turbans. It had taken us just three and a quarter hours, including a lunch stop, to arrive from Van, and the roads, contrary to forewarnings, had really not been too disastrous. Taking the ferry would have made a pleasant change but at least, now, we had the satisfaction of having seen some beautiful scenery and of arriving several hours ahead.

As we passed the army camp and the brick works on the far side, and looked back towards the shore, from which the ferry-boat had evidently left, something very odd happened. In the three weeks since we had left Istanbul the very thought had vanished from our minds, but now, unexpectedly, it was raining! Nothing spectacular, however - just a token shower to remind us that summer was over. The clouds persisted though, and on the hillside around a ruined caravanserai the black tents of nomads flapped in the wind above their protective stone walls.

Making a series of fleeting visits, as we were doing continually on our trip, it was difficult afterwards to decide how much of each lasting impression of a place reflected its genuine character and how much was due to incidental or entirely extraneous circumstances. Bitlis, for example, was to us most certainly a strange town, but for what reason? Was it the dampening effect of the rain, after our three weeks' drought, or the fact that we found ourselves running through the market, giving chase to boys who had fired at us with water pistols? Was there something bizarre about meeting cows inside the crumbling Byzantine church? Was the great statue of Atatürk which overlooked the town particularly sinister, or did the central, dominating fortress create an unusually oppressive atmosphere? Should we have expected to have stones slung at our backs by boys with catapults and to be the only tourists staying at the Turistik Otel, and probably in the whole of Bitlis? Were these the normal features of local life or had we simply picked a bad day? We certainly felt odd ourselves - Ashley not yet one hundred per cent physically and his other half complaining of stomach pains, we must have presented a sorry sight. Perhaps the water and stones were aimed at making us laugh?

There is a point on every journey, however, where morale reaches a low ebb and it just so happened that at

Bitlis ours, not to put too fine point on it, had hit rock-bottom. It was difficult to pin the causes down. Undeniably we had anxieties about the car - whenever we stopped it became an instant source of entertainment for curious young lads who couldn't keep their hands to themselves - but that alone could not have dragged us down. Perhaps forty-six days on the road was the natural limit of our endurance, or even sanity. Should we do the previously unthinkable thing and turn back now, before we were interned in some Kurdish lunatic asylum, or were we already too late? Had we been seeing Bitlis through mad eyes, implanting esoteric qualities, imagining strange events where none existed?

The Turistik Otel confirmed our fears. Each time we climbed its stairs past the wall-size poster of the Matterhorn (arguably the best feature of the hotel) and the faded one of a monstrously enlarged, chubby baby (for which the Turks seemed to have a passion) and were greeted in our room by the muddled information board, we suffered all the symptoms of chronic mental deterioration - and an agonising succession of disorientation and advanced dyslexia. However hard we tried, we could read no more sense into the notice than the following:

Turistik Otel

- Check Out time: 12 A.M.

The Full price Wilipe charged if the room is not vosoted up to 12 A.M.

- Please ask a safe deposit pox for your volu ciles othes Whe the manafene to can not be held rebonsiple.

- Pleo-se make cap planias to the giren adres belon müdüriyet.

Bitlis - Turkey
Reom No: 102
Two bed: 1600
Teshin: 150

... and we hadn't touched a drop for weeks.

There is nothing like a night in Bitlis to spur you on to pastures new. Naturally we had dispelled the treacherous thought of turning homeward, and no sooner had we left the town than we were focusing attention, with fresh enthusiasm, on our next objective - Nemrut Dagi. For weeks we had been gazing avidly at a couple of impressive photographs which depicted the unusual summit of this great mountain, and now we could hardly wait to see it for ourselves.

It was more than a day's drive away, but with Diyarbakir as a convenient interim goal we sped westwards, crossing the series of streams which flow southwards into the upper Tigris, draining the Guneydogu Toroslar, the range of mountains to which Nemrut belongs. At first we wound our way along a narrow basalt gorge where men were battering huge lumps of rock into roadstone and children offered walnuts to passing motorists. Then we crossed fertile valleys planted with tobacco and cotton, between slopes of red and green volcanic rocks. There were wide, gravelly rivers and there were tiny white wiggles of streams, depositing salts as they trickled down from high springs. We passed pretty little haystacks with thatched, sloping roofs. Flat-roofed houses were crowned with drying bundles of stripped tobacco stalks and adorned with strings of the leaves, hanging like giant necklaces from the little walls.

'Holy oil wells!' said Ashley suddenly, recalling a certain television series as we passed the turning to Batman; just a few miles from Turkey's oil production centre. From there a pipeline runs westwards to Iskenderun, nearly 300 miles away on the Mediterranean coast, close to Syria. To the south of Batman, only 70 or 80 miles away down the Tigris valley, lay the adjacent oil fields of north-eastern Syria and northern Iraq, each country pumping its resources independently across hundreds of miles of its own territory, and all because political boundaries have no regard for geological ones.

As we crossed the wide Batman River, another tributary of the Tigris, and looked beyond its single-arched stone bridge, built in 1147 and now under repair, the flat valley was a carpet of cotton plantations, rolled out as far as the eye could see - which was not a great distance and was decreasing by the minute. What had begun as a pleasant breeze - welcome now that we were below 3,000 feet again- was rapidly developing into a severe dust storm. Skinny donkeys took shelter from the southerly gusts behind hummocky hills, and when we stopped for lunch, imprisoned in our sand-blasted little refuge, we watched some weary, windswept shepherds, heads bowed against the blast, guiding their fat-tailed flocks down from the hills. One of the men broke ranks to come and look at us. We greeted one another and exchanged smiles but there was something uncanny about his visit. He wanted no food, he made none of the familiar requests for cigarettes or pencils, nor did he take advantage of the leeward shelter of the car. He simply hovered, with a look of horror in his eyes, peering in at each window in turn as though we had just dropped out of the sky from some distant planet and were drawing him towards us by some strange and irresistible force. As though entranced, he circled us for ten or fifteen minutes, succeeding only in making us increasingly uncomfortable. It was enough to put me off my lunch entirely. I began to wonder how captive animals, under public scrutiny, could possibly enjoy feeding time if their feelings were anything like mine. Ashley, munching uninhibitedly, seemed to have the secret. 'Just ignore him,' he said, reaching towards my lunch, 'and eat that sandwich before someone else does.' As if by magic, the shepherd disappeared into the haze as mysteriously as he had arrived.

Towards Diyarbakir the visibility was restricted to 200 yards and the pale sun, like a tiny white moon, peered at us dimly from the swirling grey-brown atmosphere. Breathing pure dust, not air, we battled against the sidewind to keep the car on the narrow road, made narrower by piles of surfacing grit, banked up for miles along the southern side. Soon we had crossed the Dicle (Tigris), passed the entrance to Diyarbakir's university of the river's name, and were entering the old town. With a population approaching a quarter of a million Diyarbakir, not unexpectedly, had a Turistik Otel which was somewhat larger, more expensive and more popular than Bitlis' little namesake. Consequently we chose an alternative which was nearer the centre and not far from one tier of the triple black basalt walls for which the town is famous. Three miles in length, up to 40 feet high, with five gates and numerous towers, the dark medieval ramparts loomed above the busy centre, but the spirit of the lively town was undiminished by their omnipresence. At the foot of one inner section men sat outside in the warm evening air in a pleasant little tea-garden. Not far away restaurateurs stood on the pavement, outside windows dressed unappetisingly with sheeps' heads, and made generally fruitless attempts to entice potential diners into their spicy-smelling lairs. The bazaar was interesting, lively and crowded with stalls of fresh fruit, such as melons and grapes, grown on the rich volcanic soil around the town and watered by the local springs.

The people were friendly, welcoming and. unlike Bitlis' inhabitants, apparently without catapults. We no longer felt like aliens in another world, misunderstood and unaccepted. Here we seemed to have returned from the mountainous, eastern wilderness to a more cosmopolitan and civilised world, where tourists went unhindered and hotels had hot running water. We even had our first bath since leaving home!

Our relief proved premature. In the morning we found the windscreen daubed with mud, artistically smeared by small grubby hands. However, a crowd of willing boys soon gathered and one or two, possibly with guilty consciences, helped to sponge away the dirt, while the others danced around yelling, 'OK Inglish! OK!', screaming with laughter and fiddling with door-handles, mirrors and lights in the usual unstoppable fashion. If not clean, it was all good-humoured fun, and we set off in good spirits.

Between the Tigris at Diyarbakir and the Euphrates near Adiyaman lay the lava-strewn upland surrounding Karaca Dag, an extinct volcano of 6,400 feet. There sheep and even camels found scant pasture amongst the rocks and boulders, and the clusters of low, flat-roofed houses formed sombre villages, their dark stone almost indistinguishable from the stacks of dung. Once more the basalt-dominated scenery reminded me of Iceland. Near the town of Karacadag, however, we passed lorries with great, leaning loads of cotton-filled sacks, and an oasis of tomatoes and cotton fields, fed by springs, flourished in isolation - a few green acres in a rocky desert. Men in traditional white, shoulder-length head-dresses gave an Arabic quality to the scene, compounded by the sight of camels which kindled in us thoughts of Syria and beyond. Then we were descending into the beautiful fertile valley of the Euphrates: there lay acres of rich, dark soil, freshly ploughed, and lush, green cotton plantations, close to the wide river. As we climbed away to the west we looked back over a wonderful patchwork of gentle hills and fields and then turned excitedly towards our next, loftier, goal.

At the 'Otel-Camping' in Kahta, the setting-off point for Nemrut Dagi, a smooth-talking Turk sat us down and gave us glasses of çay, indisputable signs of impending sales chat. We knew that there were 26 miles of steep, unsurfaced road lying between us and the famous summit - the question was, 'Would the car be up to such a challenge?' With our minds already half-way up the mountain, we listened with less than full attention to the man's patter, to his prediction that we should never make it in *that*, and to the remainder of the flowery speech which veiled his well-worn theme of: 'Wouldn't you rather buy tickets for my minibus trip?'

The effect was, I fear, not what he desired. Perversely encouraged by his unconvincing words, we set out in the afternoon in our own car hoping to reach the 7,054 feet summit by nightfall. It was a gruelling climb, even for the four-wheel-drive vehicles recommended, but we saw it as an unprecedented opportunity for the 2CV to prove itself. If it could struggle, fully laden, up this inhospitable mountain track, surely it could take us anywhere - from Kathmandu to the Karakoram Highway. This was a challenge not to be missed. In addition, at the peak of Nemrut Dagi stood a most astounding sight, reputedly most spectacular at sunset and at sunrise. We planned both to arrive in time for sunset and to stay until the dawn.

Four miles up the lonely track, however, with 22 miles and two and a half hours of daylight to go, our hopes were dashed. There, like a spectre in the darkness, loomed the solitary figure of a broken-down motorcycle and its helpless rider who, armed only with a spanner and an oily rag, was understandably eager to flag us down. For over half an hour Ashley struggled with the filthy chain and various pieces of the machine which should not have been, but were, detached from it. Meanwhile the young Turk, who was about as practical as a water melon, tottered about distractedly in his high-heeled shoes, scratching his head. Then, as luck would have it, a car approached, trundling down in its own little dust storm from the nearby village of Narince, and the driver (whom I could have kissed) by an almost miraculous offer of help, saved Ashley from his dismal fate.

Now it was a race against time. The track became increasingly steep as we roared slowly upwards, in first gear most of the time, urging the poor car on, winding and wending our way between potholes and boulders. Adrenalin coursed through our bodies as frantically as the 'Super' petrol flowed into the two little overworked cylinders. Together we struggled on until, after two and a half hours and in the gloom of dusk, we could see the end of the track and the cloudy windswept summit, towering menacingly above. The final slope was so steep that we were forced to weave about simply to keep up momentum but at last, within a hair's breadth of stalling, we juddered to the top, barely able to sigh with relief. We had made it - ours must be the first 2CV to reach the summit!

But as we came to a halt outside the mountain hut, we had to laugh - for there beside us was a Citroën Acadiane (a Dyane van) which had beaten us to the top!

There is something about the chance meeting of Citroën owners at 7,000 feet on a bleak Turkish mountain which promotes instant camaraderie, and in the warmth of the mountain hut-cum-café the evening soon passed in the company of the young Belgian couple and of the three resident Turks. Outside the cold wind howled around the cloud-enveloped mountain and hopes of a splendid sunset had long since vanished. At half past eight we crawled into our sleeping bags on the wooden bunks and prayed for a beautiful dawn.

We were up again at 4 a.m., brought to life by glasses of sweet, black tea, and went stumbling up the final ascent to the very top, the cold air rasping in our lungs. A minibus had already arrived and its passengers, in remarkably good spirits considering what time they had had to rise in order to come up from Kahta that morning, were hopping about the mountain top or, swathed in blankets, were sheltering from the chilling wind behind the statues. For these monuments were the essence of Nemrut's magic: here, at the mountain's summit, was an enormous artificial tumulus, nearly 200 feet tall and 500 feet in diameter, and around it, to east and west, stood the colossal stone statues of ancient gods, fashioned some 2,000 years ago to surround the tomb of King Antiochus I of Commagene. On the eastern terrace the seated figures, almost 30 feet high and built of massive limestone blocks, were ranged above us, while their toppled yet majestic heads, themselves 5 or 6 feet tall, looked with us towards the east. Now, as we huddled together in the half-light, there was an atmosphere of tense excitement. Eyes and cameras focused on the dim horizon, waiting for the magic moment when the sun would creep above the distant line. Any second now the great orb would return, illuminating the ancient figures as it had done three-quarters of a million times before ...

... and then it came. The cries went up, the shutters clicked as the first pink rays, like footlights, cast tongues of shadow on the mountain top and touched the faces of Zeus, Apollo, Tyche, Antiochus and Hercules with an eerie, rosy light. All around us the pale, cloudless sky of watery blue hung like a great heavenly sheet of litmus paper, its edges tinged with pink as though dipping below the surface of an acid world. The Turks leaped from rock to rock, yelling and flapping their arms like flightless birds, with blankets draped like useless wings across their shoulders between outstretched hands. Then, as the sun rose bringing warm relief, it seemed to draw the huddled bodies from their make-do shelters until soon we were all on our feet,

Nemrut Dagi, Turkey

emerging into the light like hibernating animals in spring. Gradually the pink glow faded and the statues became bathed in a golden light. Below us the mountains seemed to roll away into the distance, layer upon layer, casting shadows on one another like the folds of a great king's robes trailing across the landscape below a summit throne.

There was a universal mood of wonder and of joy - a sense of awe at the skill and imagination of the ancient people of Commagene and elation at the power of such a beautiful dawn to unite us, a small band of strangers, on this remote, mysterious mountain. It was an emotional blend of fellowship, achievement, privilege and sheer happiness which created one of the most memorable experiences of our journey.

We all breakfasted cheerfully at the café, swapping travellers' tales and dunking the stale bread in our tea. Then we began the descent, our 2CV and the Belgian Acadiane in convoy, rattling down the stony track together beneath a glorious blue sky. At the bottom we had to part, for they were bound for Adiyaman, we for Gaziantep.

On we went, southwards across the prairie-like landscape, passing through Urfa and then travelling westwards to cross the Euphrates again. Cereal fields gave way to cotton plantations and those in turn to orchards and groves of pistachio nut trees. All the way to Gaziantep, the 'pistachio capital of Turkey', the scenery rolled on past us as though it, not we, were moving, while our thoughts remained far away, four or five thousand feet higher, on the summit of Nemrut Dagi.

CHAPTER 7

To have landed in an establishment which not only served breakfast but also included it in the room tariff was unusual for us, and we sat in the hotel dining-room alone and expectantly to see what would be offered. The other guests had evidently either left soon after dawn or knew something about the breakfast which we did not. We were embarking on a round of postcard writing when the tray arrived and was dumped unceremoniously in front of us. On it was some tea, bread, jam, goat's cheese and olives. Had the bread been fresh, the cheese visible without the aid of a microscope, and the shrivelled olives not served in the remains of someone else's jam, it might have been a good meal. As it was, a good quantity of tea was required in order to wash it down, and, for such a volume, the two dainty glasses provided were hopelessly inadequate. The waiter was clearly unused to foreigners who started the day with the contents of three-quarter pint enamel mugs inside them, and by the time he had been asked to refill the glasses for the third time, it was obvious what he thought of us.

Having bought some groceries to use up our remaining Turkish coins, we approached the Post Office counter to despatch some letters and cards. We had some difficulty in explaining to the assistant that the UK was in Europe and not America, but she finally sold us some stamps of the correct value and we added 'EUROPE' in bold letters to the addresses, wondering where our previous correspondence had ended up, assuming all the Turkish Post Office staff were equally competent at geography.

After extricating ourselves from the Gaziantep one-way system we found that we were on the Kilis road, which, by sheer good fortune, was where we wanted to be. The Syrian border was less than 40 miles from Gaziantep and we anticipated an hour's drive. Trundling happily along at a good pace between the vineyards and the groves of olives and pistachios, we came abruptly upon a crawling queue of traffic which we joined. Partly from impatience but chiefly to satisfy our curiosity as to the cause of the tail-back we gradually worked our way up the line, overtaking whenever possible, until we reached the front. Ahead stretched a long, slow convoy of army vehicles.

Somewhat optimistically Ashley tried repeatedly to jump this queue too but the rearguard jeep reacted by swerving in front of us and finally by halting in the middle of the road. At this point a formidable-looking officer jumped down from his seat and marched up to our car. Pressing his palms firmly against the passenger door he glowered in through the side window at me and, in a monotone of controlled anger, he subjected us to a stream of broken English, from which we extracted the following: Difficult... please... work ... unpleasant... helpful... patient.' It was not hard to see his point. We gave him pacifying nods and smiles and he marched back to the jeep.

Obediently we trickled along behind them for a few miles more, until eventually the convoy turned down a dusty track and the jeep stopped again. This time, in attempting to jump down from the vehicle in a dignified manner, the officer tripped and narrowly escaped landing flat on his face to the obvious, though smothered, amusement of his junior fellow passengers, not to mention ourselves. It was clearly not his day. All the more admirable therefore was his astounding display of self-control in thanking us (as far as we could understand) for being patient and in wishing us 'Bon Voyage' or words to that effect. To produce such apparent politeness in the face of adversity required enviable discipline or the surreptitious inclusion of a number of derogatory terms which escaped our translation.

We reached the Turkish border beyond Kilis at 11.20 a.m. and managed to pass through the police and passport controls reasonably quickly. As soon as we were told to go to the customs, however, the entire operation dissolved into a state of lunchtime inactivity and, resigning ourselves to an hour's wait, we moved the car into the shade and ate some bread and cheese. Meanwhile a Syrian coach disgorged a troupe of teenage dancers who entertained us by rehearsing under the trees to the rowdy accompaniment of drums and pipes. Other victims of the midday delays sat on their luggage clapping, cheering, and opening Pepsi bottles, their caps catapulting across the dusty car-park.

After lunch a non-uniformed customs official came up, took a brief look at the car but not at its contents, and waved us on our way to Syria. The no-man's-land between the two border posts was not wide and five minutes later we saw the welcoming signs - a pleasant change for, unlike the Turks, the Syrians had taken the trouble to translate the notices into French. The prospects of easier communications shimmered like a mirage ahead.

Naturally, the Syrian border officials were out of step

with the Turks and were just beginning their lunch break as we arrived. There was no shade for the car so we propped the remains of the Sealink ferry timetables across the windscreen, opened the windows and waited. When business restarted the officer wanted to see the car's log-book and we had a short panic, exacerbated by the heat and flies, while we failed to locate it. Fortunately, after turning various bags and boxes inside out, we found it on the floor between our seats. This border post was not on the major route between Turkey and Syria (the coastal route through Iskenderun is more important) but, despite the lack of traffic, it still took us three and a half hours to cross! A contributory factor was the announcement that we must each change $100 into Syrian pounds prior to entry, but if there was one rule we had learnt to obey it was not to believe everything we were told. Ashley, having previously passed through Syria with no such restriction, and now with no intention of spending such vast sums during our planned stay of less than a week, took exception to this information. After long but remarkably amicable negotiations between the officers and ourselves an independent arbiter in the form of a German student from Damascus appeared on the scene and confirmed that it was indeed a new regulation. (It was only later that we spotted the smudged stamps on our Syrian visas which, had they been legible, would have warned us about the $100 restriction.)

Meanwhile a collection of customs men had gathered eagerly around a group of Turks whose sacks of merchandise, chiefly trousers and jackets, were lying in the dust. After a great deal of arm-waving and heated conversation (you would have thought they were haggling at an outdoor market rather than examining imported goods) the group broke up, one of the customs officials walking away contentedly with a new pair of jeans under his arm! Nearby several plump pedestrians were loading their belongings, great bundles of goods done up in blankets and rope, into the gaping boots of bald-tyred taxis - the sort of large, half-wrecked American model more familiar on the losing side of a movie car chase.

It was a relief to be back on the road again, even though the dry plains between the border and Aleppo lacked something in the way of scenic beauty. A number of curious ramshackle workshops created from the bodyshells of old buses marked the outskirts of Syria's second largest city, but the centre was greener and more attractive. We were minus a proper street map but Ashley was confident that we could not fail to end up near the citadel, nor to relocate the hotel where he and the other lads had stayed four years before - a sure sign that we were about to become hopelessly lost. To add to the confusion of the traffic, Aleppo appeared to share the belief of the Thessalonika Road Traffic Department that road signs can seriously damage your health and should be extinguished at all cost.

Having circumnavigated the public park at least three times and interrogated numerous people who spoke either no English or French, a little English or 'un peu français', we eventually tracked down a sufficiently small hotel room and a side-street parking place. Proceedings were so unhurried at the reception that there was ample time to fall into conversation with two people who were lounging near the desk. There was a sympathetic British (part-Turkish) businessman who had just suffered a gruelling journey by plane and bus from London via Amman and Damascus. While he was complaining that he had been unable to find his usual four-star accommodation, Ashley was hesitant to admit that our difficulty had been locating a sufficiently spartan hotel.

Meanwhile I was struggling to converse in French

with a floral-aproned old lady who played some part in running the place and who periodically puffed cigarette smoke into my face. Otherwise she was perfectly friendly, until I told her that we had driven from England at which she looked aghast and in a breathless ascending scale, so characteristically French, she cried, *'Mais, vous me dîtes qu'il y a une* route?!' and then sat shaking her head and mumbling to herself, *'Incroyable! Savais pas. Là!'*

Aleppo (or Haleb) is believed to be the place where Abraham grazed his cows - hence the city's name which is the Semitic term for milk. Although dairy farming is not locally predominant now, Aleppo lies in a rich agricultural area extending eastwards to the Euphrates Valley and producing grapes, wheat, barley, cotton, fruit and nuts. Owing to its historical reputation as a commercial centre between the Mediterranean and the East, Aleppo has long been famous for its textile trade, and industries such as cotton-spinning, silk-weaving and fabric-printing are still important. Damascus and Aleppo have been rivals for centuries and controversy over the origins of Aleppo continues, the Damascans naturally claiming that the capital is older than Aleppo while Aleppans maintain that their own city has the longer history. What is certain is that the earliest known reference to Haleb is found in texts of the third millennium BC while some Tell Halaf pottery of the sixth millennium BC has even been found in the city. As long as the magnificent citadel of Aleppo remains on its ancient hilltop site the mystery looks set to stay, for if there is one place where archaeologists would love to excavate it is the very mound on which the citadel stands. Here the Hittites built their acropolis in the second millennium BC and later it was the site of Byzantine fortifications before the construction of the present citadel in the twelfth century AD.

In the old quarter of the city lie not only the citadel

but also some of the Middle East's most famous covered bazaars which we were eager to see. Next morning we obtained from the Tourist Information Office a street plan, which was coded in a way guaranteed to perplex all Europeans. For instance, the unsuspecting tourist, quite reasonably setting out towards the top left-hand corner of the map (so to speak), in order to find the mosque listed 'C3', was unwittingly embarking on a wild-goose chase, ending up at 'G12'. For, strangely, the vertical grid lines were numbered from 1 to 14 towards the *left* and the horizontal lines were labelled as follows: ABGDHWZCTYK. No doubt there was some logical Arabic basis for the code and at least the west to east direction was maintained from left to right, even if the numbering was not.

Deciphering accomplished, we went on foot to visit the citadel. It was an awesome sight from the outside: surrounded by a deep, dry moat, the lower slopes of the hill are faced with huge stone slabs to form a curved and massive wall which rises steeply fifty feet or so to the upper fortifications. The entrance is equally spectacular with its solid-looking gatehouse towering above the moat on a bridge of tall stone arches. After major restoration in the sixteenth century the defences of this stronghold must have seemed impenetrable, but the citadel has suffered from numerous invasions, attacks and earthquakes and is now badly in need of the current round of renovations. The gate bears an inscription of the Mameluke Sultan Khalid, who also did some restoration after the Mongols sacked the city in the mid-thirteenth century.

We had forgotten to take our sunglasses and the glare of the hot white limestone walls dazzled us. Stumbling about amongst the tumbled masonry on the hilltop we caught glimpses of little lizards darting away from us in fright. We negotiated numerous staircases and cooled off in the shade of the old bath house - an interesting collection of little rooms, some having domed roofs so speckled with tiny round windows that they reminded us of big flour-shakers.

Outside again, we were just looking out from the upper ramparts at the monochrome view of the city's concrete and limestone buildings when a loud noise almost made us jump into the moat. It was the midday call to prayer, issuing from a loudspeaker a few feet from our ears. Two or three workmen, their heads loosely wrapped in drooping *kiffeyeh* (headcloths), put down their tools and made their way through the parched grass to the little mosque. We headed for some shade too and found ourselves above the entrance to the citadel, in a large hall of breathtaking proportions with an intricately carved and brightly painted ceiling high above us. This was undoubtedly the most majestic and beautifully preserved part of the citadel, with tall columns rising from a patterned floor of variegated marble tiles to the rich overhead designs in green, gold and red. The courtyard outside had doorways carved from contrasting blocks of basalt and limestone which interlocked perfectly like the pieces of an ornate black and white jigsaw puzzle.

As we were leaving to go to the souk we were befriended by a student of English who was determined to practise his conversation on us. Clinging as persistently as a large limpet, he was in no mind to be dislodged and the three of us moved inseparably through the narrow streets, looking at sheepskins and leather goods, brass ornaments and cooking pots, until we had all grown weary of:

'You from London? Yes, London very good place. My frien', he stay in Sussex.'

'Oh, which town in Sussex?'

'Yes, Sussex town, very nice place... you want to buy

Peanut-brittle vendor, Aleppo souk

souvenirs? I show you my frien' who sell very cheap gifts. Special price to you Inglish frien's.'

'No, thank you, we don't need souvenirs, but it was very nice meeting you...' and as we waved goodbye Ashley led me hurriedly down the nearest alley into a forest of lacy knickers. We had accidentally stumbled into the underwear 'department' of the bazaar and were surrounded by overweight women and stacks and rails of frilly red pants and large black bras which the shopkeepers eagerly held out to tempt us. We beat a rapid retreat into a street lined with shoe shops, but thereafter each time we passed local ladies modestly attired in long dresses and veils it was difficult to stop imagining exotic lingerie underneath.

Unlike the covered Grand Bazaar of Istanbul, where most of the shoppers are tourists and where carpets and gifts abound, Aleppo souk has more of a traditional layout comprising distinct zones of shops. There is an area of streets and alleys selling nothing but dressmaking fabrics, another patch with butchers' shops alone, while jewellery, sheepskins, fancy underwear and blacksmiths all have their individual locations, just as in countless souks from Marrakesh to Muscat.

Our noses soon led us past sacks full of spices, dried fruit and nuts and towards the smells of cooking. We stopped at a stall to have some kebabs; with an enormous knife the dripping meat was sliced from the vertical spit and rolled up in thin, flat, round bread with a dash of spicy yoghurt and chopped tomatoes. Just as we were tucking into this mouthwatering meal of mutton, we were horrified to see two poor sheep being dragged along a few feet from where we stood; before we could avert our eyes the knife had descended, their throats were slit, and the poor animals were skinned and strung up in the butcher's opposite.

Lunching in an abattoir was not what we had planned, and we left hurriedly to continue our tour. We soon lost all sense of direction but we were having fun, experiencing once more the magical blend of sights, smells and sounds which characterise the souks of the Middle East. We found shops with shelves stacked from floor to ceiling with nothing but big cubes of brownish-green soap. Others were selling the most revolting-looking pink sweets, and roasted chick-peas in multi-coloured sugar coatings. In another street we heard the loud repetitive 'thwack' of a man making woollen flock by thrashing a sheepskin, laid on the floor, with a long piece of thick wire. All around him were stacks of sheepskins in various shades from cream to deep brown and in the next-door shop an old bearded man, fingering his worry beads, sat cross-legged on his fleecy pile like a Chancellor of the Aleppan Woolsack.

More by luck than good judgment, we emerged from the labyrinthine lanes of the souk, past the eighth-century Omayyad Mosque, into the open air and the hooting traffic. Men with wooden barrows were peddling popular snacks, such as strings of toffee-coated walnuts which bore an unfortunate resemblance to congealed chunks of meat on a skewer. Enticed neither by these nor by the offer of a mound of luminous green confectionery, we plumped for a safe kilo of apples instead. Just outside the souk there were some barrows loaded with fresh pink pistachio nuts and shaded by umbrellas but the aromas of assorted vegetable and animal matter decaying on the ground around the market stalls, and the sight of men swinging transparent bags oozing with the less attractive cuts of sheep were enough to send us scurrying to the shade of the museum gardens where we could enjoy the apples in peace. No sooner had we settled on a wooden bench than the gardener, whom we had seen watering the bushes, suddenly decided it was a good moment to hose down the seats. The prospect of a cold shower was not entirely unattractive, but our camera gear might not have been so appreciative, so we jumped up and headed for the safety of the Hotel Afamia. We had the distinct impression that the Syrian people were going out of their way to deter us from eating.

There were other disconcerting features of the city - the blatantly military style of the khaki uniforms worn by all the schoolchildren we saw, and the large number of armed but non-uniformed men lurking in the streets. Furthermore, these were normal traits of Syrian life and not peculiar to Aleppo.

We wanted to see the coast, for it was a long time since we had bathed in the sea and Ashley, on his previous visit, had taken the fast, inland route through Syria. We took the dual carriageway as for Damascus for thirty miles or so before turning off towards Lattakia. After the monotonous traffic of Renault 12s in eastern Turkey, it was like a breath of fresh air to travel on Syrian roads and see a healthy variety of cars again.

Even in Aleppo we had noticed an interesting selection of old models such as Austin Cambridges, Somersets and ancient Mercedes.

To the south of the city, imprinted on the flat landscape, were village clusters of little igloo-style huts made of sun-baked mud and straw, as well as less attractive constructions of corrugated iron and wood. The dusty scene of stubbly red fields was only occasionally interrupted by an olive grove or a little field of maize, but as we started climbing towards the west the gentle slopes were greener with mixed orchards of figs and apples. The limestone of the hills had been gouged by a number of deep quarries, producing gravel and roadstone, and a cement works exhaled clouds of dust across the road. If the signposts had not already been in a state of dismal dilapidation we might have blamed the chalky coating for their obscurity. Fortunately the paucity of roads rendered signposts virtually redundant anyway: we were unlikely to be on a route which did not take us to Lattakia, provided it was not leading to Damascus.

We felt the car relaxing as we came over the rocky ridge and began our descent into the long, broad valley of the Orontes, spread out below us in a vast and breathtaking patchwork of greens and browns. It was the sort of view you expect from a low-flying aircraft, not a 2CV. Our sympathy with the car was so deeply rooted now that we were already looking miles ahead to the western side of the valley in anticipation of a steep climb over Jebel al Ansariye. As we struggled up from the fertile plains we were, by some quirk of boundary designation, approaching Turkey again. Despite this proximity we found the reactions of the village folk remarkably different: across the border we had generally been greeted with friendly waves or at least threatened with showers of rocks by the younger members of the communities. The Syrians simply stood and stared, or ignored us entirely. We should have been relieved by this more peaceful reception but we found those expressionless gazes, harbouring we knew not what thoughts, somewhat disconcerting.

Soon a roadside stall attracted us, not because its apples were particularly special (on the contrary, we appeared to have discovered a new source of supermarket Golden Delicious), but because of the intriguing method of weighing them. The vendor was attired in the standard style of the middle-aged rural male of this area - baggy trousers, called *cheroual* (the capacious kind with the bottom hanging down to the knees), with a western-style suit jacket topped by a *kiffeyeh* (headscarf). His scales were made of strips of old car tyres dangling from a stick and, after a spot of haggling, we came away with a quantity of fruit which was equivalent in weight (and probably in taste) to the chunks of limestone he was using as measures.

Lurching our way round the pine-clad bends, avoiding the oncoming donkeys and their riders returning from the orchards, we were now descending towards Lattakia. Patches of prickly pears along the roadside promised more tropical climes and we longed to swim in the warm Mediterranean and bask on a beautiful beach.

The reality of the Syrian coast was less romantic. A few days in Aleppo had confirmed our view that city visits were palatable only when diluted with generous quantities of more peaceful environments. Our concern for the car's safety was not least among considerations and so it was that we bypassed the centre of Lattakia, Syria's principal port, justifying our philistine evasion of its Roman ruins with the preservation of our peace of mind. Still consoling ourselves with the prospect of a pleasant seashore we followed the coast road southwards, looking out in vain for a tranquil spot.

Baniyas, marked on our map as a minor coastal town,
looked promising as a little resort but when we found on
arrival that its main attraction was a large oil refinery we
decided against lingering. On the other hand, it was a
long time since breakfast and Ashley's thoughts of food
were now taking priority over those of beaches.

Before the shops closed for the afternoon I hopped into
an egg-merchant's. (Like all the neighbouring shops, it
opened directly on to the street and would soon be totally
obscured by the thundering descent of a large metal door,
like a noisy roll-top desk.) Apart from a small cage
containing a rather scrofulous collection of hens, I was
surrounded by nothing but six feet tall tower-blocks of
stacked egg-trays, looming to the ceiling like a miniature
Manhattan. I was so overcome by the dizzy heights, and
so busy wondering how the eggs at the bottom could
possibly survive the alternative perils of cracking under
the strain or becoming fossilised before use, that I almost
forgot why I was there - despite my surroundings - but my
petty purchase of six eggs seemed suddenly insignificant.
Understandably dismayed by it, the merchant flung a
complaining chicken on the scales in an attempt to make
the transaction worth his while. Imagining Ashley's
reaction were I to return to the car with this scrawny
animal, dead or alive, I hastily paid for my miserable
half dozen and fled.

The scented smoke from an outdoor barbecue lured
us into a scruffy little restaurant for lunch. We sat at a
Formica-topped table in a sea of sawdust and waited
while the smells of our cooking köfte kebabs wafted in
through the open doors. The only other customers were
two lorry drivers who received their food long before us,
despite their later arrival, but who touchingly offered to
share their meal with us. It was typical of the countless
gestures of hospitality and generosity shown to us during

our travels in the Middle East. Happily, this is the memory of the restaurant which dominates and not our less appealing recollections of the sanitation, on which I shall not (and did not) dwell.

Disappointed that every available stretch of beach was either a deserted but litter-strewn campsite or an unattractive rocky strip too close to the road for comfort, and having almost exhausted the Syrian coast, we rolled into Tartous and decided to stop. In the first hotel we entered by the main road we were shown a good room for 54 SL (£5) but it was early, so we went to survey the rest of the town. A quarter of a mile away we found a long sandy stretch of beach which, like the hotel, was deserted. Overlooking the shore was a modern luxury hotel and further along the coast the small harbour. Despite its potential as a holiday resort, Tartous seemed remarkably quiet and neglected but then it was the beginning of October and already there were cool winds which deterred even us from bathing. However, the most striking feature of the large town was the ubiquitous construction of concrete apartment blocks: presumably in the summer holidaymakers throng there from Damascus and the inland towns (or, we speculated, the expansion may be partly to accommodate Lebanese refugees).

Back at the hotel, we were given the familiar story that the receptionist had made a mistake and that the room cost 70 SL not 54. Fortunately there was an English-speaking man who was able to point us in the direction of some cheaper hotels, so we drove down to the shopping area and decided on the best of three rather dingy enterprises - coincidentally another Hotel Afamia. Characteristically, it was in the throes of construction work, although of a relatively minor nature - in fact the chubby and cheerful landlord and his brother, stripped to their vests and shorts, were erecting a partition wall in the reception area. They were just commencing the first course of breeze-blocks when we arrived, but by the following morning the whole thing appeared to be completed, if somewhat crudely. For us there was a distinct advantage in staying in a concrete hotel with carpetless floors - we had no qualms about setting up our stove and cooking dinner, which in this instance was a memorable concoction of eggs scrambled into thick lentil-soup.

Tartous livened up considerably in the evening when the shops reopened. Our ramblings through the narrow streets took us past a host of small, expensive-looking jewellers, patisseries and tailors. Well-dressed couples were strolling arm-in-arm from one window to another or emerging from shops with beautiful gift-wrapped purchases. It was so unusual to see women, and particularly those of the unveiled variety, that, having seen no indication of a mosque in Tartous, we deduced that it must be a predominantly Christian zone. It was certainly a prosperous place in comparison with the rest of Syria, no doubt because of its Lebanese community. There was an abundance of Lebanese-registered cars (particularly Mercedes) and the Syrian secret police also appeared to be out in force, judging by the number of roaming white Range Rovers which are reputed to be their patrol vehicles. (Not that there was much secrecy about the way they were cruising round the town that evening, like peacocks in full display.) Small groups of burly men, some of whom we overheard speaking an Eastern European language, were treating themselves to slabs of syrup-drenched pastries or stocking up with tins of provisions - they were probably sailors from ships in the port.

In the morning, the ten-year-old boy who had shown us

to our room the previous evening was manning the desk. The engaging grin which greeted us was more than a show of courtesy; and his slow and deliberate attention to detail during the checking-out formalities definitely had an ulterior motive: little Ali was simply overjoyed at our interruption of his geometry homework. Even practising English was more fun than the Theorem of Pythagoras. He contrived to spend at least ten minutes, to our amusement, transferring details from our passports on to a couple of lengthy forms with results such as *'Nationalité:* Brotshesh. *Taille: 5m.'* Considering that the form was in French, his mother tongue was Arabic and he was writing in a third language whose alphabet was different from his own, it was a pretty good effort.

Tartous, although a pleasant enough town, held no particular fascination for us and indeed we should probably have forgotten all about it had not been for its subsequent (admittedly passive) role in the *Achille Lauro* affair; for just ten days after we left, the body of the American hijack victim Klinghoffer was washed ashore there and Tartous suddenly, if briefly, achieved worldwide notoriety.

CHAPTER 8

Our poor car had recently been struggling along on a meagre diet of low-octane petrol and we were intent on perking it up with a slurp of 'Super'. In Syria, however, refuelling is not a simple matter of rolling up at the nearest garage, pressing the '4 star' button and helping yourself to twenty litres. First, catch your fuel station.

It is hard to say how many of the species survive in Syria today, for their camouflage is frequently so successful that we undoubtedly passed by a few unwittingly. They certainly appeared to be rare. In a country notably lacking in road signs of any kind it is not surprising that a petrol station, endeavouring to merge into the scenery, should also be unadvertised. 'Step one' then is to look for no written indication whatsoever. 'Step two' is to keep your eyes peeled for a patch of heavily oil-stained ground. The third point to remember is that if you see a cluster of lorries at the side of the road you are probably on the right track, and if there is a car amongst them too you may even have spotted that rare mutation of the species which produces petrol as well as diesel. (Even so, at the first site we found which met these conditions, we were turned away as it was evidently reserved exclusively for police or military vehicles.) On close inspection you will find that most Syrian petrol stations consist of several dilapidated pumps and a patch of crumbling concrete. Turkish ones were outstanding in comparison - most of those along the main roads had restaurants, toilets and clear signs, even if they did not always have Super. But you can't have everything, and Syrian petrol cost only £1.20 per gallon, whereas the Turkish price was about £1.60.

In the course of our hunt, we had travelled down the coast towards Lebanon and then struck off inland, having no desire to approach Tripoli where, two days earlier, one of the Russian diplomats who had been taken hostage by Moslem extremists had been killed. Just as we turned off the Tartous-Tripoli route roadworks forced us to divert south of the main road through a little village and past a large enclosure where guns, rockets and radar scanners were pointing menacingly towards the south and west. We hurried eastwards.

The newly-surfaced road was a good smooth piece of dual carriageway and because it was Friday there was not much traffic. We were soon climbing away from the fertile coastal plain into basaltic hills, sadly strewn with plastic bags which had blown from roadside rubbish tips.

Predictably, there was no signpost for Krak des Chevaliers, the Crusader castle for which we were aiming. Ashley recognised the turning, however, and then it was a matter of winding up through the hills for about eight miles and urging the car up the final and steepest part of the ascent. Although Krak des Chevaliers stands on a prominent rocky rise of basalt and commands views over the surrounding country to three sides, it was not built on the highest ground in the area. As a consequence, not only did the castle lie hidden from sight as we approached from the west but its position also permits a good overall view of the stronghold for those camera-

Krak des Chevaliers, Syria

happy travellers who, like us, continue further up the track.

From there we could appreciate the enormous scale of the construction, with its colossal outer walls separated by a moat from the inner battlements and beset with massive round towers. There is nothing delicate about the design, no pretence about its purpose: Krak des Chevaliers was built uninhibitedly to be as impenetrable a fortress as its tough limestone and eleventh and twelfth-century workmanship could create. It is a tribute to both that after eight centuries the Krak is still uniquely imposing. Its size and setting make it, without doubt, the most impressive castle we have seen.

Scrambling over the battlements, climbing up stairways, peeping into dark holes and delving into dungeons, I was not transported back to the Crusaders' days but was reliving childhood holidays in Wales, exploring every nook and cranny of Manorbier Castle and Pembroke, Harlech and Caernarvon. I only had to step inside the great stone walls to feel again that instinct for adventure, that urge to creep down every passage as though beckoned by some irresistible but elusive shadow, or as if, in a quest for hidden treasure, I could not rest until every dark corner had been investigated. We spent two intriguing hours dodging in and out of all kinds of rooms until we had exhausted every inch of the castle. We climbed the tower of the Master's Lodge, we entered the cool Chapel, saw the soldiers' dormitories and descended to the large vaulted storage rooms with their rows of giant clay pots, long empty.

Krak des Chevaliers was built by the emir of Aleppo in 1031 and expanded and rebuilt by the Knights Hospitallers who held it between 1142 and 1271. Much of the restoration was done in 1936, but still more is required. Sadly, the whole place was dotted with litter and it seemed a great shame that the entrance fee of ten pence could not be increased (at least for foreign visitors) to a more useful sum and the proceeds put towards the upkeep of the grounds and the building. Notwithstanding the national aversion to informative signs, the benefits of one or two explanatory notices plus a board announcing the turning from the main road, and a couple of litter-bins thrown in for good measure, would seem irrefutable. After all, it is one of the most spectacular historical sites which Syria has to offer.

It was busy that Friday afternoon with day-trippers from Damascus They had arrived fresh and air-conditioned in their 'CD'-plated, chauffeur-driven Peugeots or their oil company landcruisers, but were leaving with glistening brows and with hot arms reaching into coolboxes for the cold relief of canned soft drinks. Following a battered old Land-Rover which was bursting with local children, we bounced down the hill, windows open, enjoying the wind and the dubious pleasure of our lukewarm water-bottle. Overburdened donkeys struggled up the road, passing incongruous, unfinished buildings: simple concrete constructions with a couple of completed and inhabited storeys but with reinforced pillars protruding from the top as though in anticipation of a third floor should, *'Inshallah'*, the need or the money arise.

Homs, the next large town, was heralded by hoardings along the roadside showing faded pictures of oil refineries and petrochemical works and proclaiming their Czechoslovakian sponsorship. On our left bright buses painted like fairground pieces went lurching past, with dark faces peering out through tasselled windows and horns blasting cheerfully. Homs, according to the archaeologist M. V. Seton-Williams, was 'still noted for the fanaticism and turbulence of its inhabitants', implying that their predecessors were far from peaceful. Indeed after the town was taken by the Moslems in AD 636 the population, clinging stubbornly to Christianity, was constantly rebelling until 855 when their greatest uprising took place. The Moslems crushed the rebellion once and for all, executing or deporting all Christians and demolishing every church in Homs except the one which was to be incorporated in the Great Mosque.

We found the main street blocked in the centre of town. There was nothing we could do but halt and sit it out. As though waiting in a country lane for a herd of dairy cows to amble from pasture to parlour, we were surrounded by a slowly moving mass of bodies - except that these were male and human and had just been released from the cinema. Friday afternoon film-going was definitely not a pastime for Moslem women and girls. Its popularity with young men and boys, however, was no doubt related to the scarcity of television sets rather than to the garish, hand-painted boards depicting, larger than life, the unattractive leading actresses. The average Homs man, longing to gaze freely at unattached women, was more likely to find satisfaction on the cinema screen than he was about town. Besides, nothing else was open on Friday afternoon, except for the mosques ...

... and the hotels. We toured half a dozen which ranged from appalling (even by our diminishing standards) to very good, with little variation in price. We picked a room and settled in. At about six o'clock shutters rattled open, people reappeared on the streets, and we went down to join them in our quest for bread. Like the petrol stations, it seemed hard to track down, but it was Friday and only a small proportion of the shops were open. Most were selling ice-creams, cakes or sweets, while the customers were, in general, families indulging in one or more of these coloured confectioneries as a weekend treat. Beneath the intimidating colours of icing and sugar coatings (luminous pink or green) there were some interesting mixtures of nuts, syrup and pastry or simply whole pistachios or almonds. As in Turkey, the patisseries displayed huge round metal trays stacked with slabs of the stickier cakes. Those that had escaped the dyes lightly, with just a sprinkling of green chopped nuts, succeeded in looking quite appetising. All this window shopping, however, found us not a hint of bread and it was only later that we spotted a street vendor's trolley piled high with vast bags of catering dimensions filled with half a dozen tray-sized pieces of pitta bread. It was probably a day or two old and the vendor was refusing to sell the bread piecemeal, so Ashley bought a bag and draped it over his arm like a bundle of chamois-leather (a resemblance which we subsequently discovered was not restricted to appearance).

Our plans had changed and we had decided to visit Palmyra after all. Only a week earlier we had considered that it was too far off our route and that the deviation would have entailed travelling along the same 90 miles stretch of road twice, from and back to Homs. According to our map this was the only surfaced road leading to Palmyra from the west, so that in order to avoid backtracking, we should have had to risk becoming lost or buried on or off a less reliable route across the Syrian desert.

'Now, had we had a Range Rover, this journey would have been a different kettle of fish altogether,' said Ashley longingly; and not for the first or last time on our expedition, he was swept into his rapturous dream world, emitting throaty V-8 engine rumblings and imagining himself with the power of the four-wheel drive, gliding across the sandy wastes like a ship of the desert.

'Sshh! Sshh! Keep your voice down!' I interrupted, thinking of the 2CV which, with its two little cylinders and 602cc was liable to be a bit touchy about such matters. 'Anyway, just imagine the fuel consumption.'

Then the women at the Aleppo Tourist Office assured us that there was now a new asphalt road from Palmyra running south-west to Damascus, so we decided to make the detour after all. We could only allow ourselves one day, because we wanted to arrive in the capital well before the weekend, in order to obtain our Saudi Arabian visas with the least delay.

With the prospect of several days crossing Saudi Arabia looming ever closer and in the knowledge that Ashley would be the only permitted driver there, I drove for most of our journey across the Syrian desert. It was flat and rather monotonous scenery (what did we expect?) but this was only a mild foretaste of the empty expanses to come. We were travelling across the steppes at an altitude of more or less 1,500 feet, with few natural distractions but a sprinkling of low thorn bushes and the distant range of 4,000 feet mountains to the north - Jebels Shomariye, Bil'as, Sha'ar and el Abyad. As for the blue dotted lines on our map, the reality was a north-south series of dry wadis (river beds) almost indistinguishable from the surrounding plain.

The most striking feature of the landscape was quite unnatural, however. The Syrian desert was seething with military activity, like ants on the move. There was hardly a view from the Homs-Palmyra road which did not incorporate a military camp, a tank exercise, a fleet of jeeps, a radar station or a low-flying jet. We began to wonder if we had entered a prohibited zone by mistake but, since none of the operations seemed to be directed at us, we calmly carried on across the gravel plains. We were picking up the Cyprus transmission of the BBC World Service unusually clearly and were listening to the 'Jolly Good Show', with Dave Lee Travis playing jolly bad records - not that we minded what he broadcast, as long as it was different from the limited repertoire of our cassettes.

Perhaps we were too engrossed in the music, or maybe the man was hidden behind the empty oil drums at the side of the road as we drove past, but for whichever reason we failed to spot him until we heard the shouts from behind us; suddenly we were aware of an angry figure in a red and white checked headcloth, bearing an automatic weapon and running along to flag us down. He was not in military uniform, but we had no desire to upset an armed man, whoever he was, and so we screeched to a halt. He approached to ask or tell us something, but communications were hampered by our linguistic separation; it was only when we eventually hit on a pronunciation of Palmyra which he recognised that he was content to let us go. We resolved to keep our eyes peeled in future for collections of oil drums, in case they were the accepted manifestations of military checkpoints. Fortunately, however, we had reached Palmyra before being confronted by any more.

On entering the oasis settlement we felt the relief

presumably experienced in ancient times by the caravan traders who, like us, had just ploughed across the barren desert from Homs (or Emesa, as it used to be called). Thanks to its spring (called Afqa) of slightly sulphurous water, Palmyra has always been a green oasis with groves of date palms - a pleasant watering-hole for travellers and camels. Its original pre-Semitic name of Tadmor (Palmyra is the Greek and Latin form) means the city of the dates and was first recorded as long ago as the nineteenth century BC, on an Akkadian tablet from Cappadocia. Tadmor developed as an international trade centre on the east-west caravan routes and by the first century BC, when the Romans invaded Syria, it controlled most of the trade between the Romans and the Parthians.

For 400 years under the Romans the Palmyrenes' prosperity was undiminished, as a result of this highly organised traffic. Rich citizens such as Marcus Ulpius Yarhai, honoured with statues, financed and led the caravans and owned ships on the Indian Ocean and the Red Sea. Radiating from the city were several trade routes which were protected at certain stations (for example, on the banks of the Euphrates) by troops of Palmyrene archers and which were controlled by Palmyrene commercial settlements at cities along the way. The major route was from the Mediterranean to the Arabian Gulf, via Babylon and Charax (at the mouth of the Tigris) and thence by ship to Scythia; but there was also trade with China via the 'Silk Road' across the plateaux of Asia and a certain amount of traffic to the Red Sea and Egypt. Glassware and statues were among the items arriving from Phoenicia in the west, while spices, pearls, turquoise, dyestuffs, Indian cottons, Chinese silks and a myriad of oriental goods flooded in from Scythia and beyond.

Potential profits were astounding: the Roman customs stationed on the Parthian frontier levied duties of up to 25 per cent and the values of items could increase a hundredfold between the east and Rome. It is not surprising that the Romans and the Palmyrenes were equally eager to hang on to their share of this trading power. Under the Empire its status was that of a merchant republic governed by a senator, but it gained a degree of financial independence in 129 when a certain emperor visited the city which then adopted the name Hadriana Palmyra and became a *civitas libera* ('free city'). At the beginning of the third century, it was given the title *colonia* and exempted from taxes altogether.

For all its bustling past and its present archaeological attractions, we found the place practically deserted. Approaching from the west, we came across the ancient ruins and the Afqa, now overshadowed by a luxury French hotel with an enormous empty car-park. A few hundred yards further on we came to the small romantically named Zenobie Hotel which was displaying a camping sign and looked promising. No one else was camping there but the proprietor said we could pitch our tent in the garden, just over the terrace wall - the garden being the sandy car-park shaded by some acacia trees and palms - and he pointed out the tap and showed us the toilets. Having found this site so close to the ruins there was really no reason to go on to the new town of Palmyra, so we pitched the tent and had a picnic on the terrace. There was something incongruous about sitting on metal chairs with seats of woven plastic at a solid limestone table which had started life as the capital of a Corinthian pillar.

We walked back down the road to reach the Temple of Bel, which is regarded as the most spectacular of the old Palmyrene remains. 'Small is beautiful' was evidently not a slogan which figured prominently in first-century architecture - the outer walls of this sanctuary form a square with sides of 200 m: in other words, enclosing nearly ten acres. Within this paved area there is a banqueting hall, a central cella with a ritual basin for the priests' ablutions, and a sacrificial altar, as well as an archaeologist's office and the scattered remains of a miniature railway. The handful of tiny trucks now discarded and resting in the south-east corner of the temple were presumably used to transport excavated debris to spoil-heaps nearby rather than parties of visiting tourists. (Or was this the secret means by which the Zenobie Hotel had acquired its terrace tables?)

The principal deity of the Palmyrenes was Bol (or Baal) which became Bel by assimilation to the Babylonian god Bel-Marduk. Associated with Bel (like the sun and moon gods worshipped alongside the Phoenician god Baal-Shamen) were Yarhibol (the sun god) and Aglibol (the moon god). It was to Bel and these two acolytes that the great temple was dedicated in AD32.

Bel, Baal or Bol aside, the cella or inner temple is a vast limestone edifice (Palmyra is 99 per cent limestone with the odd exotic piece of granite, which seems to find its way into most of the ancient sites of the Middle East and Turkey); it has pillars 30 or 40 feet high and an adyton (open shrine) at each end. The ceiling of each adyton is beautifully carved from a huge block of stone, one with a geometric design and the other bearing signs of the zodiac. The richness of the carving is one of the most stunning features of the temple: windows, doorways and a number of slabs, standing or fallen, are decorated with grapes, scrolls, palm trees, gods, animals and human figures. Nineteen centuries of natural sand-blasting and burial have produced remarkably little damage to the intricate stonework; but stepping back from the cella reveals its towering prospect, pock-marked by the gouging out of lead from the joints in just the same way as at

Ephesus and Pergamon. (Some of this valuable metal may well have ended up in the Great Mosque at Damascus, because when Walid I had it built in the eighth century he ordered the collection of lead from all over the Middle East).

Having paid for tickets at the temple we were free to roam over the rest of the ancient ruins, so we crossed the road and set off along the Great Colonnade which was originally more than half a mile long and, in the manner of the Arcadian Way at Ephesus, formed the east-west, principal axis of the city. A small girl jumped out at us from behind some tumbled masonry near the eastern end and insisted that we should surrender all pencils and pens immediately. She was a stubborn little ten-year-old who obviously specialised in this kind of ambush and was only deterred by Ashley's repeated *'La'* (Arabic 'No') accompanied by his efforts at looking increasingly stern.

When she had run off we seemed to have the site to ourselves: the camel-ride touts who had previously been lurking by the Temple of Naba had gone home and the only other tourists we had seen, a coach-load of Germans, had already been spirited away to their hotel. The shadows of the columns were lengthening as we walked along the ambulatory and then dodged through a gap to see the little theatre. It was well preserved and the carvings on the archways and columns behind the stage were beautiful in their detail. We were sitting on the seats enjoying the peace, with the sun warming our backs, when a couple of Palmyrene lads jolted us from our reveries by riding across the stage on a motorcycle! There was no introduction, no curtain call: they simply drove in through the stage door on the right and made a rapid exit left. Presumably the odeon just happened to lie on their short cut home. We watched in disbelief as they went buzzing away in the direction of Zenobia's Palace; then we stepped back gingerly onto the main street.

One side of the Colonnade looked like the upturned blade of a monumental sawfish with the majority of its teeth missing; the other had so few columns standing that they were like pegs in a cribbage board. Half-way up the columns that remained were the moulded consoles which once supported statues of public figures such as Marcus Ulpius Yarhai. About midway along the Colonnade, at a slight kink in its course, we came to the tetrapylon whose sixteen Corinthian columns still stand as solidly as ever, although its four statues, like all the rest, have long disappeared. So had the bikers by the time we reached what little remains of Zenobia's Palace.

If, as in my case, you had not previously heard of Zenobia you would be wondering why she had a palace built for her and a hotel named after her. Zenobia, by all accounts, was something of a Boadicea of the Middle East and she became widely renowned as a warrior queen. In the third century AD, the Palmyrenes, tired of foreign domination, decided to grasp the opportunity provided by the general instability of the Roman empire and the more specific threat from the Persians in the east to claim their independence. This they did, setting up a kingdom under Odenathus the Younger who was entitled *'corrector totius Orientis'* (governor of all the East) and who pronounced himself modestly 'king of kings'. He successfully defeated the Persian army on two occasions, but in AD267 he and his son were assassinated in mysterious circumstances. It was generally accepted that his wife Zenobia, jealous at the preferential treatment given to this son (by a previous wife) rather than to her own little boy, Wahballat, had bumped them off.

Suspicions in that direction appeared to be backed up by her subsequent ruthless behaviour. Proclaiming herself Queen, she wasted little time in conquering Asia Minor, her armies reaching the Bosphorus in 270, and in sending her forces into Egypt too. Defying Rome, she and Wahballat then proclaimed themselves 'Augusti', setting themselves up as rivals of the Emperor Aurelian who, not unnaturally, was upset. His armies came storming across from the north-west, regained Asia Minor and then took Palmyra after a few weeks' siege. The humiliated Zenobia was taken prisoner and forced to ride 'in golden chains' in Aurelian's triumphal celebrations of 274.

This was the downfall of Palmyra, from which it never recovered, and of poor Wahballat, who was never heard of again. Zenobia, on the other hand, characteristically squirmed out of trouble and ended up marrying a Roman senator who lived at Tibur.

Roman writers extravagantly described her dark beauty, her energy and luxurious lifestyle, comparing her with Cleopatra (from whom she was supposed to be descended), but Arab tradition remembers Zenobia less romantically and more succinctly as the murderous queen al Zabba. Perhaps, in my initial description, I was being unfair to Boadicea.

North-west of the palace, a ruined Arab castle sits on top of a steep hill like an eroded volcanic plug. This is the Qalaat ibn Maan which, being merely 200 hundred years old, seemed so modern (and the hill seemed so steep and the hour so late) that we decided it was best viewed from a distance. We descended instead into what was for us the most enchanting part of Palmyra - the mysterious Valley of the Tombs. It is a shallow wadi about a hundred yards wide at the eastern end, nearest the ruined city, and is dominated by the Qalaat ibn Maan to the north and the hill of Um el Qais to the south. Most striking of all are the square tomb towers, up to 60 feet tall and built of tough blocks of limestone. A low doorway, the only entrance, led us into the dark interior

Valley of Tombs, Palmyra

of one such mausoleum, where rows of sarcophagus-sized slots were carved in stone down two sides. On each of the storeys above (and below ground in some of the tomb towers) the pattern would be repeated.

Besides these massive towers, glowing eerily orange in the light of the evening sun, there were hidden in the hillside scores of underground tombs or 'hypogea'. Scrambling up the gentle scree slopes and stumbling across their rubble-filled and cave-like entrances, we narrowly escaped falling into one or two of these funerary chambers; we felt the excitement of pioneering archaeologists discovering buried treasure. Yet there was much more beneath our feet than could be seen at the surface and still more tombs further up the valley where German archaeologists were just ending another day's excavations. The sheer volume of this great graveyard was impressive, as well as the particular features of some of the tombs - some, such as the Elhabel tomb tower, built in AD108, were reserved for the bodies of whole families over periods of two centuries or more; others were once decorated with detailed frescoes and funerary sculptures. Above all, though, we were struck by the awesome silence of the place - of the dark, empty towers and the forgotten chambers; not a leaf was there to stir on the still, bare slopes as the sun slipped down slowly behind the ancient hills.

Meanwhile we were returning quietly along the road to the 'Zenobie' when we happened to pass the Afqa, Palmyra's famous spring. There was a small, sunken building to which two squatting men were enthusiastically beckoning us, presumably convinced that we wanted, or needed, to step inside for a bath. Alongside the bath-house, however, was a large, repulsive pool of sluggish water whose colour was pea soup mixed with oxtail. Whoever it was who described in the tourist guide the spring's 'clear blue, slightly sulphurous waters' and its 'medicinal properties' must have possessed a vivid imagination. As far as we were concerned, it was a place best left to the mosquitoes.

Before it was dark we cooked ourselves a meal and, as the car-park offered precious little in the way of after-dinner entertainment, we popped inside the small hotel to drink tea (beer being unobtainable) in the comfort of some armchairs. Soon a large party of middle-aged and rather bulky women burst in noisily through the door, sweeping along in their midst a couple of diminutive men who were struggling, like victims of a tidal wave, to reach the safety of the reception desk. We played our favourite travellers' game of 'guess the nationality' and narrowed the possibilities down to Russian/Eastern European. We learned later that they did indeed hail from the USSR and that their two little Syrian couriers were leading an outing from Damascus, where the Russian husbands worked. While the wives were all enjoying a rather boisterous meal (we suspected they had smuggled some vodka into the dry hotel) at a long table at the far end of the lobby, we were joined by a bunch of cheerful engineers and workmen from Homs who were temporarily employed on a local oil-pipeline construction project. They had ordered a kettle of tea which they insisted on sharing with us - thicker, blacker and sweeter than any we had tasted to date, it was surprisingly delicious.

That night the local dogs seemed to bark continually - enough to wake the entire Elhabel family from their burial tower, plus the remaining residents of the Valley of the Tombs had they still been resting there. At 5 a.m. the muezzin joined in the chorus and as soon as it was light we were up, before anyone else could add to the disturbance. We gave the car a good hose-down and were off to Damascus across the newly surfaced desert road. Military manoeuvres lacking, the uniformity of the flat landscape was punctuated only by the sight of a vast open-cast phosphate mine, a few outcrops of limestone, a couple of small drilling-rigs and a large, brown eagle which was busy clearing up a dead hare from the road.

CHAPTER 9

The outskirts of Dasmascus were more heavily industrialised than Aleppo's, but the array of roadside hoardings and the collection of Czechoslovakian factories - such as a flour mill and sugar refinery - were characteristic of the northern approaches to both cities. The dearth of directional road signs was another common feature which we had come to expect.

What I had failed to learn was that the more confident Ashley was that he could easily relocate a hotel, after four years' absence and in a crowded, signless city with no street map to guide him, the less likely was the actual achievement. In Damascus, he assured me, it was simply a matter of going downhill until we reached an enormous, multi-spoked roundabout and then of turning left to the city centre. After a fascinating but quite superfluous tour of the more modern quarters of the city, we did eventually find the great roundabout, but by then of course we were approaching on an entirely different bearing and we found ourselves flying off, like sparks from a giant Catherine wheel, in the approximate direction of Mount Hermon.

As usual, however, we found our destination in the end. The hotel was full, as were most of the twenty or thirty others in the area between the Hejaz Railway station and the old Inner City - and believe me, by the end of two hours we had visited the majority of them, scooting up a couple of flights of stairs in each to reach the reception desk, only to be told that there was no room. We were beginning to consider returning to a campsite which we had seen on the way in, at least five miles from the centre, and to wonder if we had any chance of finding it before dark, when we entered the Hotel Barada (named after the local river) as a last resort.

I was not aware that Ronnie Barker had a twin brother who lived in Damascus, but there he appeared to be, sitting behind the desk of this very hotel. A burst of fluent Arabic soon put paid to that idea but he won our hearts by producing a room for us in the nick of time, as though he could sense that if he had failed to do so he would have had a couple of nervous breakdown victims on his hands. The room we took was on the fourth floor (there was no lift) and its walls were peeling, dirty and decorated with graffiti. However, it was large enough for the stringing of our washing line and the concrete floor was clean. If we ignored the collection of empty whisky bottles, old socks and cigarette packets which were liberally scattered over the little rooftop immediately below our window, we could look out over the well watered gardens and the uniformed guards outside the Government Offices, which are housed in 'el Saraya el Kadymeh' ('Saraya' being the Persian for palace or mansion).

Our top priority in Damascus being to acquire transit visas for Saudi Arabia, sightseeing had to be arranged around the consular opening hours, and was also restricted by our eagerness to leave the city (and the Hotel Barada in particular) as soon as possible.

There was no lock-up garage for the car and although we were able to park it in a small side street not far from the hotel, Ashley was still anxious about its safety, not least because on his earlier visit he had returned to the parked Range Rover one morning to find that the police were about to tow it away. He had parked in a row of cars the previous evening in what he believed was an unrestricted zone, only to discover in the morning that the other vehicles had already fled or been towed away themselves and that his was now parked illegally in glorious isolation. Fortunately, with the help of a Syrian passer-by who acted as interpreter, Ashley and his friends had managed to wriggle out of trouble and drive the Range Rover away to safety.

From what we had seen so far, bodily removal of misplaced vehicles was still a popular pastime of the police: we witnessed several cases of a car being hauled along on its rear wheels with its front end winched up on to the back of a huge four-wheel-drive pick-up truck; and smaller cars could be seen simply bundled away to the police compound on fork-lift trucks. It was not difficult to envisage the defenceless Citroën as a victim of either fate; hence our reluctance to linger in the capital.

The manner in which we obtained our Saudi visas was somewhat trying to say the least. At first, when we arrived at the Consulate in a modern, shady avenue in the north-west of the city, we felt unduly privileged at being motioned to the front of a long and straggling queue of Syrian men who were waiting patiently for their Saudi Arabian work permits. We were soon armed with an explanatory letter, written in Arabic for us by an official outside, and were ushered into the audience chamber of the mighty Consul. I was about to reach for my sunglasses, to protect my eyes from the glare of his dazzling white robes and head-dress and his shiny gold rings, when I was forestalled. I had the distinct impression that, were I so much as to twitch a finger without his prior consent, my head would be in imminent danger of being christened, 'Off with!' Instead, when he had read our request and listened to our story, he sent us both away, quite intact, to the British Embassy to obtain letters of commendation along with confirmation that we needed no visas for the United Arab Emirates.

Our embassy was of course several miles and much thick traffic away, in what appeared to be the 'diplomatic zone', in contrast to the Saudi Consulate which was out on an unfortunate limb. While we were waiting for our request to be processed, we walked along to the Qatar Embassy, just to make doubly sure that we needed no visas in their country - as was indeed the case. Back at the British Embassy we were leafing through the large visitors' book whose first entry was in 1943 when we read the signature of Earl Mountbatten and could not resist the temptation of signing our names in the same volume.

Returning to the Saudi Arabian Consul with our authoritative letters in Her Majesty's name, at £9 a piece, we were taken aback when he gave them a quick glance and asked for our UAE visas or proof of exemption. He waved aside our protests and sent us scurrying off to the other side of Damascus again, to the Embassy of the United Arab Emirates.

On our third visit to the Saudi Consulate we felt sure that there could be no further obstacle to the granting of our transit visa. We could barely suppress our disappointment, therefore, to find that a visit to the Qatar Embassy still lay in our path. As we walked back to the car we looked sympathetically at the scores of other applicants waiting on the pavement. Some were having their photographs taken by men with ancient cameras enveloped in black cloths; others were squatting in groups, drinking glasses of tea while they waited; one was cooking corned beef, still in the tin, on his little stove; and none showed the slightest sign of impatience, even though they had probably been waiting there for days - instead there was that pervading air of fatalism and inevitability of delay, so characteristic of the east and so different from our time-conscious western world. Pondering on the lessons to be learned, we shot back to the Qatar Embassy, only to find that it had shut for lunch and would reopen at 9.30 the following morning. As lunch seemed more desirable than hanging around the Qatar Embassy, we went to have some. The crowded 'fast-food' restaurant dealt exclusively in chick peas, dished up in a vast number of guises featuring pine nuts, sesame seeds, ghee, butter beans, yoghurt, olive oil, spices, herbs and several other accessories in varying amounts and combinations. All were accompanied, whether you liked it or not, with a plateful of powerful onion salad, which, if nothing else, was guaranteed to destroy all the more subtle flavours being offered, along with the majority of your taste buds.

The following morning we duly acquired a letter from the Qatar Embassy and returned to the Saudi Consulate where we finally became the proud possessors of two transit visas. We felt like the fairy-tale suitor who has accomplished all the tasks set by the king in order to obtain the hand of the princess in marriage.

We rang the old bell and a melancholic old man shuffled to the gate in the high stone wall and let us in. He showed us to a doorway on the opposite side of the little courtyard, which was decorated with tubs of oleanders and cacti. He switched on the lights and we descended by a narrow staircase into the little Chapel of Ananias. It was cool and peaceful in this simple stone sanctuary after the hurly-burly of the hot streets of

Damascus. Daylight from two little round grilles in the ceiling supplemented the wall lamps which illuminated a tiny altar, draped in a white lace cloth, topped with a piece of scarlet cotton and two candle-sticks. The rough stone walls were arched to merge with the ceiling and the whole Chapel was only about thirty feet long; it contained a handful of plain pews and a small side-chapel entered through an archway opposite the stairs. Mounted on the walls of the side-chapel were rows of paintings depicting the life of Saint Paul. We were busy following this picture story when we were suddenly plunged into darkness. The caretaker called down to us that he would have the power back in ten minutes, so we groped our way back to the main Chapel where there was a trickle of daylight and sat on a pew, waiting, enjoying the tranquillity.

It is nearly two thousand years since Paul (then still called Saul), armed with documents authorising him to arrest Jesus' followers and possibly to bring them back to trial for heresy, set out from Jerusalem and was blinded by a heavenly light six miles south of Damascus - that at least is where a Christian shrine stands on a hill called Kaukab, or Celestial Light, to commemorate his conversion. The Chapel of Ananias, where we were sitting in darkness, was built by the early Christians near, or on the site of the house of Ananias, to commemorate the vision in which the Lord told Ananias to go and restore Paul's sight. It has not always been as peaceful as we found it: in the twelfth century Saladin turned it into a mosque, and in 1921 excavations brought to light an altar, dated to the third century AD and consecrated to Jupiter-Haddad (Haddad was the Aramean god of thunder - comparable in many ways to the Roman god Jupiter), which indicated that the Romans may have built a temple there to obliterate the Christian church. Despite these torments the little

Chapel survives as the only remaining church in the city.

We had walked to what is still the Christian quarter of the Inner City from the 'Street called Straight'. This thoroughfare runs east-west across the old walled heart of Damascus and follows the course of the original Roman *decumanus* which was about four times as wide as, and fifteen feet below, the present street. For a couple of days we were fooled into believing that the 'Street called Straight', otherwise known as the Midhat Pasha Street (in the west) and the Bab Charki Street (at the eastern end), had a north-westerly trend; but this was merely because the street plan from the Bureau Touristique had no key, which not only meant that some of the numbered sites were unidentifiable until we reached them, but also that our natural assumption that north was 'up' the plan was sadly mistaken. Add to this the fact that the streets and gates frequently go by more than one name, imagine about one hundred and fifty acres of labyrinthine lanes, some (the souks) covered over like tunnels and most of them narrow, hemmed in by jettied stone buildings and streaming with wobbling cyclists, donkey-carts and motorcycles, and you will begin to understand our confusion in the Inner City. Under the circumstances, it is remarkable that we ever reached the Chapel of Ananias.

The Romans cannot be blamed entirely for this chaos. It is true that they first walled in the ancient city to form a rough rectangle, with its northern, long side running along the south bank of the River Barada and with its perimeter punctuated by seven major gates, between two of which the *decumanus* ran. But they cannot be held responsible for the subsequent jumble of architecture which has gradually accumulated, like layers of wallpaper in an old house, without any apparent attempt to remove the redundant material. It is not their fault, for example, that the level of ancient Damascus is now buried about fifteen feet below the present streets, that very little of the original walls remain exposed, and that we had to dive underground to see Ananias' Chapel.

Hints of the Roman past emerge in odd places - doorsteps made of pedestals or chunks of column hidden in a wall - but only one of the seven ancient gates, the Gate of the Sun (Bab Charki), remains and that is at the eastern end of the 'Street called Straight'. The western extremity has degenerated into a flea-market (Souk el Kumeileh) for second-hand clothes and the original Gate of Jupiter now has a medieval replacement just to the south. Of the five other gates, Mercury, Venus, Mars and the Moon have suffered similar fates and at the site of the Gate of Saturn where Paul, escaping from the Jews, was allegedly let down over the wall in a basket, stands the Ottoman gate, Bab Kaysan.

The site of the Great Omayyad Mosque in the north-western part of the Inner City has also seen many changes. During repairs to the present Mosque an ancient relief of a sphinx with curled tail was found in the walls and it is believed to belong to an early temple to Haddad, the Aramean god. The Romans converted this original building into a temple to Jupiter, which was in turn replaced by the Christian Church of Saint John the Baptist, built by Emperor Theodosius I in 379.

It was the Omayyad Caliph Walid I who pulled down the church at the beginning of the eighth century to build the Great Mosque. No expense was spared in its construction and design: Greek architects were employed and thousands of craftsmen from Byzantium and even Persia, India and Egypt, were imported. Lead for the roof was brought in from any buildings or tombs that Walid's men could lay their hands on. Gold was used extravagantly in decorative vines on the walls, in tracery on the ceiling, and to coat the capitals of columns, and six hundred lamps were suspended from the ceiling by golden chains. White marble was used to pave the courtyard and elsewhere there was a profusion of rich mosaics and coloured marble inlay. It is easy to believe that Walid spent more than seven years' income on the building and to understand why Moslems regard the Great Mosque as the fourth holiest place on earth (after Mecca, Medinah and Jerusalem's Dome of the Rock).

The Great Mosque today is not the original which was gutted by fire in 1069 and subsequently suffered a series of restorations and fires. The existing marble inlay dates from the end of the last century after the most recent fire of 1893 during which the prayer hall collapsed. Despite these set-backs, the beauty of the present Mosque is still outstanding: its spacious, paved courtyard surrounded by cool colonnades, its walls of shining tesserae in green and gold, and its prayer hall with walls of inlaid marble and the distant, blue-green patterns of its painted ceiling.

As infidels we were swiftly turned away from the main entrance, where other visitors were engaged in depositing or retrieving their shoes, and pointed in the direction of the Tourists' Entrance where we were obliged to pay for admission and remove our footwear. Despite the fact that I had been careful to wear a headscarf and to hide my legs and arms in trousers and long sleeves respectively, I was asked to don a big, black hooded gown from a collection hanging up in the entrance lobby. I delved into this forest of dark cloth, rustling through to find a suitable size, but there seemed to be no distinction so I gave up and got inside one, whereupon Ashley lost sight of me. At five feet seven inches I count myself tall by international standards but here was I, blinkered by a drooping hood, my hands vanished halfway up the sleeves and my feet buried in a mass of excess hem. Either the designer's idea of an average female tourist was some sort of Gargantuan seven-footer, or these garments were the habits cast off by an order of uniformly giant monks.

Folding back the necessary portions, I went tripping barefoot into the open courtyard, sweeping aside the pigeon droppings as I went. A thousand years ago there would have been no pigeons there for old Christian talismans left in the Mosque from the days of its predecessor, the Church of St John, were said to have warded off 'harmful' creatures, but in 1069 the great fire destroyed the talismans and now the pigeons have a field day.

In the long prayer hall there were reminders of the Byzantine church: a richly fossiliferous marble font and the great domed tomb of St John the Baptist which looked like a model of St Paul's Cathedral. The floor was coated in a patchwork of fading, well worn carpets and dotted with faithful figures, sitting or kneeling, singly or with friends, thinking or praying amongst the tall columns. The great chandeliers seemed to dangle at a dangerously low altitude from heavy chains thirty feet long, suspended from the ceiling like the pendulums of giant clocks. Reminiscent of the citadel at Aleppo, the transept ceilings were beautifully painted in deep red, green and golden geometric designs.

Outside the blind or crippled beggars hovered hopefully. Nightshirted little boys ran up barefoot calling, 'Madame, Mister, you want souvenirs, you want postcards?' but business did not look good for the souvenir stall-holders at the eastern end of the Souk Hamidieh. There were few tourists to be seen at the entrance to the Great Mosque or, for that matter, anywhere in Damascus.

A stone's throw to the south of the Mosque we found another oasis in the dusty, busy souk and the biggest bellows I have ever seen, which might have been more at

Azem Palace, Damascus

home with a blast furnace than resting near the gates of the pretty Azem Palace. It was a refreshing spot with its green shady courtyards, its quiet pools and the sweet scent of jasmine in the air. Bougainvillaea, thick with purple flowers, draped the arcades like bundled curtains, disguising the paper-thinness of its petals. Fountains played amongst orange and citron trees and there were goldfish lurking lazily in the water. The bristling swish of a besom on the paving stones barely broke the peace.

Assad Pasha al Azem was the governor of Damascus for 14 of the 400 years of Ottoman rule and built the palace in 1749. Unlike many parts of the city, and despite a fire in 1925, it remains almost as it was then; its banded and triple-coloured masonry of alternating white, peach and black stone still looks fresh and the gardens of the two courtyards, one at the centre of the Haremlik (for the pasha and his family) and the smaller enclosed by the rooms of the Selamlik (where friends were received), are still well tended. The pasha is said to have employed every mason and carpenter in Damascus for the creation of this work of art, and the result is a colourful blend of light and shade, reflected in the variegated stonework and the intricate marquetry and inlay of the window arches and arcades. The buildings and the garden seem to harmonise so naturally that it is difficult to imagine one without the other, and easy to see why Damascus is known to the Arabs as Al Fayha or 'the fragrant'.

Inside the palace there was an interesting Museum of Folk Art and Tradition, illustrating the lifestyle of the pasha and his contemporaries. It would have been even more interesting had we been able to see into all the display cabinets, but unfortunately the power had chosen that morning to fail and we wandered about in the gloom, squinting at the shadowy glass. Some of the brighter rooms, opening on to the arcades, had beautiful marble floors and inlaid marble patterns on their walls, while others were wood-panelled and reminiscent of Tudor England, although the carved wooden ceilings were highly decorated with geometric, oriental designs and multi-coloured painting. Amongst the items we could make out were exquisite musical instruments such as lutes and zithers, delicately crafted with marquetry and mother-of-pearl.

The baths, like those at Aleppo, had the familiar collection of small marble rooms, connected by narrow passages and the little domed roofs perforated with a multitude of tiny round windows. A brave attempt had been made in a number of the rooms to reconstruct scenes from the past: dummy figures posed together awkwardly in rather tired costumes, drinking tea, preparing for a wedding, blowing glass or roasting coffee-beans. One poor static soul who had been having his back scrubbed in the baths for years still managed to look dusty. Nearby a group of moustached men in faded tarboushes (Tommy Cooper hats) were sitting in an all-male games room playing backgammon and watching shadow puppets, while next door the women were working hard at their weaving looms. 'Some things never change.' I commented, but Ashley had momentarily turned deaf.

The Inner City may be a bit of a jumble, but the Tekkiyeh Mosque although lying west of the city walls, has not escaped a chequered history. On what was previously the site of the Black and Ochre Palace of Baybars (a Mameluke sultan in the thirteenth century), Suleiman the Magnificent built the Tekkiyeh in 1554 as a convent for Whirling Dervishes. (This sect of mystics whose seat was in Konya, in southern Turkey, danced as freely then as, for tourists, they do now in their swinging white robes and fezzes which look like truncated traffic cones; but they have not always been popular with orthodox Islam and are more generally regarded as a dwindling group of heretics.) It is still a splendid mosque which, despite the two centuries' discrepancy in age, shares with al Azem Palace the same feeling of spaciousness and natural beauty so loved by Ottoman architects.

The shady gardens are now marred by the imposition of a military museum and we peered over the railings at the MiG fighters, the half-track, the auto-gyro and various other antiquities whose identities were less obscure to Ashley than to me. I was entranced by the tall twin minarets behind us, pointing skywards like a pair of well sharpened pencils above the cypresses and eucalyptus trees, and by the shaded courtyard with its duck pool and its arcades of variegated stonework. Beneath the smooth little bulges of the cupolas, which make the rooftops look like upturned orange-trays, the dervishes used to live in cell-like rooms, but now these arcaded rows house gift shops selling Palestinian arts and crafts such as wooden, glass or metal ornaments, carpets and jewellery.

We left Damascus with mixed feelings and as much 'long life' food as we could buy in the souk without seriously overloading the Citroën, our aims being to stock up for the Saudi desert crossing and to rid ourselves of our mass of Syrian currency which would be almost worthless in any other country. The provisions consisted largely of sultanas, which we bought by the kilo from a sack in the souk (and which turned out to be 50 per cent stalks and pips!), packets of dates, peanuts, apples, tins of hummus and jam and biscuits. We also found a grocer who sold tins of sardines and in our excitement at this gastronomic treat (eight weeks on the road had given us a rare appreciation of the simpler things of life), we bought up his entire stock. This was four cans, in each of which lurked a lethal chilli pepper, and all of which were covered in an accidental sticky coating - as though the top can had leaked oil over others and then all four had been dropped into a bag of sugar.

We were not sorry to have made our final four-storey ascent of the Hotel Barada, nor to be freed from the congestion of Damascan life but, not surprisingly for a city which was first settled by the Arameans in about 1200 BC and which is renowned as the oldest continuously inhabited capital in the world, we left a host of secrets yet to be revealed to us. It seemed to be a city torn between modern development and the old, traditional ways, but its hotels, unlike Istanbul's, were full of businessmen rather than foreign tourists, whose scarcity tended to increase our interest in the city. Despite its attempts to keep pace with the western world, there is no disguising its individual features and its reluctance to change - donkey and pony-traps mingle with the busy traffic and men are seen dragging huge blocks of ice along the pavements to soft-drink stalls while others, never having experienced supermarkets and shopping-trolleys, carry from the souk large bags of floppy pitta bread on their heads to act as sun-hats.

As though he had come out specifically to see us off, or perhaps to remind us exactly to whom we should be grateful for our visit to Syria, President Assad was watching us from giant posters everywhere we looked: above doorways, amidst party flags, strung across the streets and on the facade of the Hejaz Railway station. By the time we reached the outskirts, we were quite relieved to have escaped his gaze.

CHAPTER 10

It is about seventy miles from Damascus to the Jordanian border to the south, and for the entire journey there was a strong westerly wind sweeping clouds of dust across the road and hampering our steering. Progress was also hindered by a series of police control points where we were halted and interrogated briefly. I had never seen such a quantity of stationary lorries as had accumulated at these checkpoints and at the border - the first of the queues which we encountered was about half a mile long, the trucks nose-to-tail, but across the three-mile stretch of no-man's-land between the Syrian and Jordanian posts lay at least a two-mile tailback of these massive international carriers. As well as those bearing Syrian or Jordanian plates there were Bulgarian, Yugoslavian, Swiss, German and Turkish vehicles. Most were container lorries, some of which were jumbo-sized doubles with countless pairs of wheels, and all parked so closely that it was often difficult to tell where one lorry ended and the next one started: it was like an apparently endless goods train standing by for the signals to change. The individuality of some of the older Turkish and Arabic vehicles helped to break the monotony of the chain: lumbering old Mercedes and Bedfords with big rounded bonnets brightly painted, contrasted with the sawn-off faces of the modern cabs. A driver of the old school would take pride in his vehicle, trimming the windscreen with floral transfers, picking out the mudguards with green paint, the bumper with red, coating the bonnet in blue, painting stripes around the wheel arches, hanging flags and tassels at the windows and attaching at least three extra pairs of reflectors and lights until the whole thing looked more like a carnival float than the long-distance goods vehicle which it really was.

We could only guess at the contents of the containerised loads, most of which were destined for the Gulf States although some would only be going as far as Amman in Jordan, whose only other major trade route is via the Red Sea port of Aqaba. We imagined that some of the lorries might be carrying washing-machines from Italy, cotton from Syria, car parts from Germany, flour from Turkey, vegetables from Lebanon, tinned fruit from Bulgaria and, if the shelves of Syrian grocers were anything to go by, tons of soup-powder from Switzerland.

The road hauliers of the Middle East and Europe must have been rubbing their hands in glee at the continuing war between Iran and Iraq and its disruption of shipping trade in the Arabian Gulf. The risks, not to mention the insurance costs, involved in shipping a European cargo up those hazardous waters to export markets such as Kuwait have in many cases become prohibitive so that land transport is being utilised instead. Turkey, for instance, was midway through a ten-year transport Masterplan which aimed, among other programmes, to improve all its main east-west land trade routes, with the aid of the World Bank. By 1993 a double-lane motorway from the Bulgarian border through Ankara and Adana to the Syrian border should have been completed and, with Kuwaiti co-operation, the road from Mersin to the Iraqi border would be upgraded too. Even taking into account the dwindling financial reserves of Iran and Iraq and the consequent cuts in their imports, Turkish road hauliers were still enjoying a boom in this transit trade. Ironically, the ancient caravan routes were being renovated and reused, and while the new breed of desert transport may be swifter (when it is not jammed for days at an international border), camels can at least claim to last longer between refuelling stops. If the diesel runs out, maybe the 'ships of the desert' will be back in business again.

The drivers of the great army of vehicles waiting to enter Jordan were taking it easy when we passed. For most of them this was probably just a regular hold-up which they could do little about, so they were making the best of it by taking a rest. Some were sitting in groups drinking tea together on the dusty road, some were stretched out under their lorries taking forty winks, and others were bending at their offside water-tanks to fill kettles or sluice down their torsos from cool jugs. Several policemen were wandering along the queue from one driver to the next, with wads of paper but not a scrap of urgency as far as we could tell. Nobody, however, seemed in the least perturbed by the delay; nor were we worried as we sailed past towards the Jordanian border-post.

We went up to what we thought was the office of the passport control but were greeted by a sign which announced simply, as though no further explanation was required, 'Men Inspection'. I was on the point of looking for a door labelled with the complementary female version when a smart man with a neat moustache stepped out of the office. He ushered me swiftly away with low sweeps of his arms, as if I was some large, stray farm animal which had wandered on to his premises. I slunk back to the car leaving Ashley to brave the office with the 'Man Inspector' for whatever dubious duty it was his task to perform. Imagining some sort of meticulous body search, I was mildly surprised when Ashley strode back only a few minutes later, armed with a bunch of papers for the car and still mystified by the message on the door.

Having been 'stamped in' at the real passport control office and having decided not to change our Syrian currency because the rate was ridiculously unfavourable, we and the 2CV were subjected to a thorough search which involved removing all our belongings from the car so that three men could riffle through the bags and boxes, lifting out at random whatever took their fancy and piling the proceeds on a bench for us to reorganise later. Meanwhile another man was frantically examining the car door panels and poking about in the boot under the spare wheel as though he had lost something. We asked him innocently what he was looking for but he replied, 'You no have gurms?'

'Gurms?' we said.

'No, *guerns,*' looking at us as though we were demented.

'Oh, games?' we suggested, still bewildered.

'No guerns, no marijuana, no alcol!'

'Why didn't he say guns in the first place?' we muttered, irritated by our two hours' detention at His Majesty, King Hussein's customs officials' pleasure. When they were satisfied, beyond reasonable doubt, that we were not importing into their country anything more dangerous than a Swiss army knife, nor anything more deleterious to health than a box of anti-malaria tablets, and that our flask of methylated spirit was strictly for cooking purposes, we were given the 'all-clear'. Our last remaining piece of business, which was to arrange third party car insurance, was dismissed as unavailable and unnecessary in Jordan; so we put our trust in Allah and our belongings back in the car and set off for Jerash.

We reached the town in mid-afternoon and stopped in the spacious, but largely empty, new car-park beside the modern buildings of the Tourist Office and Rest House which had been installed to the south of the ancient city. Somehow I had expected that this historic site, described in such superlative terms as 'the best and most completely preserved Graeco-Roman city in the Near East' and even acclaimed in the tourist leaflet, although with a certain lack of conviction, as 'perhaps the best preserved and most complete provincial Roman city anywhere in the world', would be crawling with coach parties of tourists and armies of avid archaeologists. I was wrong and it looked as though whoever had designed the ample new facilities had been wrong too. To give the planners the benefit of the doubt, however, we had arrived there at the beginning of October which was not peak-season and in any case they had been realistic enough not to provide the Rest House, contrary to popular understanding, with beds of any kind, nor to encourage the construction of a single hotel in the modern town of Jerash. It was on receiving the last two pieces of information from the tourist police that we asked whether we could camp somewhere close to the site. We were directed to a patch of gravel just outside the South Gate in the old city walls, conveniently close to the washrooms of the Tourist Office (which was only closed between 9 p.m. and 6 a.m.). We popped our heads round the Rest House door just long enough to have a glimpse of the luxurious, empty restaurant and deserted bar and to inquire from the lonely barman the price of a bottle of beer; but when we returned later that evening to buy a drink it was to find that he had already locked up and gone home, presumably in desperation.

Thanks to the efforts of the Jerash International Project of the Jordan Department of Antiquities, particularly in 1982 and 1983 when teams from Jordan, Great Britain, the USA, Australia, France, Poland, Spain and Italy were excavating and restoring as much as they possibly could in the time (two years seem remarkably short when the aim is to uncover what nature has been busy burying for the last twelve hundred) there was more to see of the city than when Ashley was there four years earlier; but even greater amounts are still hidden on the site beneath its dry grassy mounds. The earliest pottery found there dates from 1500 BC in the Middle Bronze Age and it is easy to see why it has been for so long a popular place for human settlement: set among the gentle limestone hills of Gilead in a fertile agricultural area of the Golden River (Chrysorhoas) Valley, it is quite simply a lovely location.

The reason why the Romans developed it into a major city, however, is that it lay on an important trade route to Petra in the kingdom of the Nabateans. In 334 BC Alexander the Great had first found the village called Garshu, a Semitic name which became Hellenised to Gerasa, although for a time the place was known as 'Antioch on the Chrysorhoas', and it was soon transformed into a *polis* or city. It came under Roman rule in the first century BC and, retaining the name Gerasa, it was an important member of the Decapolis, ten cities on the empire's south-eastern frontier (now in northern Jordan and southern Syria), which collectively acted as a buffer zone between the Roman Province of Syria and the independent Nabatean kingdom to the south. The Nabatean stronghold of Petra proved a hard nut for the Romans, but Trajan finally cracked it in AD106 and extended the empire with his new province of Arabia, in which some members of the Decapolis were included, thus breaking up their association. Gerasa continued to develop for a while but the city was finally abandoned in the eighth century after a series of devastating earthquakes. It was a German explorer called Ulrich Jasper Seetzen who 'rediscovered' the city more than a thousand years later, in 1806, but until the 1920s no major excavations were undertaken.

One of the interesting aspects to emerge from the recent work of the J.I.P. is that Gerasa did not simply fall into decline as soon as the Roman era ended. Although there is no dispute that the city's heyday was from the end of the first to the end of the third century AD, there is now much evidence that it was still important during the Byzantine and Omayyad eras. Fifteen Byzantine churches have been found and several of these continued to be used during the Islamic period, while a substantial residential quarter built in the seventh and eight centuries indicates a large population at that time. Apart from churches, the other things which keep popping up all over the site (surprisingly, not mosques, of which only one has been discovered) are large pottery kilns. About two dozen of these late Byzantine or Islamic constructions have been found to date, along with cooking pots, bowls, lamps and other items similar to those discovered in other sites such as Pella and Amman. The deduction of the archaeologists is that Jerash may have been a regional centre for the ceramics industry, marketing its wares to neighbouring cities.

The Church of Bishop Isaiah is also a source of speculation: it was built in AD 559 by the Byzantines who managed in the process to recycle most of the Romans' North Theatre which had recently been ruined by a major earthquake and was not fit for much else. The floor of the church was almost entirely covered with original mosaics depicting birds, gazelles, deer, peacocks, vines and portraits of donors, while Omayyad pieces of pottery and glass found inside suggest that the church continued to be used after the arrival of Islam. Neatly stacked roof tiles, plaster patches on the floor and various plaster-containers, suggest that the church was being repaired when the devastating earthquake of AD 747 struck, precipitating the abandonment of the city.

Considering that the great oval Hippodrome is 240 m long, 50 m wide and used to seat 15,000 spectators, you might wonder how we could possibly manage to avoid seeing it; but it is also well outside the 10-feet-thick Roman city walls and the area controlled by the ticket man. Furthermore, we only had a couple of hours of daylight left to tour the rest of the city and the new museum. So we missed the Hippodrome's famous triple-arched gateway which was built in 129-130 to commemorate the visit of Emperor Hadrian who had just come down from Palmyra, having bestowed on it the title of *civitas libera*. Hadrian must have enjoyed travelling, or disliked Rome, for he spent about twelve of his twenty ruling years on foreign tours of the empire, leaving a trail of honorary monuments of which Gerasa's 'Hadrian's Arch' is but one.

What we did see were the North and South Theatres, the Byzantine churches with their beautiful carpet-like mosaics of tigers, cockerels, elephants and other exotic designs, the baths, the Temple of Zeus and the Temple of Artemis, the Nymphaeum and, perhaps most impressive of all, the great Forum, with its towering rim of Ionic columns and its oval plaza. We walked from there northwards along the Cardo, or colonnaded main street, over its huge, uneven limestone paving-stones where chariot-wheels had left ruts like trace fossils and under which the ancient drainage system still lay largely unseen. The late afternoon sun cast dark, columnar stripes across our path and made the pink and golden limestone glow against the deepening blue and the fleecy whiteness in the sky. It was all too quiet to imagine the Cardo bustling with chariots and merchants, its sides lined with busy shops and noisy with the bargaining voices of international tradesmen.

Up at the Temple of Artemis, at the heart of the great Temenos or sacred enclosure, approached by a monumental 120 m-wide staircase we began to feel dizzy. Gazing up at the towering heights of the Corinthian capitals, we wondered whether we or the columns were ever so gently toppling. In fact, we soon realised, it was only the effect of the clouds scudding by in the opposite direction. Our faith in the stability of the masonry thus restored, we were just thinking how fortunate we were not to be pestered by eager young guides, who had presumably all gone home by now, when both illusions of safety were shattered simultaneously.

A lad of sixteen or thereabouts (he claimed to have recently joined the police force) appeared from nowhere (an art perfected by many guides) and proceeded to demonstrate that the columns were indeed rocking: he wedged a couple of little stones between the pedestal and the bottom drum and the gap certainly appeared to be closing slowly and then opening a little as the column swayed gently above. Feeling sure that it must be some sort of optical illusion, but unable to see quite how, we were nevertheless so entranced that we let ourselves in for an unofficial guided tour - something we generally try to avoid, for the simple reason that there is normally little to be gained from the commentary.

Adding to our disorientation, the boy led us down some steps into total darkness beneath the temple, to the accompaniment of his excited cry, 'I show you stabble hossees, 'I show you stabble hossees!' which was no more comprehensible on the tenth repetition than it had been

Temple of Artemis, Jerash

the first time round. But on the eleventh the meaning suddenly dawned on us. What he was trying to describe was 'horses' stables' of course. Without a torch it was impossible to say what was down there but whatever it was (and he insisted that there had been a prison as well as 'stabbles', although at what date remains a mystery), it took us several minutes to grope around its passages and cells and to stumble blindly over all its stony obstacles.

It was when we emerged, blinking, into the daylight, or what remained of it, that the tour turned into something resembling an army assault course. While the junior police recruit called, 'Come, come!' and leapt about like a mountain goat over the ruined walls and the rock-strewn landscape, we struggled behind with our cameras and bags, wondering why we had succumbed to his infectious enthusiasm.

'What's that?' I gasped, as I saw him pause briefly between bounds to point out another example of earthquake devastation.

'Stabble hossees,' came the reply.

'Of course!' said Ashley, and from that moment on the useful term was incorporated into our accepted vocabulary to describe any ruin of obscure identity.

We reached the North Theatre and then scrambled down a steep, ten-foot bank into a rubbly pit in which archaeologists had obviously been digging recently. Vertical sections through hundreds of layers of deposits, with pieces of pottery and broken masonry embedded in them at various levels, indicated the scale of the problems confronting the teams of the J.I.P. The excavation work at Jerash seemed an infinitely great task.

Turning down our friend's offer of cheap coins and pottery pieces from his personal collection - local artefacts which we felt ought to remain in Jerash rather than cluttering up the back of our car- we set off back down the Cardo, to see the museum before it closed and to put the tent up before the sun disappeared. Luckily the little policeman was called into a tent near the South Tetrapylon where some Jordanian archaeologists, with immaculate timing, were brewing a pot of tea at the end of their working day. Had we not been pressed for time we might have gone beyond the city's North Gate to see the Birketein (Two Pools) where the Festivals of Maiuma were celebrated in the nude and are said to have become so disreputable that they had to be banned twice during the fourth century AD.

We visited the modern town that evening and were astonished to see in the grocery stores such foreign delicacies as cornflakes, condensed milk, cans of tuna fish and other imported luxuries. All we were looking for, however, was some bread for breakfast, and, seeing a man walking along with his arms round a big bag of pitta, we asked him where he had found it. His smile drooped with embarrassment when he had to tell us that the shop was closed now and that he had bought the last batch; but then, with a new rush of confidence, he started thrusting some of his bread into our hands. Despite our protests and his refusal to accept any money, he insisted on leaving us with two of his pancake-like loaves and even tried to persuade us to go to his home and take *chai* with him, by which time we were as embarrassed as he had been initially. We wished we had never asked. We eventually waved goodbye and made for a small, empty restaurant where we ordered hummus, salad and kebabs of unspecified meat which, judging by the hairy, black, tasselled tails of the carcasses dangling at the entrance, was probably goat. By the time it reached our plates it was pleasantly spiced, carefully barbecued and as tender as Welsh lamb. It was one of our better meals.

CHAPTER 11

We drove south from Jerash through an area of gentle limestone hills and after an hour entered the whirlpool of Amman which rapidly sucked us into its centre. The city is surrounded by a series of concentric ring roads called the First Circle, Second Circle, Third... and so on. We somehow spiralled our way inwards, hopping inescapably from one Circle to another, until we ended up in what is known as downtown Amman - literally so, for we had descended a steep slope in the process. The travel office holding our *poste restante* had moved from the centre, however, and the poor car struggled back up the hill to the outskirts where we collected our mail and purchased some 'JDs' (Jordanian dinars).

We were not staying in Amman: Ashley had been there already and so had I for that matter; twice - I had spent an hour or two at the airport on my way to and from Oman one leave, sitting on a moulded plastic chair with the cockroaches scuttling around my feet: very memorable. It was hardly an excuse now for bypassing the museums, Roman theatre and other archaeological and architectural remains of the three thousand-years-old capital city, but the truth was that, so soon after our Damascan experiences, we had not regenerated our enthusiasm for crowded streets and congested traffic.

'I know a nice little motel in Madaba which can't be more than thirty miles from Amman, so we could stay there instead. Then we could wallow in the hot springs at Ma'in,' said Ashley. It took no more to convince me and we extricated ourselves from the city, driving through the wealthy western suburbs with their splendid hillside villas and past the heavily guarded, strong steel gates of Al Nadwa Palace, the home of King Hussein and Queen Noor.

An hour's drive south of Amman across fertile prairie land lies the small town of Madaba. It rises above the plains by virtue of the mounds of earlier towns on which the present one sits. It seemed a sleepy place that morning: the museum was closed, although we peeped into the courtyard to look at some of the mosaics, and there was no sign of a hotel, nor any knowledge of one amongst the inhabitants we questioned. However, Ashley excelled himself in navigation that day and we located a motel on the southern side of the town.

I would never have guessed it was anything more than a petrol station, the bleak little concrete building behind the fuel pumps, but Ashley, swearing that it was the very place where he had stayed, asked an astonished pump attendant whether we could spend the night there. He led us into a little transport café at one end of the building and we waited while he fetched the landlady. She took her time in coming - but then in October a guest was probably the last thing she was expecting. Upstairs, she rallied round, bustling about like a mother hen, apologising for the mess, clearing away paint-cans, bemoaning the unfinished bathroom, relocating potted plants, regretting the lack of curtains, holding her palms up to her cheeks in horror at the sight of the kitchen sink which was overflowing with greasy dishes, and explaining that her preparations for reopening the motel were not yet complete - as if we had not guessed. She told us that she had been forced to close the place for two years during her son's serious illness which had involved special treatment at a London hospital. So concerned for our comfort was this hospitable woman that we had an impossible task to persuade her that, after the bed of gravel on which we had been laying siege to Gerasa the previous night, what she was offering was nothing short of luxury.

We spoke of the hot springs at Zerqa Ma'in where Ashley and his friends had bathed under a warm waterfall, an attractive prospect in view of the present alternative, which was a cold shower in a semi-tiled bathroom. At the mere mention of Ma'in, however, the poor woman went into a second frenzy, telling us that that place too was in the throes of renovation and development and was overrun with diggers and bulldozers, carving out hillsides and installing hotels and swimming pools. It was out of the question for tourists to go there. Even allowing for the possibility of her exaggeration, we no longer thought we would want to anyway. Being accompanied by the rumbles of earth-moving machinery or witnessed by a band of Jordanian construction workers was not our idea of a relaxing bath. Nor could we imagine that Herod the Great would have taken to the waters of Zerqa Ma'in (then Callirhoe) quite so readily under the present circumstances as he had done two thousand years ago, reputedly to cure his arteriosclerosis.

Ashley was by now more interested in the remedial properties of lunch than the mineral waters of Ma'in, and we settled into the transport café for a meal of hummus, tomatoes, bread and omelettes cooked expertly, in the intervals between filling up lorries, by the oil-stained pump attendant. Not completely cured of hunger, Ashley proceeded to spend the rest of the afternoon eating a bag of Syrian sultanas.

That evening, we met the three other guests, who were sharing the room next door and who were responsible for the state of the communal kitchen. This merry trio of mechanics (two Syrian and one Armenian) came from Aleppo, where they had left their wives and children for six months or more in order to work at the garage below. They invited us in for some delicious tea, which we drank from delicate glasses and stirred with such clumsy, big teaspoons that it was like trying to use a ladle in an eggcup. They had finished work not long before, at about six, cooked themselves a chicken and some rice, and now they were relaxing before collapsing into bed in preparation for a six o'clock start the following morning.

They were extremely friendly, clearly pleased to have their monotonous daily routine interrupted by the novelty of some other guests, even though conversation was virtually impossible between three men who collectively knew a dozen words of English and the two of us, who understood the same amount of Arabic. Nevertheless, our communications, which relied heavily on signs and drawings, were remarkably good. We discussed their work, compared salaries in Britain, Syria and Jordan, and then pored over a map which showed our itinerary. We learned that they were Christians, that they had previously worked in Saudi Arabia and Libya, and that they were now trying to earn as much as they could before returning to their families for Christmas. The money was good, *zayn* (here one of them held out his upturned hand, rubbing his thumb to and fro across his first two fingers enthusiastically), in all those three countries, but in Syria... (he made the same gesture much less vigorously this time). Libya had been 'OK', but Saudi, well, we only had to look at their faces to see what they thought of Saudi, but then they were tough enough men to endure anything if the reward was sufficiently great.

It was ironical that Syrian labour was flocking into Jordan to enjoy high salaries when Jordan's revenue comes largely from its own people working in even richer nations, such as the United States or Saudi Arabia, and sending their earnings home.

Nobody warned us that the generator would shut down at nine-thirty that evening, and it was sheer good fortune that I had just returned from my cold shower when we were plunged into darkness. In the morning the sunlight came pouring in through the curtainless window before the generator's rumbles had begun. We were up shortly after our neighbours and on the King's Highway without delay. This is the north-south trade route which has been used continuously for the past 5,000 years and is now flanked by two other major routes which link Amman in the north to Aqaba on the Red Sea. To the west the low-lying Wadi Arabah Highway takes a direct route from the Dead Sea southwards, and to the east of the King's Highway the Desert Highway lies along the edge of the semi-arid steppe region which makes up such a large proportion of Jordan. This easternmost route runs beside the Jordan-Hejaz railway which divides towards the south at Ma'an, producing a small branch to Aqaba while the main line, which Lawrence of Arabia spent so much effort in disrupting during the Arab Revolt, leads to Medina in Saudi Arabia.

We had chosen to go south along the King's Highway to see Kerak and then to cut across to the Dead Sea and take the Wadi Arabah Highway to Aqaba, the latter being the only one of the three which Ashley had not used previously. Between Madaba and Kerak we were travelling along the hilltops, looking down on the brown

slopes of ploughed or stubble fields and patches of small
fir trees, and in places the road cut through thick folded
sections of banded limestone and hard chert, reminders of
the period when an extended Mediterranean Sea covered
this region. In rich green wadis little fields of giant
cabbages and groves of olives were nestling amid the
darker cedars and pines, sharing these havens with
clustered dwellings.

It was our lucky day, we thought, as we tuned in to the
World Service from Cyprus on the car's radio and
received with exceptional clarity the latest news of the
Achille Lauro hijack. Our fortune was short-lived, however,
for we soon arrived at the edge of Wadi Mawjib, a great
gash in the landscape carving its way westwards from an
elevation of some 3,000 feet on the Moab Plateau (where
we were) down the fault escarpment to the Dead Sea at
1,300 feet below normal sea level. We stopped at a
viewpoint to gaze down at the deep chasm; it looked
unfathomable. In the shadowy depths the canyon floor
was obscured by rocky spurs, projecting like jagged teeth
from each wall. On the far side stacked, horizontal layers
of pale brown limestone like thick accretions of plywood
seemed to form an unbreachable barrier; and yet with the
ease of a jig-saw the Arnon River had sliced through this
block, carving out the formidable precipice. At the
intersection of the King's Highway and Wadi Mawjib the
valley bottom is about 2,000 feet below the plateau: we
felt as though we were standing at the edge of the world
and were about to leap off it. As we looked across, our
eyes became fixed on the series of hairpin bends
zigzagging unremittingly up the opposite wall of the
canyon.

We took a deep breath on behalf of the Citroën, plunged
down the northern side of the gorge, gained as much
speed as we could below the last hairpin bend, and shot

up the first few hundred feet of the southern wall like a pea from a peashooter. A few minutes later we were negotiating the fifteenth hairpin in first gear and my appreciation of the finer details of the geology was increasing steadily. In any case, I preferred to look sideways at the roadcuttings than forwards at the doom ahead. The gradient seemed impossible, but I need not have worried: the car outshone our wildest hopes and before I knew it we were out of limestone and into the basalt at the top of the sequence, with only a couple of bends to go.

It was at this point that the police had cunningly laid a trap for all unsuspecting 2CV drivers - a checkpoint which forced us to halt on the steep slope while our passports and car's log-book were inspected. However, even this temporary standstill could not thwart the car and we were soon up on the plateau again, with the wind in our sails. In the little villages the washing was drying beautifully, long lines of laundry blowing about on the flat rooftops of concrete houses. Cosy clusters of sheep, donkeys and foals huddled together for protection from the dusty gusts. The shopfronts with their metal doors rolled down for Friday closure formed dismal walls of grey along the main streets. Tomorrow they would be bright again.

By mid-morning we had reached Kerak which, being a large town, was much more lively. Just as we came to the outskirts we screeched to a halt at the sight of a little arrow indicating 'Military Passes for Aqaba and the Dead Sea' up a steep road to our left. We duly followed it, wondering whether the office would be open at the weekend. At the top of the hill we found the police station, where a young officer quickly appeared and took our passports. He said little but had a good look at the car and at our belongings through the window. Then we were asked to step inside where we waited in a crowded room on rather battered armchairs with a bunch of off-duty, young policemen and their friends, watching *Tom and Jerry* on the television. We were beginning to enjoy ourselves, all laughing together at the visual jokes, when the officer summoned us and sent us away with our passports and a piece of paper which was covered in Arabic script and decorated with an official stamp.

The town centre was packed with people busily shopping and trading as if it was a weekday and the January sales were on. Blasting above the noise on the streets were the competing loudspeakers of several mosques, issuing their Friday messages with a force intended to reach every inhabitant of Kerak, Christian or Moslem - everyone from the lads who preferred to watch TV cartoons to the plump old owner of the central off-licence, who was blatantly defying the call of Islam by marketing his range of expensive bottles and cans.

Meanwhile, the weather was taking a turn for the worse. The conditions in which we scrambled round Kerak's Crusader castle, a cold wind sweeping the hilltop and dark rainclouds bursting upon us, might have dampened our enthusiasm had they not added a suitably sinister air to our surroundings. There was a mysterious quality to the light as the sun filtered momentarily through the greyness, conjuring up images of ancient Kerak - once Kir Moab, King Mesha's capital - evoking the drama of the day when the rebel king, besieged by the armies of Israel, Judah and Edom, sacrificed his eldest son on the city wall, causing the allies to withdraw to their own lands.

The walls which enclosed us, however, were not built until 1136 by the Crusaders, who called their fortified town 'Le Krak du Desert'. Fortunately they had left a maze of passages and rooms below ground level where we could escape from the drenching rain to find all sorts of ovens, storage jars and compartments, as well as two little boys who eagerly adopted us as their new companions. They tugged us by the sleeves of our dripping anoraks from one chamber to another, leading us on an exhaustive tour of Kerak's cannon-balls, pointing at the little piles excitedly in the gloom to the accompaniment of their thunderous, but rather high-pitched, impressions of cannon fire.

Hoping for calmer waters we set off for the Dead Sea, only to be halted halfway down by a military checkpoint. Our passports and our military pass were scrutinised and then a young army officer, who had been trained at Sandhurst and was clearly proud of it, supervised the inspection of our belongings and chatted to us in fluent English about various places he had visited in the British Isles, even inquiring whether we knew Mrs Jones of Preston.

It is not hard to imagine, with the proliferation of projects such as this, that the Jordan River might soon be drained to a mere trickle and the Dead Sea become as dry as old Lake Hula to the north. However, the country's agricultural development is no longer restricted to the efforts of the JVDA (Jordan Valley Development Authority) and attention is now turning to other areas, such as Wadi Arabah and even parts of the desert such as Qa'Disi in the far south, where underground water supplies have been tapped to produce unprecedented greenery in that arid zone.

If the Dead Sea were to shrivel, at least there are no fish to complain about it: the 25 per cent salinity (five times that of the oceans) sees to that. The high salt content results from sea-floor seepage of underground water, from the sulphurous springs along the shore and from the streams bearing minerals leached from the escarpment and from the surrounding sedimentary rocks. Another

Descent to Dead Sea

ingredient of the unusual cocktail of this strange sea, asphalt, can be found floating up from the seabed or seeping along the water's edge. All these peculiar features, along with the legends and characters connected with its history, have given rise to a host of intriguing names for the Dead Sea - the Sea of Arava, the Asphalt Sea, the Eastern Sea, Sea of Lot, the Sea of Overwhelming, the Salt Sea, the Sodomitish Sea and the Sea of Zoar.

We came down to its shores on Al Lisan (the Tongue), a peninsula about six miles wide, which protrudes from the east bank in the southern half of the sea, and forms a low-lying and largely barren mud-flat with patchy scrub in the east. We parked near the road and walked out a few hundred yards across the shimmering, hot mud, crunching the salt-crust like hard snow between the islands of tough little plants. Ashley went on through the muddy pools to the water's edge, leaving me with the camera gear and his shoes, but as he disappeared into the haze, wading out through the milky blue water on the hard-caked salt-bed, he soon

Shore of Dead Sea

discovered that this was not the place for swimming. He seemed to be miles away and yet the sea was still refusing to come any higher than his knees, so he decided to return. There were large chunks of white salt in the shallow water and, had the heat of the sun not been so intense and the flies not so troublesome, we might have imagined that they were blocks of ice floating on the edge of a polar sea.

A red and green pagoda was not something we expected to see at the side of the Wadi Arabah Highway. It was about as probable a sight as a Chinese takeaway restaurant in the middle of the Sahara desert. It was no mirage though, just a small and fitting tribute to the South Koreans who built the highway through this inhospitable scrubland, which is flanked by the major fault scarp to the east and populated, as far as we could tell, by a few herds of underfed camels and a handful of bored policemen. We were warned at intervals about the animals by a series of red-rimmed triangular roadsigns bearing camel silhouettes, but the police checkpoints seemed to pop up unexpectedly all the way from the potash plants near the Dead Sea to Aqaba. The police didn't care two hoots about the contents of the car but were extremely interested in persuading us to stop for tea. Tempting though it was, we had to refuse in order to reach Aqaba that evening, as there was no intermediate stopping place.

Even so, by the time we had successfully passed through the final checkpoint and entered the town it was 5.30 and already dark. Although we would not have chosen darkness to start searching for the campsite of the Palm Beach Hotel, it was not without its advantages once we reached the place, for there were certain aspects which it was preferable not to see.

When we had first heard about the hotel its name had conjured up an image of luxurious beauty: a grassy campsite set amongst shady palm groves and the blue waters of the Gulf glistening only yards from the tent. Instead we found a small one-star hotel, separated from the main road by a dusty patch of ground which, despite our first impression, was not a rubbish tip but a place to pitch tents. Our arrival, coming, we were told, at least twelve months after the visit of the last camper, set the cat amongst the pigeons or, more accurately, the Egyptian cleaner amongst the cockroaches, although he cleverly contrived to leave the largest members of their community in the shower-room and toilet for our entertainment. Meanwhile the mosquitoes were moving in for the kill, which was briefer than they anticipated because we cooked supper in record time and rushed from the insect world to the shopping streets of the town centre.

We saw remarkably few other tourists during our four days in Aqaba and yet it had all the trappings of a western European seaside resort: bookshops and souvenir stalls, diving shops and toy shops, drink stores and travel agents. There were even glass windows to the shop-fronts instead of roll-down doors; there were brightly-lit signs above them and fresh whitewash on every concrete block. Supermarkets were selling tins of baked beans, jars of instant coffee and, luxury of luxuries, fresh milk! The cafés and small restaurants were sadly deserted save for a few local men who had come to watch the television, with one exception - a small Indian restaurant with a first-floor balcony where we joined a crowd of Asians one evening and tucked in to a feast of chicken curry and sloppy dal.

Eight pounds a night for camping at the Palm Beach seemed a little over the odds, even considering the gratuitous supplies of cockroaches and mosquitoes which were thrown in to the bargain. The little hotel we moved to on the first morning was a great improvement: while it regarded sheets as unnecessary, it did provide, for £9 a night, air-conditioning, TV and refrigerator, enabling us to enjoy simultaneously keeping cool, watching the news broadcast in English and drinking cold milk. Sometimes we would switch on the television and find an Israeli channel, for Aqaba shares the tip of the Gulf of Aqaba with Eilat, only a stone's throw away, although a visit would have been impossible. Here, where the Egyptian-Israeli, Israeli-Jordanian and Jordanian-Saudi Arabian boundaries converge, Israel and Jordan have only nine miles of coastline each. This is Jordan's single outlet to the sea. The importance of the head of the Gulf as a port location was recognised even in the days of Solomon and the Queen of Sheba, and the Romans built a military post called Aelana at the head of what they called Sinus Aelaniticus.

Jordan is fully aware of Aqaba's potential both as a tourist resort and an industrial port, joint roles which it manages to reconcile although not entirely without conflict. Windblown dust from the large new loading terminal for phosphates (one of Jordan's principal exports) has been blamed by biologists for fatal damage to parts of the coral reef whose wealth of marine life attracts so many divers, as well as snorkellers like us, to the Gulf. Nevertheless, investment has been encouraged by the tax and rent exemptions of Aqaba's 'Free Zone' (offering incentives which include up to two rent-free years for leases of more than ten years) and the modern hotels are multiplying, each laying claim to a tiny allocation of the narrow strip of shoreline outside the docks, and the tourists, we were told, are flooding in, although we did not see much evidence of them. Either they were finding that all their holiday needs were met within the five-star confines of their hotels, or perhaps they had cancelled their bookings to save their skins after reading, as we did, in a *Guide to the Middle East,* the alarming information that 'there is swimming in the Red Sea all the year round (in winter the temperature rarely falls below 200 C)'. Fortunately for us it was only October and the heat had not then reached its roasting peak.

Our hotel was not endowed with its own private beach, but we drove out of town past the cargo berths and the cold-storage facilities, beyond the Toyota import terminal (where we estimated eight to ten thousand trucks and cars were lined up, waiting for use), past the phosphate-loading area, the container docks and the police checkpoint, past the solar energy research station (a project of Amman's Royal Scientific Society) and the Marine Biology Research Station, until we reached the quiet beach which Ashley remembered. Just beyond it, to the south, was the 'tourist' beach which was in the throes of development and which we ventured on to one day. With the exception of a number of road-laying vehicles at work on the car-park it was deserted. At intervals along the sand were shade-giving constructions like bus-shelters in bold colours, and there were showers and taps and large litter bins cluttering the scene: indeed everything the 'tourists' (if only they could be found) would need in order to keep cool, wash the crystals from their skins (the seawater was extremely salty) and dispose of their soft drink cans. It was not this overwhelming array of modern facilities, however, which sent us scurrying back to the unadulterated beach to the north. Nor was it the gang of local lads, proudly showing us their bag of living cowries and a small squid which they had captured, with unashamed disregard for the conservation regulations prohibiting the collection of all such creatures. It was what we found in the water which deterred us: first there was a wide zone of spiny black sea-urchins, lying in wait for the barefooted paddler, and second the reef (only a matter of a few yards offshore) was almost devoid of life. Much of the coral itself had died and was broken up and consequently the fish and other reef dwellers had dispersed to healthier pastures. The immediate cause of the damage seemed to be the abundance of rusty cans, broken bottles, pieces of plastic and other old litter which were adorning the reef's landward edge at this part of the coast, although why such quantities of rubbish should have accumulated on the 'tourist' beach, particularly before the tourists had arrived, remains unclear. Preferring to snorkel in cleaner waters, we left the *Echinoidea* in peace.

The contrast in conditions only a few hundred yards along the reef was unbelievable. We swam amongst some of the most beautiful underwater scenery we had ever seen. Little clown-fish in their striped costumes of orange and white came swimming bravely up to our goggles, just as they had in the Gulf of Oman, and then scurried back to their personal sea-anemones, stirring the waving tentacles into a flurry of billowing curtains. Sea cucumbers like giant slugs slouched on the white sandy bottom and I saw a half-buried stonefish, camouflaged on the sea-floor and alerting me to the hazards of putting bare feet on the sand. There were dozens of little lionfish too, their long, thin frond-like fins swirling and trailing as they swam close to the coral, displaying their orange and black stripes. These were the playful creatures I had spent an afternoon chasing at Ras al Hamra in Oman, armed with a small net and with all the protection afforded by a bikini and a snorkel mask, innocently catching a couple for a tropical aquarium, only to be told by a friend afterwards of the risk I had been taking. Lionfish (or chickenfish, as they were called at the Aquarium in Aqaba), I discovered, are a variety of scorpion fish, as stonefish are, and have a poisonous array of dorsal spines. Unlike the stonefish, however, the lionfish's sting is painful but not serious and the creatures are free-swimming, strikingly conspicuous and, exceptionally pretty. There were comical little spotted box-fish too, quite harmless and shaped not unexpectedly like a tiny box, with a tail at one end and pouting lips at the other. We spent hours in this garden of coral, sharing it with the butterfly fish and the wrasses, the trigger fish, pilot fish and the schools of tiny, silvery fish which would scoot away from us in a flash of spontaneity and then, responding to some other obstacle, would turn in unison and glint across our path again.

There were Moray eels, lying in wait in rocky crevices, with their beady eyes, sharp teeth and the first smooth six inches only of their long bodies visible. Even these small ones (two feet or so) could have given us a vicious and painful bite had we come too close - I had seen it happen to Baksh, our grey-haired old Omani house-'boy', when he helped me to clear an indoor fish tank by transferring the collection of corals, fish, crabs and a slippery, two-feet Moray into various buckets and bowls. Luckily on that occasion the jaws released Baksh's thumb as quickly as they had gripped it, and the sharp teeth on the roof of the eel's mouth pierced the skin and then withdrew.

The Moray which we saw preserved in the Aquarium of Aqaba's Marine Biology Research Station would have made a different story - it was four feet long and thick as a lamp-post. I shivered to think of encountering a ten-footer while snorkelling on the reef: the alarmist story which had prevailed at Ras al Hamra was hard to forget. The size of the fabled creature was about as reliable as any fisherman's tale and seemed to alter at every telling, but the gist was that a man diving close to the reef in the Gulf of Oman had been attacked by this Moray of legendary proportions. Its jaws of dagger-like teeth had closed on his arm and refused to let go, dragging the man towards its rocky lair. The eel had cunningly and swiftly retreated into this protective den, preventing its victim from striking with his diving knife and forcing him instead to sever his own arm in order to be free. At this point in the narrative, normally a sufficiently gruesome ending for most listeners, the most imaginative storyteller would sometimes add a spine-chilling epilogue featuring a small shark attracted by the blood...

...but far be it from me to deter the hesitant snorkeller. The risks involved in swimming near most coral reefs are probably much smaller than those encountered by a pedestrian crossing the road, and certainly worth taking every time for the sheer joy of the underwater experience.

Pollution of the Gulf of Aqaba by oil has been kept to a minimum, fortunately, and all we witnessed was the odd lump of tar washed up on the beach - no more than we found on the coasts of Turkey, Oman, Britain or any other shores we have visited. We should never have guessed as we drifted over coral in the clear, clean water that less than a mile away a hundred tanker-lorries a day were unloading fifty tons of oil each via a floating pipeline into offshore storage tanks. These tanks could hold 400,000 tons of the viscous liquid before it was pumped into the great ocean-going tankers which would carry the precious cargo to Brazil or some other export market. This was just a portion of the information, the bulk of which was of a political nature, volunteered to us by a Palestinian man we met in Aqaba. He was currently employed on the 'Sherif Jetty project' to replace the floating line by more permanent terminal facilities.

'But we thought that Jordan had no oil.'

'You are right - although there are people who believe that it has been found but is kept secret until world supplies become scarce and prices rise. Then Jordan will become rich at last! I think it could be true: how is it that all these countries next to us - Saudi, Syria, Iraq, Egypt - have so much oil but Jordan has none? It is surely not possible. I think Jordan waits.

'You see the oil that arrives here is Iraq's. It cannot use its own ports in the Arabian Gulf because of the war with Iran, it cannot export all of its oil by pipeline, so Jordan helps. It is good for Aqaba, very good business, as long as the war continues. There is not so much national produce to export from Jordan itself now, and the port is not as busy as it used to be. Now, most of the ships which leave are loaded with phosphates. We are happy to have the Iraqi oil. So, every day there are tankers coming from Baghdad along the road via Amman and others going back empty again.'

Our conversation had started on familiar lines:

'Hello! Where are you from?'

'England.'

'Ah, Inglish, very good,' - and had covered the wider aspects of our travels before he asked:

'Where are your children? In England?'

'We have no children.'

'You... what? You...'

'We have no children.'

'But you are... how old?' He seemed suddenly anxious.

'Thirty-two and twenty-seven.'

'Your wife is twenty-seven?' His concern for Ashley was increasing. 'But I have six children and my wife is younger than yours,' he exclaimed, continuing to ignore me as though this was a strictly man-to-man conversation. 'She was sixteen when my first son was born, but now she is getting too old.'

'There, there,' said Ashley, turning to me with a wink and patting me on the head pityingly.

CHAPTER 12

The Citroën was an unusual sight in Jordan, where about one third of the cars were Mercedes and the remainder appeared to be either Japanese or American. An Aqaban businessman who approached us at the hotel one day wanted to buy our car since his large American monster was swallowing fuel at an alarming rate and he had been told by the Citroën agent in Amman that new 2CVs were not imported into Jordan owing to the prohibitive duty. His own company car, imported from the USA, had been subject to taxes of 300 per cent and had cost the equivalent of £40,000! The 2CV would have been peanuts in comparison.

As it happened, peanuts were among the provisions we were stocking up with in anticipation of the drive across the desert to Dubai and of the scarcity of certain items such as instant coffee in Pakistan and India. Whoever cleaned our room when we left Aqaba must have thought that we had appetites like horses', for we had refilled all our plastic storage containers and discarded, empty, a 1.8 kg tin of dried milk powder, a 2.25 kg pot of marmalade, a 1 kg tin of apricot jam and two enormous jars of instant coffee. Only the large bag of date stones, remains of the fruit which we had bought rusty-red and gorged ourselves on as they ripened to a succulent brown, was a genuine indication of our gluttony.

Equally delicious were the glasses of mint tea which we were offered at the museum by the three underworked, young caretaker-guides. We had walked down to the shore one morning to see Aqaba's castle, but it was closed and the only sign of life was emanating from the tourist office next door - Prince Feisal's residence during the Arab Revolt of 1916 to 1917. An Egyptian lad from Cairo, who was working as a temporary guide so that he could afford to continue his language studies in Alexandria, showed us swiftly round the tiny, poorly-lit museum. We had a dim view of a motley selection of rifles, swords and daggers, a sample of pots and clay lamps from Petra, and a diminutive model of a bedouin tent and its occupants.

The tea-party afterwards was clearly designed to relieve the lads' boredom (we were probably the only visitors that morning), as well as to render our visit marginally more memorable than it would otherwise have been. They succeeded in spinning out the refreshment interval for half an hour but by the time our glasses had been filled for the third time, the pot was drained and so we asked them if we could visit the castle. They offered to make us more tea but then, taking our request seriously, led us round the corner to the entrance which was decorated with the carved Hashemite coat of arms commemorating the castle's use by Prince Feisal. We were left in the experienced hands of the old curator whose muffled voice, emanating from the folds of a rather droopy *kiffeyeh,* provided a particularly uninformative and uninspiring commentary as he guided us round the ruins. He was proud of the towering eucalyptus tree which he had planted as a sapling in the centre of the sandy courtyard twenty-five years ago, but he seemed to have lost enthusiasm, during his long service, for the castle itself. He was content to mutter odd words such as 'prison' 'sleeping', 'bakery' and 'water' to explain the significance of certain rooms and wells which his tour included, leaving us to conclude that everything else was 'stabble hossees'. He did, however, manage to indicate that some blocks of granite came from Wadi Rum, while the limestone had been brought from Egypt.

Apart from the bats flitting and twittering above us in the prison cell, it was a pleasant, breezy place, only a few yards from the sea, but its crumbling walls seemed sadly to be melting into the sandy surroundings. Aqaba fort boasted none of the massive towers of Krak des Chevaliers nor the precipitous crags on which Kerak was built: younger than the Crusader castles, it had served as a fortified caravanserai for traders rather than an impenetrable stronghold against invaders, and now camouflage had become its best defence.

On 15 October, we left Aqaba and its acres of suburban lorry-parks, by the route which Lawrence used, on 6 July 1917, to enter the port - Wadi Ithm. Unlike his band of followers that summer's day, we had no sandstorm to contend with but, instead, a persistent northerly wind was channelling its strength along the valley against us so that we felt as though we were swimming up-current. It was the same wind which had been ruffling the surface of the sea for days but this was the first time we had had to pit ourselves, and the car, against it. The wadi was several hundred yards wide but its granitic sides, steep and rough, came down close to the road in places. A far cry from the massive, gentle granite such as the rounded Red Hills of Skye, these were walls of jointed, jagged rock, slashed with huge dark stripes, two to three metres wide, like great black wounds on pink skin. Some crags had been intruded by suites of dykes, criss-crossing like a bunch of giant ribbons through the rock.

Towards Al Quweirah we passed the turning to Wadi Rum and the road crossed a wider area of sand and then gravelly plains. In the distance the hills rose to peaks of three or four thousand feet but in the wadi the eroded sandstone shapes, a hundred feet high, stood proud from the plain like 'stack-rocks' in coastal waters. We stopped to see these buttes and columns and ambled through the hot, soft sand between tiny, tough plants; camels had been grazing and leaving their broad hoofprints amongst the delicate trails of lizards and birds. There was a little pile of charred wood and some discarded tin cans to the leeward side of a towering outcrop whose smooth, sculptured sides and sand-scooped hollows gave shelter from the wind or sun. Not far away the black goat-hair tents of a Bedouin camp were flapping gently and a flock of sheep was moving towards a new feeding ground of sparse, wiry vegetation.

Between Ras en Naqb and Ma'an we took a left turn and climbed up on to the King's Highway and the undulations of the limestone hills. The landscape was rocky and arid, but patches had been carefully cleared of stones and the thin soil cultivated: life was not easy for the local hill-farmers.

It was not long before we were descending towards the rocky gorges and famous rose-red sandstone of Petra. Nor was it long before we discovered, during the course of our picnic lunch, that the 'margarine' we had bought in Aqaba was in fact nothing of the kind but a strange substance with equal affinities to yoghurt and cottage cheese. Not knowing whether or not it was 'off' already, but suspecting that, if not, it soon would be if we did not get on with it, we plastered it thickly on our bread with dollops of apricot jam, or segments of a heat-deformed Edam cheese.

Happy in the knowledge that the Tourist Rest House was allowing us to camp under its trees that night, we set off cheerfully with water-bottle and cameras on the hour's walk to Petra. Everyone else at that time seemed either to be returning to the Rest House on horseback, or was already there and eagerly tucking into *musakhan* (a chicken dish) or goat kebabs, or whatever other delicacies were being served. This general evacuation did not deter us: it simply meant that we were deluged by unwanted offers of equine transport by the Bedouin guides and their growing surplus of skinny beasts. We knew that we had missed a spectacular sight which the jubilant cavalry of tourists, in their Stetsons and sneakers, had witnessed and no doubt captured on film - the rosy light of the morning sun on the famous facade of the Khaznah or Treasury - but for us there were other monuments whose colour and splendour would outshine it in the afternoon.

Petra is one of those famous places, including, reputedly, the Taj Mahal, which are quite as wonderful as everybody says they are. The colours of Petra's sandstone really do range from a rich rose-red to paler shades of yellow; and the swirling, banded patterns of the weathered rock are as beautiful as the grain of carved olive-wood. The entrance *siq* or passage, which is the winding course of Wadi Musa (the Valley of Moses where, traditionally, water gushed forth when he struck the rock), is as narrow and as steep-sided as described. As you follow its final twist before the gorge widens, the first glimpse of the magnificent Greek-style temple, called the Khaznah, really does come as a breathtaking surprise. It is easy to imagine the excitement of Burckhardt, the Swiss explorer disguised as an Arab pilgrim, when in 1812 he made the same trek and rediscovered the hidden

Cardo Maximus, Petra

city for the western world.

The most astonishing aspect to me was the extent of the city. Somehow I had expected that at the end of the *siq* there would be a cluster of buildings which we would have explored within half an hour. Not so: from the Treasury to the Qasr el Bint, as the western end of Wadi Musa, it was more than half a mile, with architectural wonders all the way. We saw the Roman theatre, climbed up the royal cave-tombs which were built to honour Nabateans and Romans but used subsequently as Christian churches, and we strolled along the paved Cardo Maximus, the main colonnaded street where long-haired, black goats were nibbling at bushes behind the columns. It was hot and still and quiet. A handful of bedouins (these were no longer nomads but had settled in Petra) had set up their tents to sell soft drinks and bottled sand - a popular souvenir in which the naturally variegated grains are stuck to the glass in unnatural but attractive designs. Like the Palmyrenes, the Nabateans seemed to have left to posterity a few of their commercial skills when they abandoned their city.

The way the guidebooks talk of the 'collapse' and 'abandonment' of Petra, anyone would think that there had been a major earthquake or some equally catastrophic event (such as the one which may have wiped out the dinosaurs) which sent the entire Nabatean population (not to mention the Romans) fleeing up the *siq*, never to be seen again. It is more realistic to imagine the 'end' as a gradual process during the fifth century AD after three hundred years of slow decline in trade which was the mainstay of Petra's wealth and importance. The Nabateans had had a good innings: a nomadic tribe from northern Arabia, they had called a halt to their wanderings in the seventh or eighth century BC and settled in Petra in much the same way as the Arameans had done in Damascus four or five hundred years before. By the fourth century BC the Nabateans had a monopoly of the caravan trade from the interior to the coast and were becoming rich.

Their kingdom expanded substantially northwards and eastwards during the second century BC and in 85 BC King Aretas III even ruled Damascus and Coele-Syria (Lebanon). They had successfully kept the Seleucids at bay and reached an understanding with the Egyptian rulers, but the Romans finally, and after much resistance, annexed the Nabatean kingdom in AD 106 and Bostra, rather than Petra, was chosen as the capital of the new province of Arabia. Although Petra continued to flourish in the second century AD, as shown by the wealth of Roman architecture which remains, competition from Palmyra, from other northern trading cities and from sea trade, began to take its toll and Petra's importance was past its peak.

We met a number of other tourists on our climb up Wadi al Deir to the famous Monastery. The guidebook described the ascent as 'an hour's steady climb', but at the risk of being beaten by darkness before we could return to the car we started briskly up the path to the Deir. The Lion Tomb and the caves of the Hermitage received a fleeting glance as we pressed on upwards. The steps were carved in the rock of the steep-sided gorge and the sun was low enough to cast shadows over most of the narrow wadi and to keep us reasonably cool. When we emerged into the sun on the hilltop half an hour later we were not sure at first if we had reached the end of the trail or if we had another half hour's walk ahead. Then we turned to our right and knew: there was the dazzling sunlit spectacle of the Deir. To our left we found another bunch of bedouins selling soft drinks and bottled sand to a German couple. Late afternoon was perfect for Deir-viewing and as we stood and marvelled the rays of the sun warmed our backs and seemed to flow into the rock-face, filling the Monastery with a golden light and illuminating the honeycombed sandstone cliffs around it. Believed to have been built in the third century AD as a temple to the Nabatean god Dhushara, who symbolised strength, it has a massive facade 148 feet high and 165 feet wide. There are two tiers of tall columns, a large central entrance and five recesses like bricked-up windows, where statues should have been. It is as though a gigantic Nabatean wedding-cake has been fossilised in the sandstone. Between the upper tier of columns and the pediment runs a carved, ornamental band with a simple design of identical discs, each about 2 feet in diameter, like a row of giant chocolate drops embedded in the icing.

From the brink of the little plateau where the Deir stood we looked out westwards over Wadi Arabah, with the rocky hillside falling away steeply and deeply just beyond our feet. No wonder that Petra withstood so many enemy attacks with those unscalable natural walls on the western side and its single entrance, the easily guarded narrow *siq* to the east; nor was it surprising that the city was 'lost' to all except the local bedouin population for so many centuries.

Until that evening at Petra we had been under the impression, following the disparaging comments of our friends, that as a demonstration of insanity our ambition to reach India in a 2CV was difficult to surpass. It was with a mixture of surprise and sympathy, therefore, that we came across an Englishman who had cycled all the way from Folkestone. As if that wasn't mad enough, he was intending to carry on pedalling to Johannesburg which he hoped to reach in six months' time! His journey itself provided ample cause for commiseration but when we saw his emaciated condition, resulting from a month's dysentery initiated in Nevsehir (in Turkey), we wondered how he could possibly continue to lose weight at the same distressing rate and survive. The imminent dissipation of his cycling muscles would leave him stranded in the Nubian desert or somewhere equally inhospitable. He was in a pitiable condition: I wanted to fold him in my arms, say, 'There, there,' and take him home to Folkestone. But then I realised that it would take more than an upset stomach to send any of us, mad travellers, scampering prematurely back to England. There was Ashley to think about too, of course - it was simply not safe to leave him alone with a car at his disposal while I was 3,000 miles away returning a stray cyclist to his nest. Ashley would have grabbed the steering-wheel with both hands and spent the rest of his working life, or at least the car's, gleefully driving through every country of the world: I would never have seen him again. Under the circumstances, I decided to restrict my pity for the cyclist to offering him some supper, which he refused, and a mug of coffee, which he accepted, relishing the prospect of its powdered milk. We reassured him that stores brimming with such gastronomic delights were awaiting him in Aqaba.

I was relieved to learn, during the course of the conversation, that he did not intend to cross the Nubian desert but was hoping to take the ferry up the Nile instead. This seemed a wise decision in view of the experiences of Neil Clough, an earlier cyclist on the England-South Africa run, who had written a book about his journey which we had all read. He had found that the only practical way of traversing the Sudanese sands between Wadi Halfa and Abu Hamed was to push his bicycle along the railway track for ten, gruelling days, during which he was tormented by flies, almost expired from heat and lack of shade, and very nearly died from dehydration. Insanitary and overcrowded though it was said to be, the Nile ferry was a relatively attractive alternative. The cyclist's route from Jordan to South Africa interested us, because driving through Egypt, Sudan and Kenya to Tanzania was one of the many possibilities we had entertained during the planning stages of our trip. Even though he would not encounter what would have been our major problem - obtaining petrol - we knew enough about the difficulties in store for him to admire his sheer courage at undertaking such an adventurous journey.

Twittering early birds in the branches above the tent woke us the following morning but ceased their chatter abruptly as soon as the sun was up, by which time we were rising too. It was not long before we were bouncing back up the hills to the King's Highway and then northwards as far as Shaubak before cutting across eastwards to the Desert Highway. Backtracking though we were to Amman, in order to arrive at the western end of the good straight TAP (Trans-Arabian Pipeline) road to take us across Saudi Arabia, we were avoiding the Kerak-Madaba road by choosing this alternative.

The Desert Highway slices through the sandy plains like a jointed series of Roman roads, offering a relatively swift passage to the heavy vehicles which dominate the traffic and to 2CV drivers who can find no reason for hanging around anyway. It is fortunate that the most monotonous landscape often accommodates the fastest roads for, apart from a couple of signposts to some phosphate mines and the sight of an overturned Iraqi oil tanker which had plummeted down the embankment, spilling black oil into the gully, we saw little in the way of interesting scenery, and the only diversion arose from a road-widening project where a dual carriageway was being constructed. For a short, freshly-surfaced stretch, the traffic, lacking directions to the contrary, was enjoying a free-for-all. The majority appeared to be in favour of treating each side of the carriageway as a normal two-way road and had obviously plumped for one side or the other by the toss of a 10 fils coin. A minority of vehicles, with suitable tyres, had chosen to ignore the road entirely and were steaming up on the outside, generating mini-sandstorms as they went and hampering the progress of the workmen still further. It was not surprising that most of the labourers had abandoned work altogether and were squatting in clusters for tea.

Later we passed a small house in front of which a dozen men were sitting drinking *chai,* until we came into view, whereupon several of them jumped up and began beckoning and gesturing wildly that we should join their party. Unfortunately, Ashley being all for pressing on, we disappointed them, but it was another example of spontaneous, Jordanian hospitality. The checkpoint police, some of whom the Folkestone cyclist had found to be 'a touch' too friendly, were always offering us tea, and a young man in Aqaba had insisted on giving us soft drinks (canned by a well-known Japanese car manufacturer) while he talked to us. In these instances the conversations were always introduced by courteous expressions such as 'Welcome to Jordan/our country!' or *'Ahlan wa sahlan!'* and laced with anxious inquiries about our opinion of the country's beauty and of the people's hospitality, both of which we were quick to praise. We found the concern and generosity of Jordanians and Syrians alike refreshingly genuine after several of the eastern Turkish gestures of friendship, which masked some ulterior motive such as a parting request for one of our more valuable possessions.

The Desert Highway rapidly deteriorated after the widened section, and by the time we had reached and successfully by-passed Amman we were glad to be on the smoother surface of the road to Azraq, where our joints were less likely to be dislocated.

The prospect of Dubai now lay ahead like the crock of gold at the end of a rainbow. According to Ashley, all we had to do was to dash briskly across Saudi and Qatar, stopping only for borders and petrol ('And water?' I added anxiously) and in next to no time we would be swimming in the clear waters of the Gulf, or drinking chilled beer in an air-conditioned apartment. I had to remind him that what had taken three alternating drivers of a Range Rover two days to cover in the reverse direction would not be the same gentle cruise in a 2CV with a single helmsman. (Women were prohibited from driving in Saudi Arabia.)

Nevertheless Dubai was our next major goal and Ashley, being eager to reach it as soon as possible, was raring to cross the border into Saudi that afternoon. Our stop at Azraq (the last town on our route through Jordan) was therefore intended to be a brief one: long enough for me to stock up with fresh provisions and exchange the remainder of our coins for edible items, while Ashley filled our collection of water containers from a convenient tap in the main street. With more time we could have visited the Qasr (castle) and the Wetlands Reserve where the fresh water of Azraq's oasis attracts thousands of migrating birds.

I duly bought a great stack of flat loaves, a kilo bag of fresh Melba-like toast, an assortment of apples and cucumbers and some cheese, and then crossed the road to buy some eggs. When I held up six fingers and then pointed at what I was after the little shopkeeper hurried into the back and returned with half a dozen trays. We soon cleared up the misunderstanding, which was now becoming familiar, and he offered me a seat and a carton of banana milk, fresh from the 'fridge. We chatted for a while until his English vocabulary had been exhausted and, as Ashley was waiting on the other side of the street with the car, I stood up to go, explaining that I would take the remainder of the drink to him. Little did I know that this would give rise to a lengthy exchange of good wishes, thanks and other heartfelt sentiments so prolonged that a casual observer might have thought that ours was a lifelong friendship, not a fleeting acquaintance based on half a dozen eggs and a carton of milk.

Meanwhile, Ashley had been speaking to a French courier who had just driven three female passengers up from Aqaba through the largely roadless eastern desert in a four-wheel drive Renault van. Their last stop before Azraq had been only seven miles away at a wildlife reserve where, the Frenchman told us, we should certainly be allowed to camp. Since it was the only one of its kind in Jordan and would give us the rare opportunity to see the pale Arabian oryx, it seemed to me an infinitely more fascinating prospect than another customs search. He-who-would-be-in-Dubai took some convincing before he finally and reluctantly gave in and we soon set off for Shaumari. One of the three young lads who were living and working at the reserve sold us tickets and showed us where we could camp in the sandy car-park. The other two were engrossed in a game of table-tennis outside their bungalow and indicated that they would show us the reserve when they had finished, so we sat and watched them while we chatted to the third. When the game did end the pair simply pointed us in the direction of a large concrete watch-tower and recommended that we take our binoculars.

From the top, buffeted by a strong cool wind, we looked out over the large fenced area of flat desert and began to scan the enclosures. The reward for an hour's vigilance was the sighting of three gazelles who were hiding sensibly amongst the thickest bushes in their pen. The only other visible wildlife were a pair of ostriches, a wild ass and a couple of well fed Arabian oryx; all would have been better seen from ground level as they were in separate enclosures close to the tower and were obviously relatively tame. One oryx was born in San Diego Animal Park, USA, in 1974 and was having a lazy life in which food was supplied at regular intervals. We could not help feeling that he would have looked a great deal trimmer and healthier had he been amongst the fortunate ones who had been set free either in Jordan or in Oman as part of the reintroduction scheme initiated in the 1970s. It was a sad fact that such a fine species of antelope had once been hunted to extinction in Jordan, chiefly for the supposed aphrodisiac properties of its long, straight horns.

In 1962 the international 'Operation Oryx' had been set up to save the Arabian oryx *(Oryx leucoryx)*. The idea was to capture wild ones, to establish a breeding zoo-bank and to build up a stock which could be liberated in new national parks and sanctuaries in the Middle East. By 1969 the wild population, restricted to Oman, was thought to be below 200, but herds of 16 in Arizona, 7 in California, 23 in Qatar, as well as collections in Kuwait and Saudi Arabia, ensured that reintroduction could be started. Thanks to the Shaumari Reserve the oryx, the wild ass, several species of gazelle such as the Dorcas and the rhim, and other indigenous and once plentiful creatures will continue to live in the Jordanian desert where they belong. To know that we were supporting a significant contribution to wildlife conservation more than compensated for the dearth of animals on view. After all, Shaumari was not a zoo (as the three Jordanians there had emphasised in an effort to pre-empt our disappointment) but a place where the animals could be protected while living in their natural habitat. This at any rate was the gist of my consoling words to Ashley, who was beginning to mutter:

'I told you so. It was a waste of time coming to Shaumari to look for animals which refuse to be seen. We could have been over the border and halfway across Saudi by now.'

To have pointed out that the wind which was currently trying to blow us off the top of the watch-tower was an easterly, which would probably have prevented us from even leaving the customs post, let alone reaching the middle of Saudi Arabia, would have been wasted breath on the one-w.-w.-b.-i.-D. It was paradoxical that at the outset of our journey we had predicted that I should be the one always anxious to move on to the next place and to adhere to our schedule (rough though it was), and that Ashley would be so nonchalant that the odd week's delay would not have perturbed him in the least. In practice, however, it was more often Ashley who was eager to be on the move whereas I wanted to see whatever seemed interesting en route. You might think that either we had completely misjudged our own temperaments, or the journey had changed us dramatically; but there was more to it than that - such as the fact that Ashley had been this way before (even if not to Shaumari nor eastern Turkey) and had, as the saying goes, already 'bought the T-shirt and read the book' and was now having to sit through 'the film'. It was also significant that we had written from Aqaba to our friend in Dubai to tell him to expect us on 21 or 22 October and neither of us wanted to disrupt a time-plan which was going to affect other people.

CHAPTER 13

By 8.30 the following morning we had left Jordan and were at the Saudi border post of Al Hadithah. It was quiet and spacious with extravagantly large modern buildings. We parked in the shade of one of them and entered the large block of conveniences by what we believed to be the appropriate doors, only to find that we had both emerged into the same vast and vacuous room. Along one side was a long row of private cubicles, apparently identical, and since there was no one else there to be shocked or offended by the presence of one or other of us we speedily made use of the luxury facilities which included, alongside the holes in the ground, little water-sprays in place of the usual taps and jugs which did duty for toilet paper in most of the countries we had visited.

The immigration building was another large, silent hall but was half-filled with rows of apparently dumb people awaiting the return of their passports. When we walked in, their collective gaze was averted from the blank screen of dark reflective glass which faced them, and they watched us fill in our forms and take them to this panel in search of someone to hand them to. It was unnerving enough walking up to the black wall with the gaze of a hundred speechless Arabs fixed on us as though we were actors in some silent movie, but when we spotted a letter-box chute and posted our passports and forms to an apparently disembodied hand which was vaguely beckoning from the bottom of it we burst into spontaneous laughter. It was all like some ridiculous dream! We endeavoured, for the sake of those who could not share the joke, to suppress our mirth, but it was one of those absurd cases in which the harder you try, the more uncontrollable your giggling becomes. We stood, like two naughty children, shaking quietly with our backs to the audience, until a little man relieved us by opening a door and passing out our stamped passports. We hurried out with them into the hot fresh air.

Next-door there were some offices with more obvious signs of activity, so we went to find somebody who could translate our Arabic entry stamps into English and tell us how long a transit period we had been allowed.

'One week,' replied a senior uniformed official with excellent English. Lounging in an armchair in his office his colleague, in casual white *dishdasha,* was fingering his string of worry beads. When he heard our names he looked up with the enlightened air of one for whom a bell has just rung, and announced that he had received a telex message from the Saudi Arabian Consul in Damascus. Ashley and I exchanged worried glances.

'He has instructed the officers at this post and at Salwah to give you every possible assistance when you arrive in our country and when you leave for Qatar.'

We looked at the imparter of this news with a mixture of relief and surprise. Was that just a friendly smile in the telex-man's glinting eyes, or could he be quietly smirking as he clicked his beads, amused by our reactions? His face was frustratingly inscrutable.

We drove along for the customs check and were ordered to unload everything from the car onto extensive benches. The white-robed Saudi Arabian officer snapped his fingers and waved his hands to enlist the help of members of his army of blue-overalled Sri Lankans, Indians and Pakistanis who were employed as cleaners, mechanics and general assistants. Every box and bag of ours was opened, their contents were disgorged and every item was examined; no book or bottle was left unopened, no tub of food unsniffed in the relentless and thorough search for drugs, arms, alcohol and pornographic material.

Meanwhile the car was taken to an adjacent bay where, to our horror, it was partially dismantled in the same pursuit: the seats were removed, the door panels examined, the fuel tank guard and the air-filter were taken off, the mats were lifted and the mechanics even tried to take out the floor plate which runs the whole length of the car. Ashley was nearly at his wits' end in his attempt (constantly thwarted by the customs official, who repeatedly ordered him to return to the baggage benches) to keep his eye on the team of heavy-handed, large-spanner-wielding mechanics who were attacking the 2CV. With one mindless action, they could have accidentally undone weeks of careful preparation. By the time our baggage had been thoroughly scrutinised, the last tourist brochure leafed through, we felt as though we had just witnessed the ransack of our house - and that in effect is what had occurred, for our little car and its contents did represent, for the duration of our journey, home.

When the car had been reassembled and restored to full working order we still had to repack it from mounds of our jumbled possessions which had been liberally strewn about the benches as though by a toddler emptying a box of toys. The officer responsible was already riffling through his next victim's belongings, but it was small consolation to know that everyone was treated as we were: we had already reached our own conclusions about the real content of that suspicious telex message. The supervisor of the mechanics, a Bombay man, was sympathetic, chatting to us as we repacked and enjoying the opportunity to voice his own disapproval of Saudi customs officers in far stronger terms that we either felt or would have dared to express in earshot of an employer. The Bombay man would have hit it off famously with the Syrian mechanics in Madaba and many of the other immigrant workers in Saudi who were consistently disparaging about the country and yet were happy to be paid to work there. There is no doubt that the bad feelings sprang, in part, from jealousy of Saudi Arabia's wealth.

As for our own annoyance, it was only a passing reaction to the apparently careless abandon with which the search was carried out, and to the three hours we had wasted at the border. We had no objections in principle to the meticulous examination of vehicles entering a country, but if there was one virtue we had yet to learn from our Asian friends it was patience. Presenting the Indian with a couple of English paperbacks which he clutched to his heart in gratitude, we set our watches forward one hour and raced off up Wadi Sirhan.

That at least was our intention, but we had forgotten to take into account the beastly easterly which was hell-bent to see that our transit visas expired long before we had reached Turayf, let alone the border with Qatar.

We suspected that it was not unlikely that such a man of authority as the Saudi Consul in Damascus held sway not only over the granting of visas but also over Saudi Arabia's meteorological conditions. Surely it was not coincidental that each time the road took a slight bend in direction the wind swung round reliably to meet us head on. There was only one thing which would calm our suspicions, give the car a rest and cure all our current irritations: so we stopped for lunch. The Edam was almost spreadable. We sat in the car listening to the World Service and, for a time, we were glad of the wind which kept us fanned and thwarted the local flies.

For the first hundred miles, from the border to Turayf, we were travelling through scenery which, Ashley emphasised, was exceptionally interesting by northern Saudi standards. After all, there were lava-capped hills some of which, such as Zatab Ash Shamah, were over 3,000 feet; we passed a number of little oases, one with an old castle camouflaged against the sandy desert; we saw herds of camels and the dark goat-hair tents of a bedouin camp; and there was even a *lokantasi* (a Turkish transport café) for long-distance lorry drivers at one of the petrol stations. The shredded truck tyres and car wrecks which littered the roadside at frequent intervals were, however, not unusual: they were to haunt us for the next thousand miles.

At Turayf the road meets the TAPline (Trans-Arabian Pipeline) which was initially constructed in 1950 and now runs from Dammam on theArabian Gulf across a thousand miles of predominantly desert land to Sidon in Lebanon. The TAPline has a capacity to transport nearly half a million barrels (about 17 million gallons) of oil per day from the oilfields of eastern Saudi Arabia to the Mediterranean coast. We also intercepted at Turayf the link road from the main Baghdad-Amman highway and from then on we were on the TAPline road. We bypassed the town centre but passed a number of modern mansions and a new housing development site for 'Internal Security Officers'. Turayf has its own airfield and was obviously an expanding town. It is only twelve miles from the Syrian border, to which we had been running parallel, and we

TAPline road, Saudi Arabia

were forced to slow down on encountering a series of enormous ramps with flashing traffic lights, culminating in a police checkpoint where our passports were examined with suspicion and the car with interest.

The TAPline road must make even the greatest Roman civil engineers writhe in their tombs with envy at its sheer, uninterrupted straightness. Apart from one or two minor kinks, the road and the pipeline stretch more or less as the crow flies from the north of Jordan all the way to the Arabian Gulf in a south-east by easterly direction, almost clipping Iraq's southern border as they go. Fortunately the wind had abated by the late afternoon and we cruised along at a comfortable 50 m.p.h, stopping only to refuel at Al Jalamid where we discovered that the national petrol price was a staggeringly cheap 36 pence per gallon.

At 5.45 p.m. the sun packed up for the night and we shortly followed suit. We dived off the road on to some firm sand and drove a few hundred yards before pitching the tent and cooking a meal by the car's sidelights.

Hundreds of moths came to gatecrash the party, and the arrival of a mammoth, hairy spider, so alarming that at first I suspected Ashley of a practical joke, made a suitable climax to the evening's entertainment. I watched in horror as it trotted past the cooking stove and under the car.

'If 'that's the size of the local arachnids, I'm glad we decided to sleep in the tent instead of under the stars,' I gasped, but Ashley was already scrabbling on his stomach beneath the sump guard, trying to get a closer look at the beast.

I had no intention of joining him.

After that, we turned the lights off and found that the stars were becoming progressively brighter and our night vision improving so rapidly that artificial light was soon unnecessary. The sky was like a dark velvet pin-cushion studded with myriad diamond-headed pins, and, like thousands of people before us, we were drawn helplessly into a contemplation of infinity. However many times it has been done, we still could not stop ourselves indulging in a brief marvel at the mystery and the staggering volume of unexplored space. Meanwhile, the lights of a hundred-strong convoy of Jordanian lorries were sweeping along the road in a bright, relentless stream. We had seen the fleet paralysed at the border earlier in the day, but now it seemed that nothing could stop their onward march, night and day, to Riyadh or the Gulf.

Periodically fishing moths out of the cold, rationed inch of water in the washing-up bowl, we washed our shivering bodies from face to feet and brushed our chattering teeth. It was only half-past eight but in the last two hours the temperature had dropped like a stone and we crawled eagerly into the downy comfort of our sleeping bags.

At 6 a.m. we were up just before the sun and, as it was

still rather chilly, we even switched on the car heater for a while to thaw my feet, which are notoriously over-reactive to temperature changes: for most of the trip they had been red and swollen like a pair of fat lobsters, but now they had temporarily reverted to their more familiar impression of a couple of ice-blocks. The sun soon warmed the air as we sped along the straight, flat road, keen to put as many miles under our belt as possible that day.

Every minor change in relief and every slight interruption of the monotonous landscape we greeted with disproportionate appreciation. A sandy hillock thirty feet high became a mountain; a little road cutting, exposing a narrow band of horizontally bedded limestone and chert, assumed the importance of a major geological discovery. I even began to count the shredded remains of lorry tyres and the abandoned cars by the roadside - for readers whom the subject fascinates, there was an average of one tyre remnant every fifty yards and a relinquished vehicle every mile! (Bearing in mind that these desert victims are never cleared away, I should be interested to hear from any future TAPline road travellers whose own counts would indicate the rate of accumulation!) How long will it be before the desert is turned into a scrap yard by the hypnotic power of this straight road, which sends dazed drivers tumbling down its embankments? When will some enterprising soul start recycling the tons of scrap metal?

Somewhere between Al Jalamid and Ar'ar, the pipeline disappeared underground, and simultaneously we entered a wonderful series of gentle bends in the road. Ashley was just changing down a gear or two, quite unnecessarily, to negotiate these novelties when we became aware of a large car approaching rapidly from the rear. To be precise, we were being followed by the kind of megalosaurian Pontiac which made our 2CV look as vulnerable as a white mouse. Not only that, but it was bearing down on us with menacing speed, its headlights flashing from the gleaming chrome.

'Why doesn't he overtake? There's plenty of room, no one coming.'

We hadn't seen another vehicle for miles - not a moving one anyway.

'I think he wants us to stop,' said Ashley and, as I turned round and we pulled in, I saw that the flashing lights were emanating not only from the vicinity of the radiator grille but also from an impressive rooftop array. The khaki-uniformed cop stepped out of his parked green and white vehicle which rocked gently when he slammed the door. He could have been Clint Eastwood the way he swaggered up to the window, gun on hip, the Pontiac still flashing in the background.

As soon as he opened his mouth, however, the illusion was shattered. A stream of incomprehensible Arabic issued forth and 'Pazzaporta' was the only word we caught. We duly showed them to him but his look of consternation merely deepened as he perused them.

'Who is this?' he asked Ashley, while nodding in my direction.

'Oh, she's my wife,' Ashley replied, a little too casually for my liking. 'Name?' again to Ashley.

'Ashley Earwaker.'

Perplexed silence for a moment as he tried to square this with my passport. 'No, *bint!*' nodding towards me.

'Yes, that is my *bint,* my wife.'

'Name of *bint?*' From his look, it was clear that he suspected Ashley of more than non-co-operation. There was no doubt in the cop's mind that this Englishman was a kidnapper of white slave-girls and that I was his latest victim, being dragged against my will across the Arabian desert.

'Mrs Earwaker,' admitted Ashley at last and, under his breath, 'Of course. Why don't you read the passport?'

'Ah. Madame? *Bint?*'

'Yes, Madame Earwaker. Wife. Madame.'

The light had finally dawned that we were married and the suggestion of a smile flickered momentarily across the policeman's face. Then he turned abruptly and marched away with our passports to his car. The awful possibility that we had been conned flashed through my mind.

'Just a minute!' I said, getting out of the car in protest.

'Don't panic,' said Ashley, casually. 'Remember he's got a gun.'

'But he's got our passports!' I countered, jumping back in the car all the same.

'Everything's OK'.

Clint was coming back.

The policeman had roused his colleague from the padded comfort of the Pontiac's back seat where he had been lying dormant and hidden from view, and after a few words they had decided to return our passports and set us free.

'I bet that was the telex message at work again.'

'He should have known that we were married, then.'

I glanced at my passport and suddenly realised the cause of the confusion: my passport had been amended in 1983 by the Passport Office in such a half-hearted way that 'Miss N.A. Rigby' still appeared as my title on the front cover, with 'Mrs N.A. Earwaker' added in diminutive letters above. It certainly did not look very convincing.

There were four police checkpoints to confront us that day, two at Ar'ar, where Ashley was surprised to see that new houses and shops had sprung up in the last four years to make it a sizeable town. At the first a row of smart Toyota jeeps and Nissan Patrols stood gleaming beside the barrier; at the second the policeman, for reasons best known to himself, assumed that we were Turkish until proved innocent. Then, at Rafha, we rode uncomfortably over a set of ramps before grinding to a halt at the barrier. Ashley's discomfort was exacerbated when he instantly recognised the place as the site of the famous 'spotlight tumulus'. When they had passed this way before, Ashley and his friends had been staggered by a three feet-high mound of confiscated car spotlights, for which the checkpoint policeman clearly had a maniacal appetite. It had taken the three of them a good half-hour to dissuade the obstinate man from adding the Range Rover's extra eyes to his collection. The performance was not one which Ashley was eager to repeat, nor did he relish the thought of losing a part of the car's anatomy the fitting and securing of which had involved so much hard work. Besides, it was no consolation that our spotlights had successfully survived the marauding hands of countless Turkish boys if they were then to be hacked off here in one fell swoop by an official kleptomaniac.

We were fortunate. We cast our eyes in vain for the glistening heap and guessed that the guilty policeman had probably been led away by little men in white coats. His replacement glanced briefly at our passports and returned sensibly to the shade. The fourth checkpoint was similarly trouble-free - in fact, coming as it did in the late afternoon, it made a timely break in our game of I-Spy which was becoming decidedly stressful. Having exhausted all exterior possibilities, after S for sun, sand and sky, R for road and P for pipeline, we had been struggling through the visible contents of the car for the last fifty miles or more, and tempers were getting frayed. Furthermore, we were unable to pick up the soothing tones of the World Service, nor could we agree on a cassette to play.

Lunch had been a disaster too. Ever since breakfast we had been looking forward to it and Ashley naturally needed a break from the wheel. We had turned off the road, scaled a gravelly ramp over the pipeline and stopped. Immediately we were swarmed upon by hundreds of flies which appeared as if from nowhere. We tried shutting the windows, but the heat was stifling as our only air-conditioning was generated through the open windows by the motion of the car. Just before we reached melting point we had managed to consume a couple of hard-boiled eggs and a cucumber and were on the road again, flicking the most obstinate flies out of the windows as we went. The rest of lunch was not exactly appetising as the Edam was approaching the liquid state again and the thin bread had only to be released from its bag to be turned instantly to toast by the strong, hot wind - which was having other effects too...

At first we were intrigued by the two brightly-painted, three-storeyed livestock lorries which overtook us, but for the next few miles, until they were out of range, our noses were overwhelmed by the windblown smells of several hundred sheep and goats on board. Then there was the time we were approaching a large lorry-park just as the vast numbers of Jordanian trucks, which had been changing tyres and being serviced there, decided to get back on the road; the quantities of dust which their wheels sent billowing into the atmosphere and storming towards us turned us rapidly into a moving sand-dune. These incidents were as nothing, however, when seen against the background of our chief problem with the wind - the car was simply incapable of doing more than 45 m.p.h. in its battle against this natural force. We could do nothing but practise patience. Nevertheless, the sun went down about twenty-five minutes earlier than the previous day and, encouraged by this sign of significant eastward progress, we stopped soon afterwards. Although the breeze was sweeping sand against the tent that night, it also carried warmer air and, unlike the previous evening, it was pleasant to wash in cool water and to let the wind dry our skin.

We were so eager to be back on the road early the following morning that we failed to notice, between us and the asphalt, a patch of soft sand in which we promptly became stuck. Fortunately several large strips of lorry tyres were conveniently to hand, and with these improvised sand-ladders and our shovel we were soon out of trouble and laughing at our stupidity.

When we reached Al Nu'airiyah, we were only twenty-five miles from the Gulf coast and longing for the beaches of Dubai. Before turning off the TAPline road to go south to Hofuf we filled up with petrol and found that the wind had caused our consumption to increase by about 15 per cent. True to form, the enemy veered from a south-easterly direction to a south-south-easterly one as we turned, and remained almost dead against us as we headed for the oil-rich province of eastern Saudi Arabia.

Compared with the northern gravel plains which we had seen for the last two days, this eastern lowland region bordering the Gulf was like the Garden of Eden. The sandy area, called Al Hasa on one of our maps (we had three, of differing scales, with marked disagreement on roads, regional names, settlements and international boundaries), was dotted with little plants and shrubs; there were oasis settlements at frequent intervals and numerous herds of grazing camels, some with calves. We even found a tree to park beneath for lunch, although the flies quickly drove us away again.

It will take a long time for the bedouin people to catch up with the twentieth century - nomads for thousands of years, they toy half-heartedly with the idea of settlement without any real commitment. We passed small, attempted villages whose only gesture of permanence was a collection of wooden and corrugated iron huts and which consisted otherwise of traditional goat-hair tents, flocks of sheep and goats, odd camels and donkeys and the ubiquitous Toyota and Datsun pick-up vans.

As incongruous as the juxtaposition of Japanese vehicles and bedouin tents might be, we had become accustomed to it in Oman, but the sight of a cornfield in the middle of the so-called desert was almost unbelievable. The corn had been harvested weeks before we passed by, but even the acres of stubble and the stacks of straw bales were enough to make us look twice. There were rows of gleaming tractors and other bright new farm machinery, obviously freshly imported from Europe. Vast areas of desert had been fenced to create fields, which were being irrigated by centre-pivot sprinklers, enormous metal-strutted gantries on wheels. These sprinklers were several hundred yards long and rotated, like the hands of a clock, about a central point, so that they covered an enormous circular area in one cycle. The task (not to mention the cost) of making the desert green is stupendous when you consider how much water must be input to offset the colossal evaporation losses, but it had obviously been successful here, and agricultural development in Saudi Arabia is bound to advance dramatically, provided enough money continues to be invested in these ambitious schemes.

Between Ayn Dar and Hofuf we were in the heart of the oilfield province and pipelines were two a penny. They radiated over the ground like the spokes of giant bicycle wheels, from several gleaming gathering stations, each with a shimmering gas flare and an assemblage of large, silver pipes and tanks. The geometry of the roads from Dhahran, Dammam and Doha on the coast, and from the inland towns of Nu'airiyah, Haradh and Riyadh, is not as simple. Most of them follow radial paths at first, but instead of converging simply at Hofuf they come within twenty miles of it and start dancing round an imaginary maypole, criss-crossing as they go. Not only did our maps disagree on the precise configuration of these roads, but also the layout had changed since our latest (1984) map was published. We have no idea, therefore, exactly how we approached Hofuf, but by following the new road-signs (fortunately in English and Arabic) we came in approximately from the north, just as it was beginning to get dark.

We stopped for petrol and caused the Pakistani pump attendant considerable alarm.

'You are taking a very big risk, sir,' he said, nodding anxiously towards the car where I was sitting.

Ashley turned to see which particular risk he was referring to - was it the vulnerable, soft roof or our heavy load, or were we so tired that we had failed to notice a flat tyre?

'Your wife, sir...'

'Oh, her. Yes, she can be a bit of a hazard at times, but...' My clenched fist appeared at the windscreen.

'You know women are not allowed to drive in Saudia?'

'But I've been driving the whole time.'

The attendant looked again at the car.

'Oh, sorry!' he said, 'I was thinking that your car was left-hand drive but, of course, it is GB. OK, sir!'

Hofuf we remember as a large university town, rapidly expanding with new buildings, and teeming with traffic lights, all biased towards red. Despite these obstacles we soon emerged on the south-eastern side, passing the university's 'Date Research Centre' and 'Agricultural and

Veterinary Research Centre', numerous modern suburban mansions, and collections of corrugated PVC greenhouses identified as 'farms'.

It was half past five, dark and rapidly approaching our bedtime, as we left the built-up area and began scanning the roadsides for signs of a track or some firm sand for camping. On and on we went across a sea of soft sand for what seemed like hours to two hungry, weary souls. We were almost on the point of making the ultimate sacrifice of backtracking to Hofuf and finding a hotel when, at last, up popped a promising set of tyre tracks, to starboard.

Soon we were digging into sardines, under a bright moon, and socialising with the neighbourhood's large beetles. A solitary but outsize ant, which looked as though it had just eaten all its friends and relations but was still game for a dish of dessert, made straight for the oily tins. Already over half an inch long and with the girth of a large cabbage white caterpillar, it was obviously going for a world record in ants' dimensions and was odds on to break it.

By contrast, the scorpion we saw the next morning was so pale and tiny that we suspected the monstrous ant of depriving the poor thing of most of its food supply. I was happy enough that it was that way round: the vision of an approaching scorpion three or four times the normal size would have sent me scurrying faster than the arrival of the giant ant would. To judge by the wealth of little animal tracks which appeared overnight in the sand around us, we must have been camping in the middle of a popular hunting ground: it looked as though hundreds of small mammals, lizards and insects had been chasing about all night, no doubt hotly pursued by our voracious friend.

We entered Qatar near Salwah, which is only a mile from the coast and was extremely humid that morning. In the sticky heat we were asked to unload the car by the customs officer, who was only marginally less meticulous in his search than the Saudis had been. Two hours after we had been allowed into Qatar we were already leaving the country at Sauda Nathil, at the eastern end of the isthmus which separates peninsular Qatar from the mainland.

It was all very well leaving Qatar, but for the next sixty-six miles we were at a loss to know which country we were in and what time of day it was. Our previous experiences of no-man's-land had generally been two or three miles between the exit point of one country and the entry to another. On this occasion, however, we drove for one and a half hours from Qatar before we came to the United Arab Emirates. Had it not been for Ashley's recollection of boundary demarcation problems in this part of the world, we might have seriously believed that we had missed the border post accidentally. In fact when we reached the UAE customs post at Al Silah at twenty to two we were told that it was really twenty to three and that after our official exit at Sauda Nathil we had then driven across thirteen more miles of Qatar, followed by forty within Saudi Arabia and thirteen within the UAE. Feeling bewildered, we nevertheless knew that it was fruitless to consult our multifarious maps for confirmation; we simply took our informant's word for granted.

Arranging ten days' car insurance at the border had seemed a straightforward task until we came to inquire whether it would be valid for me to drive too. The Palestinian insurance agent had his doubts but made every effort to clarify the situation by spending the next thirty minutes on the 'phone to his company's headquarters in Dubai and Abu Dhabi, while we enjoyed the cooling influence of his air-conditioned office and two cups of *chai* Lipton, served by his assistant, who came from Kerala in India. My three days' deprivation from driving was beginning to give me withdrawal symptoms, and when at last I was told that my entitlement to grip the wheel was restored, I did so eagerly, feeling as though it would be downhill all the way to Dubai.

Figurative hills were about all we could hope for on that final stretch of *sabkha* (salt desert). Whereas sand-dunes had appeared amid the hummocky terrain between Sauda Nathil and Al Silah, the remainder of the road to Dubai ran across a proverbial pancake. There was little traffic and only the kilometre-stones indicating the diminishing distances to Abu Dhabi, and one or two hotel advertisements, relieved the monotony that afternoon. The mounds of soft sand amongst which we camped that night were not dunes but part of some roadworks involving huge earth-movers which had left conveniently firm tracks over a small area somewhere between Ruwais and Tarif, nearly a hundred miles west of Abu Dhabi.

The sun had set at 5.55 p.m., fifty minutes earlier than on our first night in Saudi Arabia. Between these two stops we had travelled 1,100 miles in three days and now we were only 180 miles from Dubai. On the eve of our arrival at the port - our final destination on the southern side of the Arabian Gulf - we were as cheerful as schoolchildren at the end of term. If anyone had seen us that evening they would have naturally, but mistakenly assumed that we were under the influence of alcohol rather than the strain of a few days in the desert. They would have seen me staggering drunkenly along the tyre-tracks in the moonlight, pretending to be driven by hunger and thirst towards a mirage of fruit cakes and fresh, cold milk; and they would have witnessed Ashley ceremoniously lifting a deformed Mars bar from the steel chest and delicately removing the wrapper as though he were unveiling a long-lost piece of treasure. Naturally there was no fruit cake on the menu that night, nor any milk but the powdered variety, and the treasured Mars bar, which we had bought in Damascus at great expense, was years past its best.

Early the next morning, 21 October, we awoke to find ourselves shrouded in a heavy sea-mist which had drenched the tent, dampened the sleeping bags, and covered the car in condensation. While we were warming ourselves with mugs of coffee and wondering when the sun would break through the fog to dry our camping gear, a rumbling noise reached our ears and from out of the gloom appeared an enormous orange monster, and then a second. Our own surprise at being disturbed at 6.30 a.m. by a couple of bulldozers already at work faded into the mist, however, compared to the wide-eyed alarm on the drivers' faces at the ghostly apparition of a white 2CV, a luminous green tent and two lunatics hiding amongst the sand-heaps.

CHAPTER 14

During the day evaporation from the surface of the *sabkha* concentrates the seawater solution present in the pores between the sand grains and causes crystallisation of minerals such as gypsum, aragonite and halite (common salt). These crystals bind the sand surface into a hard, salty crust which we had been walking on the previous evening. Now the humidity was so high that the *sabkha* surface was soft and damp to a depth of an inch or two, but when the sun began to come through, the crust would reform. These cycles of evaporation and solution, including occasional flooding of the coastal *sabkha* by seawater, create not only a flat, salt-encrusted terrain: we also saw beautiful patterns of polygonal cracks where the crust had dried out excessively; there were large clusters of desert-rose (tabular crystals of gypsum) projecting from the salt surface; and we found some areas where the cracked crust seemed to have lifted itself up into little angular ridges, each one a foot high and like two rows of roof tiles, resting against each other to form a tunnel of triangular cross-section. (This region, once known as the Trucial Coast of Arabia, is the prime example of *sabkha*.)

By about nine o'clock the mist had cleared and we

had reached the end of the dual carriageway's roadworks and diversions. We passed the turning to Abu Dhabi, drove sixty more miles, and then for the last twenty to Dubai the roadsides became increasingly densely packed with hoardings advertising a wide variety of Japanese products such as air-conditioners and four-wheel-drive vehicles. At midday we were entering the city (more accurately the sheikhdom) of Dubai and wondering how we were going to find our friend's flat with only an outline of a street plan, when the word 'HILTON' appeared in large letters on the skyline, like a message from heaven, and we came homing in, knowing that if we reached the hotel we would be close to our destination.

We parked our dusty little wagon in the car-park amongst the rows of shining Mercedes, and waved hopefully to a little Indian man who was working his way up the row, polishing the car windows. Up the steps we bounced to the hotel reception and asked at the desk for directions to our friend's address. There was a moment's hesitation, during which we detected a hint of bewilderment in the receptionist's eye: had we spoken in a language which he could not understand? Impossible - this was the Hilton, after all. Then we looked at each other and realised what a strange spectacle we presented: there was Ashley in his shorts, T-shirt and sandals, here was I in crumpled blouse and skirt, and both of us desert-worn and weary, with sand in our hair, skin coated in dust and yet the effrontery to stroll into this refined world of suited businessmen and exclusive perfume shops. Under the circumstances, the receptionist's horror was remarkably controlled. He treated us with undue courtesy: a copy of a street map was rapidly produced and, having ushered us politely to the doorway, he seemed exceptionally eager to give us the necessary directions. The operation was so swiftly executed that we were back at the car too soon: the chamois-wielding Indian was still several Mercedes away from cleaning the once-white 2CV.

Nine days in Dubai flew by, as all good holidays do. The apartment was luxurious, the sea was invigorating and the beach's white coral sand was warm and soft. We were entertained by friends and spoilt by the variety of European and Indian food available: we drank cold milk as though we would not see it again for months (as indeed was to be expected in Pakistan and India) and savoured the simple, long-forgotten flavour of toast for breakfast. I found that I had almost lost my taste for beer, which was probably a good thing, considering the prospect of more ale-less weeks ahead, but Ashley readily emptied a few cans of chilled Dutch lager.

We had a pile of mail awaiting us, and the use of a telephone; there was ample time and hot water to launder our entire wardrobe (such that it was), and I was startled to find myself enjoying the novelty of ironing our clothes. 'All things in moderation,' I thought, and soon put a stop to it lest the pleasure should become a habit. Between these frenzies of domesticity and periods of gastronomic delight we swam in the sea, attempted to windsurf, and even had a game of squash. A great deal of time, however, was taken up in arranging the car's shipment to Karachi. Upon this crucial crossing of the Arabian (or Persian, depending on your point of view) Gulf hung, after all, the continuation of our travels, and much as we were enjoying the pleasures of Dubai, the onward journey was uppermost in our minds.

We had gone straight to the offices of the Pakistani National Shipping Corporation on the afternoon of our arrival, to inquire about the date of the next sailing to Karachi. In London we had discovered that this shipping line was the only one to run regular car services

between Dubai and Pakistan. Although none of our
series of letters forewarning them of our arrival in Dubai
and of our intention to ship a 2CV appeared to have
reached their destination, the PNSC staff were extremely
helpful. In fact, they were able to inform us that a ship
would be leaving in five days' time, sailing via Damman
and reaching Karachi on about 6 November, giving us over
a fortnight before we would need to fly across to pick up
the car. We sat in the tiny office with Mr R. of Bombay,
drinking tea in the pleasant draught of an electric fan, and
were caught between the loud volleys of two telephones,
one on his desk and one on his colleague's behind us,
which startled us alternately. Our heads turned with the
mechanical regularity of a tennis umpire overseeing a
particularly prolonged rally of championship men's
doubles. Between the frequent interruptions, however,
we posed the majority of our most pressing questions,
concerning such matters as insurance, customs clearance
and security at the ports.

At first Mr R.'s answers were reassuring and his replies
of 'No problem' inspired us with confidence in the
experience and competence of PNSC. However, when we
inquired about pilfering at Karachi docks (having been
warned in Britain that it was inevitable) and he once more
wobbled his head from side to side saying 'No problem',
we began to smell a rat. We had the distinct impression
that for 'No problem' (which was Mr R.'s favourite
phrase) we should be reading, 'Oh yes, sir - this is a
very big problem but I am not intending to admit it, nor am
I pretending I can do anything about it. So, let us all keep
smiling and hope that it will go away.'

It was an attitude which I, even in my limited
experience of dealing with Pakistanis and Indians in
Oman, had learned to recognise. There I would inquire in
a shop whether a certain item was in stock, to be told

cheerfully by the assistant, shaking his head, 'Yes, madam,' which really meant, 'No, but we don't want to disappoint you. We can order one for you.' It was fruitless to ask, 'Will it be here next week?' or, for that matter, any question designed to elicit the answer 'Yes' or 'No', because you could guarantee that the latter reply was taboo in such circumstances. The solution, therefore, was to compose an unambiguous question such as, 'When will you have one in the shop for me to collect?', take the answer and add on a few days for good measure.

In the case of Mr R. of Bombay and the pilfering at Karachi, we also had to reword our inquiry carefully: 'We have heard that things are likely to be stolen from the car while it's waiting at the docks. How long must it be there before we can collect it and who will give us insurance for that period?'

This time his smile broadened and, instead of the standard phrase, he admitted: 'Oh, yes, sometimes there may be a little pilfering - but what can you expect, when poor dock-workers see rich cars coming over with headlights and all these things which are worth so much food for their families? This is why... excuse me (the telephone)... Yes, so, you see, we are not liable for loss or damage at the port - oh no, sir - and insurance companies are only covering loss by sinking of the ship and they are not covering the car at Karachi. This is also why you must be taking away any valuable things and any mirrors and lights which may be pilfered. That is what you can do. You cannot collect the car straight away because it must be cleared by customs and all these things, which take one day, maybe two days.'

We agreed to come back to see him a couple of days later, so that he could tell us more definitely the ship's docking date at Karachi and we could book our flight accordingly. When we did revisit him, however, he was none the wiser, but while we were discussing payment of the fare and various handling charges his colleague suddenly announced that he had a friend (it sounded ominous from the start) who had a launch which was leaving for Karachi tomorrow with a space for a car. This would be much cheaper and the car would be there by 28 October and ready to collect on the 30th. Would we like to inspect the boat at Sharjah in the afternoon and, if we were in favour of it, deliver the car by ten o'clock that evening? Since we had nothing to lose and the possibility of a large number of dirhams to gain, we consented to be back at the office at 5 p.m. to be driven to Sharjah. Meanwhile we stripped the car of its easily removable, exterior items - spotlights, headlight units, wipers, wing mirrors and reversing light - and packed a number of valuables into the padlocked chest, while the remainder of our vital possessions, such as water-filter, radio, camera gear and cooking-stove, were to be taken on the 'plane with us.

Predictably, the driver arrived late (by an hour and a quarter) but we eventually reached Sharjah, half an hour's drive up the coast, met Mr A., the launch's owner (a middle-aged, white-capped Pakistani from Peshawar), and were shown some of his country-craft - old wooden boats of about sixty feet, with room on the deck of each for about a dozen cars. 'Our' launch, the *Al Sagar,* would arrive tomorrow morning.

It was a gamble choosing the little *Al Sagar,* instead of a full-blown PNSC cargo vessel, but the savings in time and cost were the deciding factors. Mr A.'s confident announcement that he had never taken out an insurance policy in his life (trusting instead in Allah) did little to allay our fears for the car's safety; but then he had (apparently) not lost a boat in his fourteen years of trading in the Gulf and, in any case, we were taking out insurance for the unlikely event of the *Al Sagar* sinking. As for pilfering, it was just as likely to happen whether we used the ship or the country-craft.

Naturally there were other snags. As requested (and using an alarm clock for the first time since leaving England!), we arrived at Sharjah at eight the following morning to load the car onto the launch which, as these things happen (or rather don't), had failed to arrive. We sat patiently on sticky vinyl armchairs in the hot little office of the trading company not far from the water's edge and were plied with cups of tea while we waited. Outside was a collection of dusty old Japanese cars which were to be carried to Karachi too. These were the bread-and-butter of the company's trading activities: Mr A. had agents in Japan who organised the shipment to Sharjah and Dubai of these second-hand but re-conditioned vehicles, which were then shipped to Pakistan at Karachi for sale to those who could afford them.

By eleven o'clock there was still no sign of the *Al Sagar,* which was being held up at the customs in Dubai. We escaped round the corner to a travel agency to visit a Sri Lankan friend whom Ashley had known in Oman. (A Tamil with a Sinhalese wife and two young children, this unfortunate man no longer dared to return to Colombo, where he had hoped to retire, and instead was applying for emigration to Canada.) It was Thursday, the beginning of the weekend, and when he finished work at lunchtime he drove us back to the wharf.

The weekend was having other effects: since the *Al Sagar* had not cleared customs before noon, it would now be unable to depart before Saturday morning which meant that it would arrive in Karachi at the start of the following weekend, only to be held up again. If we were lucky, *Inshallah* (God willing), we might expect to collect it on 2 November. This was bad enough news - the longer

Raising the 2CV, Sharjah

the car was standing idle at Karachi, the greater the risk of robbery - but then Mr A. casually added in passing that the launch would have to stop at an Iranian port en route to pick up some cheap diesel which was about a quarter of the Dubai price. 'Fine,' we thought, and left hurriedly before he could think of any more means by which we should never see the car again, in addition to the mounting list of possibilities - namely, theft, being washed overboard in a storm, and becoming a victim of the Iran-Iraq war.

That Saturday morning, at 8.30 we were watching anxiously as our denuded car was hoisted up over our heads in a sling by a large crane and deposited on the deck of the country-craft amongst the piratical crew-members. I was busy photographing the operation while

Ashley supervised the sling-fitting and the securing of the car to the deck, deliberately emphasising his concern for the car's well-being to the team of Pakistanis, who loaded it, as a result, with the utmost care. It was given a good position at the stern, in the shade of a little blue-painted poop-deck, and I was trying to take a shot of the car on board when the crew eagerly lined themselves up in

Loading 2CV onto Al Sagar, Sharjah

the foreground for a group photograph.

The only uniform features of this cheerful bunch of Pakistanis were the mahogany colour of their skin, their flip-flop footwear and their curly toppings of thick black hair, although even this was hidden by one of them under the red, white, yellow and green stripes of his woollen hat. He was dressed in a brown shirt and matching *shalwar*. (These pantaloons looked as though they were made by taking a long, full skirt, slitting it back and front from the hem to the knee-height and stitching the two halves into short legs, leaving the remainder of the garment as a collection of loose, brown folds). Next to him was a rather coy man, dressed in outrageous clothes: a shirt whose upper portion looked like a snowstorm on a dark night and merged at navel level with a dazzling oriental design in orange, blue, red and white. Below this work of art he sported a pair of baggy cotton shorts in a blue and white fabric which was undoubtedly intended for the pyjama market. The third man's attire was another suit of *kurta* (long-tailed shirt) and *shalwar* in grey-blue, while the fourth wore a *sarong* (loose skirt) in

Al Sagar crew, Sharjah

orange and black, tastefully set off by an oil-stained, whitish T-shirt. The young character on his right had a hint of Filipino about him - a swashbuckler from the South Seas with an evil grin which showed in his eyes and formed creases in his cheeks beyond the tips of a long moustache; he had a white scarf around his forehead as a head-band, and only his brown *dishdasha* (a robe like a nightshirt) spoilt his piratical image.

With a crew like that, it promised to be an interesting crossing - if only passengers had been allowed on the *Al Sagar* we would have jumped at the chance. When we had asked PNSC about travelling by boat ourselves, however, we had been told that Karachi's port charges were so high for incoming passenger boats that it was now virtually impossible to find a vessel which would take people there.

The fact that we had arrived in Sharjah at 8 a.m. and seen the car loaded at 8.30 a.m. seemed a little too good to be true and we would have credited it to our forethought in bringing copious reading and writing material - in the same way as carrying an umbrella tends to ward off the rain - had we not spent the following four hours awaiting the arrival of the customs officers.

Sitting in Mr A.'s office again, amongst boxes containing Chinese kiddies' tricycles and Japanese cassette players, we were revived hourly by cups of sweet, black tea carried in from a tea-shop round the corner. An assortment of employees came and went, some handing in bills of lading, others using the telephone or having a cup of tea, and most of them shaking hands with all who were present, save, in some instances, the only woman in the room. (The customary handshake on such occasions is not the firm palm-to-palm greeting to which we are accustomed: it is little more than a fleeting touch of the fingers accompanied by the words *'Salam alekum'* and a reciprocal *'Alekum salam'.)*

Our precious 'Carnet de Passage' having been restored to our safekeeping by the customs men, we hailed a cheap shared taxi (like the Turkish *dolmus)* and waved goodbye to the 2CV. We were dropped in the agglomeration of modern office-blocks and towering hotels on the north side of Dubai Creek, the deepwater channel 16 km long to which Dubai owes its nickname, 'the Venice of the Gulf'. We visited the new indoor shopping complex called Al Ghuirair, with its upmarket stores and bright, clean restaurants, but they were closed for the midday siesta. Had they not been, Ashley said, he could have imagined himself to be in Houston, Texas. Not far away, and yet separated by centuries, was the souk, where small-scale traditional trade, most notably in gold, continues to this day. Gold smuggling and trading once made Dubai rich, and jewellery, in both gold and silver, is still highly prized among Arabs and sold by weight rather than workmanship.

Arabia, for me, is characterised by this juxtaposition of old and new; the name conjures up images of Toyota vans parked by Bedouin tents, of veiled women herding their goats along the verges of a dual carriageway, of a ruined medieval castle adjacent to a satellite-tracking dish, or an electric air-conditioner outlet beside an ancient wind-tower. (Dubai has many of these ornate structures - the world's first air-conditioning - protruding above the old rooftops like large, square bell-towers with flat tops and open sides. They act like chimneys, drawing the hot air up and out of the buildings.)

Oil-rich countries, such as Saudi Arabia, Oman and the Emirates, have been exposed to several centuries of western development in as many decades, and the effect may be compared with superimposing twentieth century New York on Tudor England. It was no surprise, therefore, to be walking along the edge of the Creek with a row of tower blocks housing hotels and international banks on our right and a collection of wooden dhows and launches on our left. While computers were frantically printing out the current exchange rates for the dirham behind fifteen storeys of reflective glass, barefooted Indian or Pakistani carpenters were calmly repairing wooden hulls using traditional tools such as bow-drills, hammering in hefty nails and then carefully sealing the joins by caulking. Some of the crews had curled up on deck with towels over their heads for a post-prandial nap, or were sitting in their sarongs on packing-cases drinking tea together. As we were walking by a sailor unashamedly hopped into one of the cradle-like, wooden toilets which swing from the sterns the dhows. On the quayside cargoes of boxed or crated electrical goods, food and toys waited under the hot sun for loading on to vessels or lorries. There was no sign of hurry: the boat might sail tomorrow, *Inshallah,* but if not, the day after would do just as well. Who could say when the customs man would arrive anyway? As we strolled along, the alternating sounds of hammers tapping, paintbrushes slapping and bursts of laughter and chatter waned and crescendoed, with the occasional blast of pirate Indian pop music from a portable Japanese cassette player.

We reached the ferry landing-area and crossed the Creek on one of the fleet of open passenger-boats. For the equivalent of five pence each, people squeezed themselves on to the large central bench which ran almost the entire twenty-foot length of the boat, until the ferryman, sitting in a hole in the middle, decided there was no more space and set off for the other side. It was good to catch the breeze in our hair and feel its coolness on our faces and it was fun when the boat bounced over the wake of a passing launch, sending the passengers jostling together. All too soon the boat had reached the other side and everyone clambered over the other seven or eight moored ferry-boats, using them as stepping-stones to reach the quay. We loved the boat-ride but the faces of our fellow-passengers expressed only the unmistakable boredom of all commuters.

In the souk on the southern side we haggled with money-changers and succeeded in disencumbering ourselves of our Syrian pounds before walking back to the apartment, guided by the (then) tallest building in the Middle East, the thirty-two-storeyed, 1979 Trade Centre, which was close to where we stayed. The roundabouts and central reservations of the dual carriageways were oases of green in the dusty city. Some of the grass was watered by automatic sprinklers, but a band of Pakistanis was also employed simply to direct hosepipes at the greenery for hours on end, and the grass was growing so well that other workers had to be engaged to cut it. The fresh smell was an unexpected delight and we thought nostalgically of our garden in Kent and, less longingly, of plodding up the slope pushing the lawn-mower. Suddenly an unbelievable sight brought us to a standstill:

'Did you see what I saw?' we both gasped simultaneously.

We had just witnessed, amidst the dense traffic of predominantly Japanese cars, the spectacle of one of them cruising by with nobody at the steering-wheel. Was Dubai the home of the Invisible Man or had we been out too long with the 'mad dogs' under the 'midday sun'? We mentioned the incident to our friends, who naturally accused us of lunchtime drinking, but later admitted that what we had seen was one of the driving school vehicles with dual controls, which included two steering-wheels!

The earth's shadow passed briefly across the moon on 28 October and we knew that we too should be moving on. It was tempting to stay in Dubai, to continue to enjoy the good food and company and the beautiful beaches - we had even been dreaming up enterprises which would enable us to settle there: growing strawberries hydroponically was one idea and, less seriously, Ashley had suggested building a brewery to produce real ale. Such a project might be welcomed by the young British expatriates whom we had seen bopping the night away at 'Thatchers' discotheque, but as far as Sheikh al Maktoum was concerned it would probably go down as well as a pork chop at a Jewish wedding. (Alcohol in Dubai was already relatively easily available, compared with its neighbours such as Saudi Arabia and poor Sharjah which had, shortly before our arrival, been declared 'dry' as a condition imposed by the Saudis when they agreed to offer financial aid to the ailing Emirate and to build Sharjah a magnificent mosque.)

We felt duty-bound, however, to go and rescue the 2CV from the dangers of Karachi's docks and 30 October had just begun when we arrived at Dubai airport for our 3.50

a.m. flight. We thought we would be the first to check in, but we found a queue of passengers and stacks of luggage already waiting. Most of the men were Pakistanis, their heads done up in a number of variations on the turban theme. They had probably been working in the Emirates for a year or more, for they were returning home bearing a multitude of trophies, such as Japanese radio-cassette players and large digital watches, in the same way that Chinese workers going back to their families from Hong Kong carried television sets or electric food-mixers. A number of portable stereo sets had been dressed in gaudy, homemade covers of bright pink, purple, luminous green and orange, and now, as they dangled from shoulder straps at the sides of middle-aged men in *dishdashas,* I was reminded of ageing hippies. One of the younger men was carrying a brand new rifle which, much to our relief, was not allowed into the aircraft cabin.

Of the non-Pakistani passengers, the majority appeared to be Filipinos returning to Manila, which was the final destination of the flight. We were later told in Karachi that these Far Eastern workers are now leaders in the cheap labour market and that the Arab countries are beginning to employ them in preference, for example, to Pakistanis. This could only be bad news for Pakistan, with its already high unemployment rate and its need for foreign income. However, if the number of Pakistani immigrant workers was declining, we were not aware of it in Dubai: they were everywhere - serving petrol at the pumps, cleaning the apartment, changing our money in the souk and taking it in the supermarkets, sitting beside us on the ferry and kneeling towards Mecca on the grassy, well-tended roundabouts. With such a large proportion of the population coming from Pakistan and India, and such a long history of trade between the Gulf states and the Indian subcontinent, it is hard to imagine Dubai, Oman or their neighbours without these well established immigrant communities. Most of the work is done by them and the majority of the shops, restaurants and small businesses are run by them. Dubai was a good introduction to the countries we were about to visit.

CHAPTER 15

At about 6.30 a.m. we were descending towards Karachi and looking down on the web of channels and islets which form the Indus delta. The early morning mist was floating eerily in ribbons above the winding waterways, highlighting their pale, sinuous paths. This was the end of the river's remarkable journey of almost 2,000 miles from its source in Tibet. Here the meltwater from the snowfields of the Himalayas and the Hindu Kush mingled reluctantly with the Arabian Sea, just north of the Tropic of Cancer. The great river, after draining an area of 372,000 square miles (three times the size of Great Britain and Ireland), and irrigating millions of acres of farmland in the provinces of Sind and Baluchistan, seemed to have spent all its energy now and was yielding itself gently to the sea. Yet for thousands of years the inhabitants of its fertile valley have been dominated by its power: dependent on its summer floodwaters for the irrigation of their farmland but fearful of its destructive force. Mohenjodaro, one of the two known cities of the Indus civilisation, was devastated by exceptional floods more than once, and countless homes have been swept away by the Indus' merciless momentum. Even the name, derived from 'Sindhu', the

Sanskrit word for ocean, acknowledges the river's power. Below us, however, the delta looked deceptively calm. We filled in our disembarkation forms, and those of a couple of illiterate Kenyans beside us, and fastened our seat belts for landing.

It was already warm and humid when we stepped on to Pakistani tarmac, but inside the airport buildings the conditions were pleasantly cool and surprisingly efficient. Having heard so many conflicting reports about the need to acquire visas before or on arrival at Karachi, we were happy to be greeted by a smiling immigration officer who said, as he stamped our passports with loud, confident thumps on his desk, 'Welcome to Pakistan! As members of the Commonwealth you may stay as long as you wish!' (a surprising greeting considering that Pakistan withdrew from the Commonwealth in 1972). One of our fellow passengers obviously intended to remain longer than we did: having already collected a mountain of luggage from the revolving conveyor belt, he then put paid to a popular saying by claiming his kitchen sink as well. Chuckling to ourselves, we sailed through the 'green' exit with our lightweight rucksacks, camera bag and holdall, and found an unofficial taxi to take us to the city centre.

The traffic was pandemonium. To appreciate the contrast with driving conditions in Dubai (which was busy enough in the rush hour), imagine first swanning about in a peaceful swimming-pool and then being lifted out abruptly and plunged into a tropical river seething with maddened piranhas and trembling with the simultaneous blasts of a hundred brass bands. Darting around the taxi was a swarm of cars, buses, motor-bikes, donkey-carts, autorickshaws, tongas (horse-drawn carriages), lorries, bicycles - in short, of every conceivable vehicle - to the cacophonous accompaniment of horns, hooters, bells and shouts, which made Hyde Park Corner at 5.30 p.m. on a weekday look like tranquillity itself.

By the combined navigational and driving skills of the two lads in the front seats, and perhaps by a stroke of good fortune, we arrived at the Hotel Columbus in one piece. I jumped out and spoke to the man who was sitting on a chair at the gate, but he mumbled something about the place being closed for a year. Thus ended our hope of staying in the hotel where Ashley had previously had a room while working in the city. The driver and his friend offered to take us to an alternative hotel and so we set off once more into the hurly-burly. They had more difficulty locating this one but when the friend turned to us, shouting incomprehensibly and pointing excitedly at a driveway, at first we took it to be the hotel entrance until we realised that we were not stopping.

'What did he say?' I yelled above the ambient din.

'Oh, stabble hossees, I think,' said Ashley, reverting to the terminology of Jerash.

The place we had just passed in Club Road was in fact the Karachi Gymkhana, founded in 1886 by the British as a sports-orientated club and still maintaining its exclusivity by an astronomical joining fee.

We hurtled on through the sea of traffic and eventually came aground on the pavement outside the Metropole Hotel which, although it had seen more glorious days, was still too grand for our pockets. We paid off the taxi and set out on foot to Saddar, an area of shops, markets and, more relevantly, small hotels. One of them, which stated amongst its regulations that guests should hand in all ammunition and weapons at the reception desk, looked promising but the room we were offered was a hot, dark, windowless cell. We settled instead for a back room at the Gulf Hotel, which for 200 rupees (£9) a night provided us with a double room and shower, air-conditioning and a ceiling propeller-fan. We were lowering ourselves down gently from the luxuries of Dubai.

A cool shower, a few hours' sleep and some food revived us and we walked to the Tourist Office where leaflets, street maps, information and encouragement were showered upon us, as though we were the only visitors of the afternoon (which may indeed have been the case).

'You are wanting to drive to Peshawar and then up the Swat Valley to the extreme north of Pakistan? No problem.' (We had heard this somewhere before.) 'There are good roads all the way.' (It sounded unlikely.) 'And you will be finding Tourist Rest Houses at all these places marked on the map. Then you must visit the hill stations of Gallies and Murree - very, very beautiful, many trees and not so hot as Karachi. And Lahore, you must be going to Lahore and to the ancient cities Mohenjodaro and Harappa. The Punjab is very beautiful also and...'

We only just reached the Indian Consulate before it closed at 4.30 and listened sceptically to the news that there was absolutely 'no problem' in obtaining our visas: we simply had to take away two forms, return them completed in the morning and collect the visas in the afternoon. It sounded much too good to be true and certainly did not concur with the information we had received from the Indian Embassy in Abu Dhabi: that we required letters of recommendation from the British Embassy, that the visas took at least three days to come through, and that we should need special permits in order to enter Punjab.

The next morning we were not unduly surprised, therefore, when the consular procedure did not go as smoothly as planned.

'I am very sorry,' we were told by another official, 'you will have to go to Islamabad to get your visas. We can only issue visas for entry to India by air.'

When we questioned him further he said that, owing to the unrest in Punjab, the border at Amritsar was only open on three days per month -the 2nd, 12th and 22nd - which, since we had heard this news from England too, we tended to believe.

The office of Amer Traders, owners of the *Al Sagar,* was in old Karachi, hidden amongst the stalls of the Machi Miana Market towards the port area. It was nearly three miles from the leafy consulate gardens in Fatimah Jinnah Road but we set out on foot for, although we were eager to hear news of the car, we suspected that there would be little point in hurrying there. We strolled through the shady green park of Babh-e-Jinnah named after the founder of Pakistan, formerly Frere Hall, which was built in 1865 in honour of Sir Bartle Frere, Commissioner of Sind, and now houses a library. Under a tree a group of men were squatting together around a radio and listening attentively to the English commentary on the Pakistan-Sri Lanka Test match. We sat, eavesdropping for a while, on a bench and watched a playful striped palm squirrel skipping over the lawn and scurrying up a tree-trunk.

The long, wide Chundrigar Road, leading to the port, was hot and noisy with traffic and we were glad to take brief shelter in the offices of a couple of insurance companies halfway along. At the first, the idea of insuring our car at all was dismissed with horror, an attitude with which we found some sympathy, having already gauged the standard of driving in Karachi. The second company, 'Adamjee', which announced itself all over the city as the biggest insurance company in Pakistan, sounded more hopeful and indeed we were given a quote by the obliging manager. He also gave us rough directions to the Amer Traders office, but when we asked him to show us on our street maps his bewilderment was total. He was another example of a widespread inability to map-read amongst people east of Istanbul.

Nevertheless, we soon found ourselves negotiating the Machi Miana Market and located the little staircase leading to the office. We climbed the dirty concrete steps stained red with splashes of betel-juice, and emerged onto an inward-facing balconied landing with small offices ranged around it. Below us we could see the market stalls from which a blend of noises and spicy smells came drifting up. A number of loiterers on the landing, surprised by our arrival, stared disconcertingly at the two intruders and then, in response to our inquiry, told us to wait in a tiny office. When the man from Amer Traders finally arrived his tidings offered little encouragement. His English was so poor that we wondered whether we might understand his Urdu more easily, and he seemed decidedly uncertain about the arrival of the launch: 'Maybe you will see the car, four or five November.' (It was then 31 October.)

It was all very gloomy news for us but he broke into a broad, wicked grin (revealing a large gap in one set of teeth) as soon as we asked about handling charges.

'Five hundred rupees for the port,' he said, 'and then extra expenses - ah, this is 300 rupees,' rubbing his hands in anticipation.

'What is this 300 rupees for?' we demanded.

'Accha! 300 rupees for extra expense, yes.' His eyes glinted above his gap-toothed grin as we repeated the question to no avail. We stood a greater chance of wringing water from a block of granite than extracting an explanation, and so we added another unanswered question to the growing list of fruitless inquiries which was already endangering our sanity.

We had experienced similar frustration at a cinema the

previous evening with the ticket man, who insistently replied, 'This film is finishing 9 or 9.30,' when all we wanted to know was what time the next day's show began. Only his well meaning smile and expression of child-like innocence prevented me from bashing him over the head with the bunch of bananas I happened to be carrying.

This time I had no bananas and anyway, the man's colleague arrived in the nick of time to save us from despair. He seemed to have a better grip on the English language. The launch was expected tomorrow evening *(Inshallah)* and would be unloaded two days later. He would telephone us at the hotel when it was ready and we would only have to pay 500 rupees to the port as handling charges. Encouraged by his plain speaking, we said 'Goodbye' and dived down the stairs into the hurly-burly below. Squeezing between the fruit-stalls, the cart-loads of offal, the scooters and the cross-legged street-vendors, we managed to find an autorickshaw willing to take us back to the hotel.

Like a disturbed nest of ants, the entire city seemed to be on the move. Our lives were in the driver's hands as we clung to the iron rails and the three-wheeled vehicle careered jerkily through the chaos, dodging between the traffic and buzzing along one-way streets like a bat out of hell. However wide these backroads were, every one of them was automatically reduced to a narrow passage which threaded its way through a clutter of street-vendors, parked vehicles, pedestrians and animals. I was so fascinated by the constantly changing scenes, by the flashes of colour and the perpetual commotion, that my fear soon turned into exhilaration. As we bounced along, my eyes tried desperately to keep pace with the rapid succession of new sights: it was like watching a fast-moving film on a wide screen from the front row - there was simply too much to take in.

Our room was beautifully cool and calm, and I realised that the excitement of the busy streets was enjoyable only as long as we could escape from time to time into a haven of peace. In the same way, I had been able to withstand the extreme summer temperatures in Oman more easily in the knowledge that, every now and again, I could refresh myself in the sea or under a cold shower. In Karachi, each quiet respite renewed our enthusiasm to take on once more the mad but fascinating world outside: the traffic, the crowds, the noise, the begging children and the problems of communication. 'If anything wears us down,' I commented in my diary, 'it will be our constant struggle against misinformation, however innocently given, and our continual efforts to reshape questions until they succeed in teasing out straight answers.'

With the old banana-man, however, we had no such difficulties. On the first day we picked him out amongst the other street-traders near the hotel by the superior quality of his fruit. He was not touting loudly like his competitors, with their apples and guavas, their bananas or pomegranates: he stood quietly by his barrow, his face half-smothered in a thick, grey beard, his eyes sadly clouded with the onset of glaucoma. Customary haggling established a firm understanding between us on the basis of a dozen bananas for four rupees and, from that day on, no words were needed: we simply approached the barrow, exchanged smiles and did the deal.

Eggs of indeterminate age were also readily available, and a bakery opposite the hotel produced some beautiful brown loaves which, unlike the white ones, were not sweetened but, like them, tasted overwhelmingly of coconut oil. There was even Marmite for sale, although at four times the British price. Karachi's tap water is probably quite safe to drink but, since the same could not be said for the rest of the country, we thought it a good time to put our water filter into action and make a habit of it. Tap water in all the previous countries of our journey had caused us no ill effects, but in Pakistan we were not prepared to take the risk. We had to admit that we had been lucky until then: our only trouble had been Ashley's bout of 'Turkish trots' in Van.

Friday in Karachi was quite pleasant, we agreed, as we walked through the city to the National Museum: the traffic was reduced to a safer level and the streets were relatively peaceful. There was time to look up at the brilliant blue roller birds on the telegraph wires and at the circling brown kites overhead without the imminent risk of a collision with another pedestrian, and we could hear the chattering congregations of finches in the mimosa trees and the 'caw-caw' of crows instead of the hubbub of hoots and horns.

The museum was housed in Frere Hall until 1951 when the modern building was opened in Burns Garden - pleasant surroundings of palms and well-watered lawns. We walked up the museum steps into the vacuous hall and were greeted, just inside the entrance, by a large notice which announced 'God effaceth and establisheth what he pleaseth', below its Urdu translation.

Pakistan's history boasts one of the oldest civilisations on earth - that of the Indus. More extensive than that of Mesopotamia or Egypt and earlier than the beginning of China's dynasties, it dominated, from 2500 BC to 1700 BC, an area far greater than the Indus Valley alone, stretching along the coast from the Gulf of Cambay (now in India) almost to Pakistan's present border with Iran, and reaching as far north as Lahore in Punjab. Two great cities, Harappa near Lahore, and Mohenjodaro near Larkana in Sind Province, were identified in the early 1920s and many of their more portable relics have found their way into the protective cases of the National Museum, while the brickwork ruins continue to crumble. Mohenjodaro, in particular, is threatened by river erosion and salinity problems; Harappa's deterioration was accelerated in the nineteenth century by a team of ignorant railway constructors who, thinking that the bricks would make good ballast for track-laying between Lahore a Multan, proceeded to demonstrate it.

The Indus people, to judge by the museum exhibits, were well organised. They grew wheat, barley, peas, melons, sesame, dates and even cotton; they stored their grain in large public granaries; they had standard weights, such as cubes of banded chert, and they used little steatite seals carved with inscriptions and animal designs to stamp bales and other commodities. They baked many of their bricks in order to withstand the frequent floods; they built brick drainage systems with inspection holes; and there was a fair degree of literacy. They were imaginative people too: one of them, for example, had carved a seal with a grotesque composite creature made up of a human face, an elephant's trunk, the horns of a bull, the forequarters of a ram and the hindquarters of a tiger!

We were so absorbed by this extensive range of 4,000-year-old relics - elaborate toys and figurines, copperware, jewellery, painted pottery and a rare fuchsite vase - that we didn't notice one of the museum staff creeping up to us, until he opened his mouth and we almost jumped through the glass in surprise. He had come to let us know that they were closing the museum for prayer-time and that it would not reopen until 2.30. Disappointed, having arrived only twenty minutes earlier, we trudged back to the hotel to make some lunch. In Burns Garden families, evidently forewarned of the closure were picnicking peacefully under the trees, while three noisy boys raced about, hurling a dead crow at one another as though it were nothing but a handful of

Shopping street, Karachi

seaweed.

There was no evidence of a ban on Sunday - or rather Friday - trading in Karachi. We passed a host of street-stalls, including a broad pavement plastered in second-hand books and magazines. Fascinating titles, such as *The Empire Forestry Guide 1933* and *Love, Sex and Marriage,* nestled bizarrely amongst Enid Blytons and 1967 *National Geographics.* We had already spent several hours browsing in Karachi's book shops amongst similarly well-shuffled publications and had fished out a number of topical paperbacks, including *The Siege of Krishnapur* by J. G. Farrell and *A Short Walk in the Hindu Kush* by Eric Newby, which, though old and faded, had not been read; they had simply been sitting on the shelves for several years, waiting for a buyer. The Pakistani prices were arrived at by multiplying the British ones by a constant factor, so that old paperbacks still marked '3/6d' could be bought for 3 or 4 rupees.

Today the shops were closed, however, and the street-traders were having a field-day instead: besides the books, there were barrowloads of pomegranates for sale, mounds of chopped sugar-cane, Japanese watches, second-hand clothes, toys, cooking pots and reels of cotton; there were wooden chairs and mirrors set up on the pavement by enterprising barbers; and there were betel sellers with their mortars and pestles, crushing and mixing the dried, brown betel nut (the fruit of the betel palm, *Areca catechu)* with shell lime and perhaps a dash of some aromatic flavouring, and wrapping little portions of the blend in individual 'pan' leaves (from the betel pepper plant, *Piper betle).* Betel chewing is such a popular pastime that its gruesome consequence, brick-red saliva, stains mouths, walls and pavements all over Karachi and a large part of the rest of the continent. It is so widespread an Asian habit that it is estimated to be indulged in by a tenth of the world's population!

Just as we had started to eat lunch in our room, repeated raps at the door announced the arrival of the grinning room-boy, curious as ever to see what the strange foreigners were doing. We were already accustomed to his unnecessary visits and their impeccable timing, guaranteed to coincide with our shower-taking or meals, and this call was not unexpected. The only element of surprise lay in what excuse he would have dreamed up today: oh, of course - he wanted to satisfy himself that the electric lights and ceiling fan were still in good working order, and so we watched him casually pulling the switches, while he surveyed with wide eyes our display of western paraphernalia such as water filter, Swiss army knife, road maps and insect repellent, which were currently strewn across our beds.

Walking back to the museum, we noticed a squatting man wearing a rather pained expression on his face and with his left arm apparently stuck down a hole in the road. It was only when we came closer that we realised he was simply cleaning out the drains and was not the victim of some surreal accident. Like the pervasive emission of gobs of chewed betel, he was just part of the Karachi scene. Although travelling in the east we were beginning to register less shock at the unexpected, there were certain eventualities which it was difficult to take for granted, such as the local practice of using us as photographic subjects. Outside the museum, for instance, an autorickshaw pulled up and a young couple with two small children trussed up in their Friday best popped out of the confining seats like a cork from a bottle and, seeing us, immediately ran up to take our picture. I suppose at the time we felt slightly flattered and mildly surprised, but in retrospect, I wondered if they had taken us for two of the museum pieces.

That afternoon our cultural enlightenment moved from the realms of the Indus civilisation through the introduction of Buddhism in the third century BC and the ancient Kingdom of Gandhara (comprising Peshawar, Swat, Buner and Bajaur) to the Moghul invasion and beyond. Outstanding in my memory and hanging on a wall of the museum was an unbelievable piece of Moghul craftsmanship - a rug woven entirely from fine strands of ivory. It was beautifully intricate.

Nearby there was an interesting section devoted to the 'Freedom Movement' and the life of Quaid-I-Azam (Supreme Leader) Muhammad Ali Jinnah about whom I previously knew very little He was born in Karachi in 1876, I learned, studied law in England and worked at Lincoln's Inn before moving to Bombay, where he became involved in the Muslim League and finally achieved the 'Pakistan Resolution' of 1940 and the establishment of Pakistan in 1947.

There were numerous pictures of this rather austere and wiry-looking man (both in the museum and on the walls of restaurants, shops and offices throughout the city) and it was while gazing at some of them that we were called once more to pose for a photograph. This time, two lads insisted on standing by us and our four fixed grins became gradually more strained as the third lad struggled to get his camera the right way up and to squeeze the group into his frame at the restricted range available. Naturally, he had every right to take photographs of foreign visitors, in the same way that we had been photographing people throughout our travels; but was there more to it than that? Was there, for them, something prestigious about posing as friends of white people or was the act no more significant than the photographing of an American tourist next to a Beefeater in London - a simple statement, 'I was there'?

Outside the museum gates, as the late afternoon sun was casting long shadows along the main road, the man with the mobile 'Falooda' stall who had been dispensing cool glasses of that peculiar, syrupy, pink, vermicelli-laden milk-shake, was preparing to go home. Suddenly a tennis ball whistled past, nearly clipping him on the ear and going for six over the museum wall. A boy in white *kurta* (long-tailed shirt) and billowing *shalwar* (pantaloons) raced by, nipped through the gates into the Burns Garden, and the ball came shooting back into the road, landing just short of a motorbike which happened to be passing. The motorcyclist continued to weave his way between the young fielders, teenage umpires and cheering supporters of the scoring batsman and then negotiated the next wicket along the road.

Cricket practice on a Friday afternoon seemed to be a compulsory activity for every Karachi boy between the ages of eight and eighteen. The streets, as well as every spare patch of ground, were packed with improvised pitches, and the cars, tongas, motorbikes and buses simply had to find their way through the muddle: the game must go on. We stopped to witness the enthusiastic play and four little boys, who were further down the batting order, swiftly encircled us, singing and calling, 'What is your name, sir?', 'Photo, photo, photo!', 'Rupees, rupees!' and 'What is your name, madame?' When we had all introduced ourselves to one another they ran off laughing and we turned towards Saddar. Ashley had just commented on the lessons in dedication to the sport which could be learned here by English cricketers, and was wondering whether the Pakistan selectors recruited their Test sides from the streets of Karachi, when a well dressed lady with three small children walked by. A moment later the two boys, no more than four and six years old, ran back to shake Ashley's hand and then scampered back delightedly to their smiling mother, who took their hands once more. We were touched by the spontaneity of the simple gesture.

Further on, we exchanged *Salam's* with a uniformed sentry as we passed the smart white Coastguards Officers' Mess, which stood out from the other buildings in Sarwar Shaheed Road like a lily in a dirty pond. The young cricketers had gone home and now the crows and kites were wheeling in vast numbers above crumbling, old walls of yellow stone - even the colour suggested decay. In the absence of traffic there was a foreboding quietness, foreign to Karachi, lingering in the air. The lonely man at the corner, with his weary old horse and tonga, tried hopelessly to offer us a ride for the third time that day, but we were almost back at the hotel.

CHAPTER 16

Fearing that Amer Trading would forget to telephone us about the car, we tried to call them, but either they were out or their telephone was out of order. We gave up and went to post a letter at the nearest post office. There was no public entrance - simply a window on to the street with big, vertical iron bars rusting across the opening. We pushed the letter through and someone inside weighed it on an ancient pair of scales, scribbled something on it and then slid it, with a pile of other letters, under a cabinet which looked suspiciously like its final resting place.

Mr Rajkoti (BA Eng. Lit., Karachi), branch manager of Adamjee Insurance, was pleased to see us again and delegated the long-winded paperwork of our third-party policy to his juniors while we three sat in his air-conditioned office for nearly an hour, drinking cups of coffee, thick with evaporated milk, and talking about matters linguistic and dietary. His diabetes, for example, troubled him greatly in Karachi, where so many local foods contained sugar, he told us in excellent English. He had been educated in a strict Catholic missionary school and was in favour of retaining English as the first language of Pakistan, on the grounds of its widespread international use and particularly its prevalence in technical literature. The present school system, nationalised by Bhutto, provided a choice of English- or Urdu-speaking schools which, Mr Rajkoti agreed, was a good compromise.

Our next port of call was the Automobile Association of Pakistan, housed in a tiny, one-man office, perched on the third floor of a large building by an open-air landing which was served by an ancient cast-iron, spiral staircase. We found Mr Rizvi nestling amongst his collection of yellowed pamphlets, like a hamster in a straw-filled cage. He had an old black telephone (the sort with the plaited cord) and a number of AA handbooks from the 1960s, but no road maps of Pakistan, which we were after. What he lacked in material resources, however, Mr Rizvi made up for in his eagerness to help: there was a map shop in West Wharf Road, he told us, and then went on to warn us of the perils of importing a car to Karachi. We should expect to allow at least four days from the docking date for unloading and customs clearance, and should be prepared for countless bureaucratic delays, endless to-ing and fro-ing between offices, and numerous miscellaneous fees along the way. Much easier, he suggested, to appoint a clearing agent and retain our sanity than to attempt the customs formalities ourselves. Anything to speed things up, we agreed.

'I know you people are not used to these procedural delays in Europe and America,' he sympathised. 'But it is not the same here.' He sighed sadly. 'One man does one job and then you must go to find another for the next form and a third for his signature and so on. Everything is taking days instead of hours. If you live here all your life, you get used to these things. You have no choice,' he added resignedly. It was all rather depressing.

'Something has been puzzling me,' said Ashley, on a more cheerful note. 'What on earth is the rule for negotiating roundabouts in this country? Do I give way to traffic from the right?'

Mr Rizvi's face brightened. He rocked back in his chair, gripping the desk edge with both hands and laughing quietly.

'Oh, sir,' he said, 'there is no rule. Only the law of the jungle!'

Apart from the leafy potted plants which graced its hall, there was nothing jungle-like about the international bank across the road. It must be one of the most luxurious commercial buildings in Karachi: a modern tower-block whose exterior gleamed with pink, polished granite and whose well-ordered interior rested in a bed of deep-pile carpet. Outside on the dangerously uneven pavement beggars congregated daily. Some of the best-dressed men in the city worked inside, most of them in western suits and ties, while the slender, female employees glided across the open-plan areas in their more traditional dress of fine *shameez* (the female equivalent of the *kurta)*. Everyone was too polite to tell us that the bank had been closed for transactions since 11.30 because Saturday was early closing. Instead we were systematically passed along a chain of desk-bound officials, until one suggested that we kindly return on Sunday. We had to: it was the only bank in Karachi where we could obtain cash on our credit card.

As we stepped out of the bank into the real world the next morning, our pockets bulging with wads of battered rupees, a fork-lift truck was removing an illegally parked car in a nearby sidestreet. A camel-cart, laden with sacks of cotton, stepped out of the station yard not far away and ploughed straight across the main road, causing a sudden crescendo of hornblasts, which made the pavement shoe-mender look up briefly from his last. We made our way once more to the 'underworld' of Amer Traders and the Machi Miana Market, dodging the now-familiar obstacles, such as. open man-hole covers and banana skins, and turning down the persistent offers of taxi-rides and autorickshaws. To our dismay, we were greeted at our destination by the gap-toothed half-wit of Thursday's encounter, but he summoned a friend, who was hanging around on the landing, to interpret and we learned that the launch had arrived the previous day (only two days late!), that our car would be unloaded the following morning (we found this hard to believe), and that by the evening it would have cleared customs and be ready to drive away (we almost laughed at his optimism).

'You come *here,* ten o'clock!' ordered our friend as he stabbed his desk-top repeatedly with the tip of his chubby forefinger, 'and you bring the 800 rupees!' he added, breaking into his wicked smile, as we said, 'Goodbye.'

We called in at the dockside Aero Stores - no, we weren't on the trail of chocolate bars - to buy some road maps. Invited to sit down at the desk, we were then deluged with the whole gamut of Pakistani maps, each spread out in turn and smothered by the next, until we were up to our necks in the things. We protested that all we wanted was a national roadmap but the unrelenting lady only returned to the shelves to fetch yet more reams

of irrelevant cartography. There was a map for every spatially variant feature of the country, from rainfall to population and from geology to flood control; every national statistic which could possibly be represented by the Survey of Pakistan was in that stack of paper. On the basis of those maps alone we could have spent a month in the Aero Stores and written a new textbook on Pakistan's geography - indeed, we were convinced that

Man Cure Clinic, Karachi

the woman's efforts were directed towards persuading us to do so. Educational as it would have been, however, we had neither the time nor the inclination for such a study and left the shop with our meagre purchase of a road map of the entire country and a more detailed one of the North-West Frontier Province, while the poor woman set about her afternoon's work of restoring the contents of the shelves.

We trekked back the three and a half miles to the hotel, past rows of shops with old wooden balconies and modern signs announcing 'Dolly Stores', 'Abdullah's Garments' and 'Bonanza Modern Wool House'; past festoons of telephone wires and an esoteric establishment called the 'Man Cure Clinic'. We were just in time to join a crowd of men in the hotel reception area and watch on television the closing play of the one-day cricket match between Pakistan and Sri Lanka. As requested, our room had been cleaned and the room-boy had even gone so far as to change the bed-linen in our absence, so that Ashley's bed now had a 'clean' bottom sheet artistically decorated with a large brown tyre mark, and my sheets were so liberally speckled with moth-holes that I might have been sleeping in chicken wire - an impression undiminished in the bathroom the next morning by the shower of feathers and other, less desirable, bird matter which I received from a pigeon alighting on the window ledge. It was not a good omen for the day.

The Amer Trading office at ten o'clock the next morning was littered with the usual collection of miscreants and dirty tea-cups. We joined them. The air was hot and heavy with boredom. Everyone seemed to be waiting for the 'phone to ring. Entertainment was restricted to the spectacle of one of the inmates - a bearded young fellow - playing at origami with a scrap of silver paper from a cigarette packet; he wore a dark woollen waistcoat over his *kurta* and *shalwar* and, with his winter hat and thick blue socks, he looked as though he had just come down from the mountains of northern Chitral or Kohistan and had not had time to change. Everyone else was perspiring away in the clammy heat. It was never clear to us who these silent people were: employees, customers or just hangers-on? We all simply sat and waited. After half an hour, the ageing tea-'boy' swept up the dirty cups, which returned, minutes later, refilled with sweet tea.

At eleven a competent-looking man, the clearing agent, arrived to attend to us and, after filling out several forms and scrutinising the 'Carnet de Passage' and our passports, led us out into the narrow streets, past market stalls and camels, to the old Customs House (next door to it is a great modern building which, when completed, will replace it). We waited in the cool hall while the agent dispatched a boy to get some photocopies. Towering above us on the wall was a huge wooden panel with hand-painted letters which listed, like the past presidents in an old club, the archaic customs allowances for tourists entering the port: they included 'one perambulator... one pair of binaculars [sic]... and any honorary gifts presented to a person in foreign countries', but there was no mention of a cassette recorder or a 2CV.

When the boy returned, the quality of the four photostats necessitated much inking-over to effect their legibility. Ushered upstairs to the 'Preventive Department', we found ourselves transported back in time to the 1950s. It was a world where smart customs officials with military moustaches sat behind heavy, ancient typewriters, beneath flapping propeller fans and amongst mountains of yellowed paper files and ribbon-bound documents. Wardrobe-like metal cabinets overflowed with more stacks of paper, while messenger-boys scurried between offices separated by flimsy partitions of thin wood and glass which shook and rattled dangerously with the opening and shutting of doors. Stacked up high in a dark corner, on top of a filing cabinet, was an old tennis racquet, some books, a camera and an assortment of other, presumably confiscated, articles.

Mr Akbar Ali, who had been talking to the agent for some time, imprinted the four forms with a large purple stamp and so put an end to the day's proceedings and to our faint hope of seeing the car that evening, informing us that the Customs Department would begin examining the *Al Sagar* and its cargo the next day, *Inshallah*. Despondently we returned to the hotel and nearly strangled the room-boy when he came to check (what would he think of next?) the number of curtain hooks on the rail.

The streets in Saddar were seething with people that afternoon when we went down to the main post office. Policemen had cordoned off one thoroughfare and were desperately trying to keep back the crowds from a religious procession of the minority Shi'ite Moslems (mourning the death of the Prophet's nephew Husain), by maintaining a no-man's-land between the two groups. We slipped through with others into this gap to reach the post office, which was conveniently quiet. Rejoining the crowds, we sensed an increased tension in the air. Previously latent hostilities had surfaced and we heard raised voices and shouts above the chanting of the procession. Suddenly violence broke out as the people pushed forward and the police began using their sticks to beat back the onlookers. Some resisted; others, terrified, ran back down the street, spreading panic, like wild-fire, amongst the crowd. Caught in the frightening rush, we clung to each other as we were swept back along the road by the moving mass. It was only a matter of seconds before we escaped from the throng down an alley to breathe easily again, but it was an experience not easily forgotten. I realised how rapidly and automatically such rumbles of fear and antagonism triggered by an isolated incident of violence, can be transmitted like shock waves through a dense crowd.

We were duly back amongst the Amer Trading cronies the following morning. With unprecedented haste, we were whisked away in a taxi to the port by a couple of lads who spoke no English. At the gate police were stopping dockers and sailors on their way out and checking the contents of their carrier bags - nothing but fish, it appeared. The two lads spoke to an official behind bars, but to no avail. Following our escorts blindly, we jumped on a bus to the 'PASSISSUING OFFICE' *(sic)* where we spent half an hour filling in forms and waiting for signatures before returning, still passless, to the Amer den.

'It is taking too long to get your passes for the port,' the agent told us. 'It is better that you are waiting here while my people are getting the car examined by the customs.'

'But I must be there when the car is checked, to make sure it is not damaged,' said Ashley, thinking of the treatment at the Saudi border and expecting worse.

'No need to be worrying, sir. My people will look after everything, and anyway the customs are only checking chassis number and engine number and these things. No problem.' His head waggled ominously. 'This way *Inshallah,* you will have your car this evening. If you wait for passes, it will be taking two days or three.'

'OK,' we conceded, eager not to prolong our stay in Karachi indefinitely, and the agent disappeared, saying, 'It should take only half an hour *Inshallah.'*

We were waiting in the office for four hours.

Cups of tea and a steady flow of visitors came and went. We read *Dawn,* one of Karachi's English newspapers, from cover to cover and shifted about on the hard wooden seats. At midday an old bearded man shuffled in with a towel under his arm and all but the tea-'boy' and ourselves drifted out silently. The newcomer sat down at the desk, opened out the towel to reveal a copy of the Qur'an, and began chanting quietly to himself. As if by clockwork, five minutes later the devout visitor rewrapped his book, left the room and the mob trickled back. More cups of tea followed.

By two o'clock we were restless, hungry and annoyed. Even our gap-toothed friend, who was having his usual battle with the telephone system, had caught our impatience and was bashing the receiver buttons in despair. On the point of giving up in favour of food, we were forestalled by the miraculous arrival of one rather hot and weary clearing agent and another lad, in whose sole care we were swiftly dispatched to the Customs House.

On a heap of files and papers, at the bottom of which was a document tagged 'Urgent', a large, yellow volume entitled *1969 Customs Act* lay prominently on the desk of Mr Akbar Ali. If there was anyone in Karachi who acted by the book, it was Mr A. A. and he had clearly been studying this one in search of all the possible legal impediments which he could add to the already substantial catalogue of delays to the clearance of our little car. Slowly and deliberately, his eyes and his guiding finger moved down the pages of our documents which the boy had handed to him. Evidently the customs men had been through the entire contents of the car and had subsequently written down a list of all they could remember, in random order, like contestants in a television game who, having memorised the items on a conveyor belt, call out: 'Electric kettle... bathroom scales... tea-set... teddy-bear...' Mr Akbar Ali was confronted with an inventory of less exotic items, such as inner tubes, bars of soap, foot-pump, torch and toothpaste, but his mental filter, responding to page 677 (or more) of the *1969 Customs Act,* was systematically segregating all of the car's spare parts.

'The customs men tell me you have all these spare

parts in your car,' he informed us, finally. 'You know that it is not allowed? I'm afraid you will be paying duty on all these things. If not, they will be confiscated. We cannot allow people to sell spare parts after personally importing them.'

We remonstrated simultaneously: could he not understand that our car was so unusual in Pakistan that finding spare parts for it would be well nigh impossible? Did he really believe that we would try to sell things which were so vital to our own survival? Would he not take the same reasonable precautions if he were to drive 9,000 miles from London to Dubai?

The commendable patience with which he listened unflinchingly to our tirade could only have been born of great experience: how many people before us had been driven to this desperate defamation of Pakistan's customs legislation, for which Mr Akbar Ali could hardly be held responsible? Yes, he had heard all this many times. Expressionless, he summoned a middle-aged colleague to whom he began methodically to dictate a letter, his eyes fixed, as though entranced, by the lolloping blades of the propeller fan above. The letter, as formal as a testament, began:

'To the Assistant Chief Collector, The Customs House, Karachi.

Dear Sir.

I hereby declare that I, Ashley Earwaker, and my wife have imported our Citroën car on the...'

It went on for a full page to describe our journey and intentions to leave Pakistan within one month, included a solemn oath that we would not sell any item of spare parts while in the country, and culminated in the crucial plea for tax exemption. When the secretary eventually laid down his pen we sighed with relief- but the matter was far from complete. Ashley was obliged to copy the entire letter in his own hand and to sign it. Then Mr Akbar Ali signed it. After that we had to wait to see his immediate superior for a third signature. Finally we were ushered into the spacious office of the Assistant Chief Collector, a relatively young man, whose walls were plastered with enormous poster-photographs showing ingenious methods of concealing smuggled goods in false compartments of luggage, in flasks, sandals and all sorts of interesting hiding-places.

Meanwhile Mr A. A., we suspected, had been scanning the pages of his favourite work, for when we returned he was quick to point out that there was a stamp lacking on one of the documents (or one of its copies - I was beyond caring: they were all spattered with stamps and signatures). Helpless, we could only take his word for this omission and watch in desperation as he sent our young escort scuttling away through the streets to the Amer office to get the paper stamped. Our patience was, by this stage, on the point of collapse: were we, we asked the inscrutable Mr Akbar Ali through clenched teeth, going to see the car today or after Christmas?

'Today, *Inshallah,*' came the inevitable reply, the very wording of which precluded all hope of fulfilment.

The boy returned, the paper was signed again, and we were led to another official for what we prayed would be the final examination of all the documents. Incredibly, they were found to be in order and we skipped back with the lad to the Amer office, thinking that, after all, we were going to be reunited with the car. Then the final bombshell dropped.

'Before you can pick up your car,' announced the agent, 'you must be getting a form exempting you from port charges of 1500 rupees. I am very sorry, but it is 4.30 and the office issuing this form is closed now. Please, you can come back at nine tomorrow morning and there will be no more problems... *Inshallah.'*

'No problem?!' we screamed. Having already spent a week in Karachi waiting for the car, and with the likelihood of remaining there indefinitely increasing with every utterance of the word *Inshallah,* we were mad with frustration and, incidentally, irritable with hunger. In fact, not to put too fine a point on it, my fist was poised to smash a few more gaps amongst the grinning dentures of a certain friend of ours. Had it not been for the timely interception of Ashley's parting flood of invective, aimed at the enemy, I might by now have had my ears cut off, or be languishing in a Pakistani prison, on charges of assault.

We climbed aboard a bus which, for three pence each, took us about two miles back to Saddar, with an ever-increasing rush-hour load, until we were extruded near the Empress Market. The buses and the lorries of Karachi never ceased to amaze us: the extravagance of their decoration was matched only by their degree of dilapidation. Some of the Bedford trucks were forty years old if they were a day, but there was an assortment of ages and marks, from old GMC to modern Isuzu. To see them chugging along, heavily laden, gleaming in carnival procession, dripping with brightly coloured tassels and badges, and topped with great vertical shields of painted metalwork above the cabs, made even an ornate Turkish lorry look like the back-end of a bus. They reminded me of pictures of the jeepneys of Manila. Some of the buses conformed to a bizarre, barrel-shaped design which only strengthened the impression that they were bulging at the seams. The tyres? It was best to forget about the tyres until we were several thousand miles away and unlikely ever again to set foot on a Karachi bus. They had gone beyond the stage of losing their tread and had worn down through the rubber to the canvas in many cases, while cracks and splits gaped ominously like excruciating wounds.

Women were segregated from men in a relatively small portion at the front of the bus. I found myself on a bench seat opposite the driver, squeezed between two rather skinny girls whose fragile bones seemed perilously close to disintegration at every jolt and bump along the route. In addition to the potholes, of which the large chasm in the floor near the gear-stick made me only too aware, there were lateral hazards, owing to the tendency of the buses to jostle one another like dodgem cars. The conductors, meanwhile, bashed the metal plating with their palms at every stop, yelling their destinations repeatedly and as incomprehensibly as newspaper touts in order to attract more passengers, although how anyone could hear above the hoots and roars of the other traffic remains a mystery. As for the male passengers themselves, leaping on and off and clinging to the outside like squirrels to a tree, they were more like professional acrobats than tired men returning home after a hard day's work, a category which accommodated more aptly the one Englishman on board.

Alighting in Saddar, we were still entertaining the possibility of a cinema outing but our hopes were dashed on discovery of the unappetising selection of bloodthirsty films, such as *Rambo, Part II, Super Inframan* and *Return of the Himalayan Man,* whose gruesome heroes were currently displayed in garish, hand-painted posters above the Odeons and Regals of Karachi.

Nine o'clock the next morning found me and my paperback confined to the Amer office again and Ashley undergoing a hair-raising experience on the back of a motorbike in the pursuit of exemption from the infamous port charges. It came as no surprise to us, by now, that the office for which he was making should be illogically located some three miles from the port itself, as though put there for the sole purpose of causing maximum inconvenience to clearing agents and their clients.

At 10.15, nevertheless, he returned, the charges waived. Someone slipped down to the port to pay the wharfage and unloading charges for us (800 rupees, Mr Rizvi had informed us) and we should have the car by 12 *Inshallah.* Meanwhile, could we hand over the money - 800 for wharfage, 500 for unloading, and 800 for services rendered?

'What...? You told us to bring 800 rupees and that's all we have with us. There. The rest you must wait for.'

At 1 p.m. we were still sitting in the office when someone summoned us to go down to the port to wait for the car to be driven out to us. We could hardly believe our luck. We sat expectantly at the port gates with our escorts in the sweltering Mazda, watching eagerly every outgoing vehicle and pedestrian. Suddenly a familiar face appeared - swarthy beneath a white headband: it was the 'pirate' from the *Al Sagar*! Grinning, he recognised us too, came up, shook hands through the car window and went on. Any minute now, we thought. It was like waiting at the school gates for your child to be let out at the end of term. There was just one snag: we were at the wrong gate, someone kindly informed us after half an hour. It was only to be expected.

At the correct gate we stood in the shade for three quarters of an hour and were just on the point of giving up hope altogether when there on the horizon appeared a white... well... was it... ? It was hidden behind a lorry... no... yes... YES! ... here comes the car! ... Hurray! ... It's our 2CV!

It was held up at the gate for a further inspection of its engine and chassis numbers, but then it came through. The first thing we noticed was that something heavy had been dropped on its roof, bending one of the aluminium bars out of shape, although the hood itself was fortunately unscathed. What genuinely distressed me, however, was the state of the interior: one look at the chaos of our belongings was enough to make me dissolve into tears. Had I not been at the end of my tether after yet another long hot day of untold frustration, I should have had more control; but seeing the random manner in which the customs men had clearly thrown back our goods into this, our precious home, I felt nothing but despair. Tools, spare parts and grease-gun were entangled with packets of food, clothes and books, most of which were either dirty, bent, torn or all three.

Naturally Ashley's principal concern was with the condition of the car itself and he insisted on returning to the hotel to make a thorough check of the exterior and under-bonnet matters before Amer received the additional sums which they were now demanding. As for the car's contents, there was no alternative but to remove the entire jumble from the car to our hotel room, sort and clean them, note what was missing and return the remainder to their rightful boxes. This we did, much to the consternation of the hotel staff who looked aghast as we entered in a welter of paraphernalia. Fortunately it was a hotel where tolerance exceeded smartness, or we should have been thrown out of the premises instantly. As it was, our room for the next few hours was converted into a cross between a bomb site and a jumble sale. There was sugar in our shoes, washing powder amongst the books, jam in our clothes and grease on just about everything. When we had performed our laborious task, we conveyed buckets of soapy water repeatedly to the car, restoring it inside and out to something resembling its former self, and hoping simultaneously to wash away the remains of the salty seaspray before it spread its rusty fingers across the metalwork.

CHAPTER 17

Free at last from the fetters of bureaucracy, we escaped from Karachi before the morning rush-hour could ensnare us. Gleefully we sped along the 'Super Highway' towards Hyderabad, gladly paying the eight rupees' toll for the privilege of a smooth, straight run eastwards. The level pastures of the Indus Delta were sprinkled with gently grazing cattle and interrupted by fields of rustling maize; small channels where egrets waded in blue water flowed between banks of lush green vegetables. Shepherds and goatherds, migrating back to their villages, looked strangely warlike, carrying heavy axes amongst their harmless flocks.

We skirted Hyderabad, turning left a hundred miles from Karachi to follow the western bank of the Indus River northwards. The road was just wide enough for two lorries most of the time, but the surface was abominable. Sudden diversions into the soft dust avoided sections of road-mending where, through the drifting, reddish clouds, we could make out teams of men digging sandy ground or carrying shallow bowls of gravel on their heads. In the brown villages the colours of the women's dress were as rich as jewels against the simple brushwood shelters and the huts of mud and stone. We saw camels, hauling their loads of logs with elephantine passivity across timber yards, while men nearby shocked us with their bright red turbans like beads of fresh blood. In one village a young policeman and his friend flagged us down excitedly, but for no legitimate reason - unable to speak English, the policeman simply stood and grinned at us while his friend invited us with gestures to join them for tea and then started pointing eagerly at various articles in the back of the car while begging with his other hand. It was time to move on.

On our left now was the edge of the folded Kirthar Range, whose central ridge forms the provincial boundary between Baluchistan to the west and Sind to the east. Sind, long known as the 'unhappy valley' on account of its meagre rainfall and irrigation-dependence, had become notorious for its recent subjection to additional misery, particularly in the districts of Dadu and Larkana, for this was bandit country. From the shelter of the Kirthar Hills armed dacoits had regularly been descending by night, like wolves, to their victims in the valley, and the Karachi newspapers that November were plagued with reports of their exploits, such as in *Dawn*:

'DADU: Armed dacoits looted ornaments, arms and other articles, worth thousands of rupees, when they attacked Bilalwalpur, a village 35 miles from here, on Sunday night.'

'LARKANA: The judicial inquiry into the firing incident near Nazar railway crossings, Larkana, that claimed the life of Syed Amir Ali...'

'RAWALPINDI: ... The unrest in Sind, Mr Jatoi [veteran politician and member of the National Assembly from Sind] said was on its peak. Sindhi youth, he said, were terribly disturbed by the present state of affairs in the country. It would be unwise to describe the present

Camel-driven irrigation, Pakistan

situation in Sind as normal, he said.

'The only question being widely asked by the people of Sind is 'for how long they have to live in the present situation'. This showed how infinite communication gap was [sic] between the rulers and people, he said.'

'DADU: Public and district administration should make joint efforts and evolve strategy to curb antisocial activities in Dadu district. This was stated by the Deputy Commissioner, Dadu, while speaking to people during his visit to villages Ismail Barbar and Bilawalpur. The D.C. urged them to face the threat posed by dacoits, unitedly. In this regard he said the Government would provide all possible help to people and arms licences would also be issued to them.

'It may be mentioned that he visited the villages to offer Fateha for a zamindar [land-owner] who was killed by dacoits a few days back.'

We were not eager to delay in this troubled region, least of all at night, any longer than was required by a visit to the ruined Indus city of Mohenjodaro. In the brightness of daylight and the company of traffic, however, we felt safe.

At midday, north of Amri, we stopped in the shade of some steep rocks to change the oil and to refit a number of the car's parts which had been removed for the shipment and which we had thought safer to keep hidden until we had left Karachi. Across the road by the river was a patient camel, trudging round in a circle to operate an irrigation water-wheel decked with pitchers. We were peacefully contemplating the timeless quality of this scene, unchanged for centuries, when an enormous lorry, bejewelled in chrome, rumbled past and a missile hurled from the cab landed at our feet. The driver was still waving and smiling from his window as we pulled from the dust his mysterious offering: the May edition *of Australian House and Garden*! Buses also roared past, tooting loudly, their passengers sprouting at all angles from the roof-racks; and several cars, seeing our bonnet raised, stopped to see if they could help. One family generously insisted on leaving us a gift of oranges; another, less kindly, gentleman claimed to be a Saudi Arabian visitor with a penchant for collecting foreign currency notes - that was his excuse anyway for asking to swap his 100 rupees for ours which bore different serial numbers! He soon disappeared when he realised that he had overestimated our gullibility.

The fairground-style lorries, ploughing southwards along the road, were staggering in every sense of the word. Some were piled high and swollen with maize-stalks to twice their normal height and width. Others with high sides grumbled by under even greater loads: each had a hessian-bound mound bursting out of the top and over the sides like a giant, bloated mushroom, while strapped onto the back of the lorry there was an enormous pendulous sack, bulging and swaying far beyond the vehicle's width.

Bedford truck, Pakistan

Soon we were bouncing along the uneven road once more, hurrying to reach the town of Mehar before nightfall. A minibus hurtled past us with a full load of passengers inside and at least twenty more happily hanging off the sides or balancing on the roof. Ahead a loaded lorry slowed down in a village, to the delight of two small boys who ran up behind, tugged at the loose sticks of sugar cane and skipped away, laughing, with their easy loot. We passed men riding camels, lurching their way slowly along the roadside, and water-buffaloes ploughing between the lush green paddy-fields. As bright as poppies in a cornfield, the vivid colours of the cotton-picking women bobbed amongst the soft white bolls. Nearby on wooden watch-towers - platforms raised on stilts above the maize fields - boys sat vigilantly guarding the crops against predators.

The pools and irrigation channels were brilliant with bird life: egrets herons, dazzling large kingfishers, plovers and ibis; while in the tall trees sat hoopoes, rollers, kites, doves, mynahs and bee-eaters. After the wastes of Arabia and the chaos of Karachi we were invigorated by the wealth of colourful images and enchanting scenes - such as the curious habit adopted by the local men of disguising themselves as haystacks and emerging from the reedbeds when we least expected it, to trot across the road!

In the distance the smoking chimneys of little brickworks protruded ominously from the plains, like the barrels of artillery guns pointed skywards, and horse-drawn carts laden with bricks periodically blocked the narrow village streets.

When we struck the village of Khairpur Nathan Shah the main street was crowded and weekend celebrations were already in full swing: it was Thursday afternoon, and with the prospect of a public holiday on Saturday (an annual festival in honour of the Indian Muslim philosopher-poet Iqbal's birthday) making it a long weekend, the fun had already started. Loudspeakers trembled with discordant music; skinny horses and traps, all brightly decorated with beads and garlands, jangled by; the fruit stalls were fluttering and glittering with flags, tassels and ribbons; there were shops selling luminous-coloured sweets and cakes, tea-shops and barbecues cooking corn-on-the-cob; and everywhere we saw swarms of brightly dressed women, men sporting coloured sequined Sindhi caps (pill-box style with a notch cut away at the front), and happy children dancing across the street with headless hobby-horses. It was a day for rejoicing!

The trouble began when we reached Mehar and found that the Tourist Rest House, which was marked on our map and where we intended to stay before going on to Mohenjodaro the following day, was closed. (We learned later that the army had taken it over.) Since it was growing dark and too late to continue to the next town, Larkana, which was forty miles away, we went to the police station to ask if we might camp there. In their dusty walled compound the young constables, reluctant to interrupt their game of volleyball in order to help two foreigners, told us we should have to go to the hotel at Larkana. Unwilling to risk driving in the dark along this dangerous stretch of road, we found that our only option was to camp at the '24 hours' petrol station on the north side of Mehar. It was guarded by an armed *chowkidar* (night-watchman) and manned by some hospitable lads who brought us cushions, chairs and jugs of water, while we waged war on the mosquitoes. The swamp, on the other side of the forecourt wall, was bristling with the vicious brutes and they came swarming towards the floodlights with a multitude of their friends and relations, plastering the tent and dropping into our sardines. Fuming mosquito-coils, cans of fly-spray and lashings of insect repellent lotion were powerless against the invasion. Lacking an entomologist's appreciation of the environment (every conceivable species of flying insect seemed to be represented), we made it our sole ambition to isolate ourselves in the tent from the rest of the living world.

First, however, we spent half an hour in the building at the invitation of the friendly pump attendants, one of whom, a young medical student, knew enough English to converse with us. He acted as interpreter for the others, who looked on in awe and occasional amusement, the *chowkidar* stroking his curled moustache, his beady eyes dark beneath his bright pink Sindhi cap, while the boy, whose nickname was 'Donkey', grinned at us through enormous teeth. Despite the unglazed windows, we suffered few bites within those concrete walls: presumably the insects were deterred by the action of the large propeller fan. By ten o'clock we were safely inside our cosy cocoon, sharing it only with a handful of murdered insects, and threatening each other with a fate worse than death should one of us have to get up in the night, thereby opening the flaps to more mosquitoes.

At 2 a.m. we were disturbed by the *chowkidar,* who was circling the tent, poking it with his shotgun and muttering incomprehensibly. Sleepily we told him to go away, but when he persisted, raising his voice angrily and trying to force his way into the tent, we realised his evil intentions towards me. Startled, we scrambled into our clothes as the gun was thrust threateningly through the tent flaps.

Storming out of the tent, Ashley tried to wrest the gun from the *chowkidar.* After a struggle he did so, but there was no time for him to fire it into the air for already the *chowkidar* had pushed me back into the tent and Ashley had to haul him out. As I picked myself up horrifying shouts of abuse roared around me while the two battled barefoot in the dust. Ashley shouted at me to hit the man over the head with the hammer and, terrified of the implications but driven by panic, I wielded it but was stopped in mid-air by the *chowkidar*'s accomplice running towards us.

I climbed, trembling, into the driver's seat of the 2CV but was unable to lock myself in by shooting the exterior bolt (by reaching through the window) before the *chowkidar* was at my side, battering on the door and violently shaking and turning the handle. For what seemed like hours I pulled on the door-strap as hard as I could and almost collapsed with relief when he accidentally shot the bolt and gave up, running towards Ashley instead, who was now fighting with the second man.

'Go, go, go!' yelled Ashley to me, but the accomplice rushed in front of the car and pointed the gun directly at me. I gulped, put my foot down and the man fell away as the car moved forward, while the *chowkidar* rushed, inexplicably, towards the building (perhaps, we guessed later, to fetch ammunition?), leaving Ashley to run beside the car. As I turned out into the road Ashley moved to the other side, trying to keep the car between himself and the armed man.

Suddenly I heard a shot and turned, terrified for one moment...

... but Ashley was still running. I slowed down and he climbed onto the front bull-bar, clutching his right arm as we made our getaway. The men, without transport, were soon left behind, so I pulled up and Ashley got in. They had peppered the car with pellets and hit Ashley in the arm, but he had pinched out the lead shot which luckily had not penetrated deeply.

As we fled in the darkness to Larkana the nightmare continued: we knocked down a dog which ran madly into the road, we lost our way more than once, and we were stopped in a village by uncomprehending policemen who finally let us go on. I was shaking like a leaf, remembering the reports of dacoit attacks and hoping we would reach the safety of the police station soon. Suddenly an armed man stepped out from a parked van into the otherwise deserted road as we approached. I screamed to Ash, 'Whatever you do, don't stop!' and, as we continued, we looked over our shoulders only to see that the van was giving chase. Soon it had caught up with us (oh, for a fast car, we thought) and as it overtook we noticed the 'Police' sign along its side. It pulled in and half a dozen armed and uniformed men jumped out to flag us down. We had no alternative but to stop.

My nerves felt as though they had been through a shredding machine. This was what we had dreaded: a hold-up by Baluchi bandits in disguise. Now they would rob us of what remained of our possessions and probably shoot us to boot. They approached the windows, crowding round the car, some in thick greatcoats, several in berets, some clutching rifles and others shining torches in our faces. I refused to open my window. Ashley opened his and a mouthful of Urdu came at him, but there was no violence, there were no more gunshots.

These were genuine policemen of the Highway Patrol, protecting us from the very bandits whom we feared. Our relief was matched only by our frustration at the language barrier between us and these suspicious men It took at least ten minutes to explain, through increasingly desperate gestures, that we had been involved in a fight at Mehar, that Ashley had been shot and we were anxious to reach Larkana, urgently to report the incident to an English-speaking officer and to dress our wounds. Nothing could remove from their faces the bewildered expressions of men who, at three o'clock in the morning, had just met a mad British couple covered in cuts, bruises and multifarious wounds driving in the most peculiar vehicle ever seen in Sind, along one of the most dangerous roads in Pakistan. Astounded though they were, however, they did let us continue to Larkana and they followed closely behind until we reached the town, where they overtook again and led us into the police compound.

Despite extra sweaters, we now sat shivering from cold and shock in the office of the Chief of Police, waiting for him to appear. The group of armed policemen near the door stood whispering amongst themselves, or simply staring at us in disbelief. One of them brought us cups of tea - hot, sweet, very milky, tasting of woodsmoke and exceptionally soothing. It was just what the doctor ordered.

The Chief of Police, displeased at being woken so early, listened to our tale and took a brief, written statement from us before disappearing home to bed, expressing the intention of returning at a more reasonable hour. His constable, instructed to keep charge of us, brought into the office a couple of charpoys and blankets for us, but we were in no state to sleep. Instead we sat together, dressed our cuts using our own first aid kit, made frequent sorties to the toilet (each time having to ask permission and being led past the prison cell where two wretched inmates clung to the bars in wide-eyed fascination), and steadied ourselves with copious quantities of tea.

At one stage I broke down uncontrollably, suffering from what must have been a combination of delayed shock and extreme relief, blubbering like a baby at the realisation of our narrow escape. We were lucky simply to be alive, together and in safe hands. Never had I felt so overpowered by simultaneous emotions - love, hate, fear, anger, relief, joy, misery - which rushed feverishly through my mind in wild combination, a flash flood of feelings, uprooting rationality in its unrelenting and merciless course. Only gradually did this storm subside, giving way at last to a calmness of thought, as though the sun were filtering through grey clouds. Our decision came as naturally and inevitably as this new light. There was no doubt, only sadness in our mind. We could not continue our journey: we should return home as soon as we could.

The Chief of Police at Larkana, however, had other ideas. When he returned at 10.30 a.m., he had already been on the 'phone to Mehar and to the Sind headquarters of the police and, because we were foreigners, our case had achieved what he called 'priority status'. There was no possibility of our leaving before arrests had been made. The Inspector from Mehar was on his way over to collect us shortly, *Inshallah,* and to take over the case. After two hours (which the Chief spent listening to the cricket commentary on the radio), the Inspector arrived and, over fried eggs, fried bread and more tea, we related the tale again. At first we protested at the thought of returning to

Mehar while the *chowkidar* was still at large and armed with his shotgun, but we soon saw that we had no choice in the matter: we had to go. I travelled in the Inspector's car with two armed guards sitting in the rear, and Ashley drove the 2CV, accompanied by another armed policeman.

The journey, which we had made only hours before, could not have undergone a greater transformation than if we had awoken from a bad dream. As we returned to Mehar the valley was radiant beneath a deep blue sky, with happy children playing in the lush paddy-fields, men and buffaloes bathing in pools, and women washing or picking cotton amidst an unforgettable array of exotic birds. The whole beautiful scene was infused with sunlight, which seemed to penetrate the very souls of these people: surely poverty here was easier to bear than in the slums of Karachi.

For almost two days we were held by the police at their Mehar compound until the culprits had been arrested and identified by Ashley - I could not bear to set eyes on those men again. We were questioned repeatedly and at length by the Chief of the Mehar Police and by the Sub-Divisional Magistrate. The *chowkidar* finally gave himself up in the village cemetery after his family had been taken hostage by the police - a practice apparently widely used in Pakistan. Meanwhile, we were given the Inspector's room in his guarded residence, which was built in 1916, a relic of the Raj. His room was simply furnished with two charpoys and an electric fan, the windows barred and the doors bolted. (One of his predecessors, we were informed, had been murdered in this compound.) His was an unenviable job, separating him for months at a time from his wife and children in their Punjab home, maintaining order in this difficult region; but next year it would be someone else's turn. His manservant brought us food, heated water for us to wash with, and besieged us with mosquito coils in the evening.

Such generous hospitality, verging on servility, embarrassed rather than consoled us. That the police felt responsible for our safety and anxious to redeem their reputation we could understand, but it was disturbing to hear from the Magistrate that, as British subjects, we deserved special consideration, in view of 'Pakistan's long-standing debt to Britain'.

Exhausted that night, but tormented by mental turmoil and the yelps of dogs outside, we did not sleep easily. In vain we had waited up, as requested by the Chief of Police, in order to identify the men whom he had hoped, *Inshallah,* to arrest that evening, but it was not until the following morning that the culprits were tracked down. We had breakfast on a concrete verandah whose outlook was an eight-foot wall just a few paces away. We were encouraged by frequent promises of imminent summons to the Magistrate's court, but the minutes turned into hours and each hour felt like a day. We passed the time by reading and dressing the cook's old sores and cuts which bedevilled his feet.

At last we were escorted to the Chief's office and the end of our incarceration seemed in sight, but the path to freedom was still littered with obstacles. I was not aware, until then, that the assault had intensified in me a revulsion for violence of any kind. When the police, bent on retribution, brought our aggressors into the compound, the sound of beating and anguished cries triggered my gut reaction. It was this instinctive distress, rather than a more reasoned objection to the brutality (such as the injustice of punishment before trial), which made me plead for a halt to the flogging and which even overrode a strong natural desire for revenge. By then we were anxious to leave.

A police van transported us to the Magistrate's court,

where a doctor examined Ashley's gunshot wound and a second identification, followed by cross-questioning, took place. Then our statements were remade and copied by a painfully slow and inaccurate typist. This was the outcome of Ashley's version (mine was almost identical):

I do hereby state that:
My name is: Ashley Anthony Thomas Earwaker
Father's name: Thomas Earwaker
Caste: Earwaker
Religion: Chiristian
Age about: 32 years
Occupation: Jeo-Physiciest
Residence: Bank Cottage, Lodge Lane
Westerndam Kent
U.K.
That I, with my wife Nicola Anna Earwaker are tourists in Pakistan. We left Karachi in our car on the morning of 07th November, 1985 and reached Mehar at about 5.00 P.M. We understood from our road map that there was a Rest House at Mehar, but we were told in the Town that there was not. We went to the Police Station and asked there if we could camp in our tent for the night, they said nNo. As it was getting dark and we did not want to drive to Larkana in the dark, we stopped at the P.S.O. Petrol Pump station just North of Mehar and asked there if we could camp. They said that we could camp, so we put up our tent. We went to sleep at about 10.00 P.M. and were woken at about 2.00 A.M. by the armed watchman who was trying to get into our tent. We said 'please go away' but he did not, and he tried again to get into the tent. He pointed the gun at us, we got out of the tent. He then pushed my wife back into the tent and tried to rape her. I struggled with the watchman to stop him, but he called out to another man, who came to help him. This second man took the gun and pointed it at me. While

both men were taking me over to the buildings, my wife got into our car and locked herself in. The watchman ran back to the car and tried to get in, but when he realised that the. door was locked, he ran back to the building. I walked away from the other man, who had the gun, and went back to the car. I did not have time to get into the car because the watchman was running back towards us. The second man, with the gun was standing in front of the car. My wife started the enginee and moved off in the, car. I ran along by the side of the car. Then a shot was fired at us and one bullet hit my right arm. We went down the road and then I got into the car and drove directly to Police Station at Larkana at 4.00 A.M. There we narrated the incident to the Incharge of the Police Station who immediately rang up to Police Station Mehar. At about 11.00 A.M. Inspector of Police Station Mehar reached at Police Station Larkana and he brought us back to Police Station Mehar where F.I.R. was lodged. I know the accused now present in the court who are same.

Cross examination to accused Altaf Hussain Jatoi _

Nil though chance given.

Cross exam: to accused Abdul Haleem Khattee Soomro

It is incorrect to suggest that you have rescused us, but you also pointed gun at us.

Before me

Sub-Divisional Magistrate, Mehar. Certificate.

Certified that the above statement has been recorded in his presence and hearings and it contains all of whatever stated by him.

Sub-Divisional Magistrate, Mehar.

We declined an interview with a newspaper reporter and, as we left the court, hid our faces from the photographer who was lurking outside. In the dust of the police compound, a dirty collection of our camping equipment and other belongings, which the guilty parties had flung over the petrol station wall into the swamp as soon as we had left, was spread out to dry in the hot afternoon sun. The police had kindly dredged the articles from the mire but we had to leave many of them: the down sleeping bags were damaged beyond hope and we were eager now to abandon my geological hammer.

By the time we were allowed to depart under armed escort for Karachi our patience was running out. We felt a desperate need to leave the sickening affair behind us, but each step of the proceedings - the statements, the questioning, the doctor's examination, the identifications and, finally, our release - had been heralded by that well-known oriental promise of inaction, 'In a few minutes, *Inshallah,*' followed by a delay of several hours. To echo the sentiments of Eric Newby after his spell in the Hindu Kush, we longed to be back amongst 'people who mean what they say and do it'!

Nevertheless, it was a moving moment when we drove out of the compound at Mehar. We had shaken hands warmly with all the police who had helped us and Ashley was embraced like a brother by the Inspector and the Chief of Police. It was a small but united band of men who stood to attention as we left. They had treated us with great respect and sympathy in the best way that they knew, and we were grateful.

The relay escort, which led us back to the 'Toll Plaza' on the Super Highway to Karachi, fulfilled the promise of 'VIP' treatment too. For the whole journey we followed a small police pick-up van carrying three or four armed guards, and each time a change-over took place at a district boundary the next van was waiting for us. At the final change near Hyderabad the local Police Chief even came out to meet us. The entire operation could not have run more smoothly, and by 9.30 we were back in Karachi, with mixed feelings.

CHAPTER 18

'No loving in the streets!' yelled the white-uniformed policeman above the roar of traffic. We hesitated before crossing the busy road, suddenly aware of our indiscretion. We smiled: holding hands seemed a trivial offence after the traumatic events which had forced us to return prematurely to Karachi.

When we had left the city two days earlier, the thought that we should be back so soon could not have been further from our minds. Yet here we were, once more entangled in the bureaucratic net of the Pakistani port, endeavouring to ship a small white car back to Britain. Unwilling to offer the kind of inducement which might have accelerated the customs formalities, we were forced to accept the delay. Even the powerful Pakistani National Shipping Corporation, whose container vessel, the *Cosmo Ocean,* was to carry our Citroën 2CV was a slave to the Karachi customs officials. For five days we shuttled between countless offices under a deluge of certificates and documents, waiting for stamps and signatures or for the relevant person to arrive. There were no short cuts through the frustratingly long-winded procedure. Sextuple copies of a form, completed for a few rupees by a pavement typist outside the Customs

House, had to be signed individually, three times by us and at least half a dozen more by various officials in a number of office blocks.

There was a moment when the regulations looked impossible. Ashley needed a port pass in order to accompany the car into the customs area (women were not allowed to enter under any circumstances) but there was one snag: before the pass could be issued, a signature was required from an office *within* the port area, which Ashley was not permitted to enter until he possessed a pass! The only solution to this 'Catch 22' dilemma was to track down a port official who knew the gatekeeper and was willing to act as an escort.

Finally we had the sniffer dogs to contend with. Understandable official concern over the illegal drugs traffic from the North-West Frontier Province through Karachi had led to the introduction of these specially trained animals from the United States - evidently in insufficient numbers, for there was a two days' delay before they came to trample through our car.

Meanwhile we had other business to attend to. We had already been to the British Embassy dutifully to report the incident which had led to our imminent return home, but beyond a sympathetic ear we had encountered a wall of disinterest. Far greater concern had been shown earlier by the police and the national press. Our air tickets to London were supplied by a wily refugee from Afghanistan who, under the auspices of a major travel office, was running a private agency for a friend of his, quite openly undercutting his employers' air fares. We might have bought our tickets from a retired major, the manager of another travel firm which we visited one evening, but he was less interested in selling tickets than in the opportunity for a good chat.

'Come and have some tea in my office,' he said, five

minutes before closing time. 'I'm in no hurry to go home.'

An obedient young lad soon brought in a tray of Lipton's *chai* and some biscuits.

'I like my staff to be disciplined,' said the old man. 'That's what an army training does for you, you know.' His neat grey moustache and his clear round eyes seemed to dance a little as he smiled. 'I have a great deal to thank the British for: my commander taught me almost everything I know.'

'When did you leave the army?'

'After the war - our war, I mean. I was a prisoner in India from '71 to '74 you see. A terrible time. I wanted to forget it all and start again, so I came to Karachi, along with millions of others of course. Sometimes I escape from the city and up to the north - we run tours to Gilgit and Chitral for people who can stand a jeep ride in the mountains. It is peaceful there, away from the city crowds.

'Overpopulation is our biggest problem, as you will have noticed! The girls marry at thirteen, even as young as twelve, and have babies while they are still children themselves. You see, the difficulties are increasing all the time. We simply can't provide enough food or jobs for a country with seventy million people.' He spoke as though he felt personally responsible for their plight and yet with a degree of fatalism commensurate with his years. 'The danger in a crowded city is that a little unrest can so easily escalate to widespread violence, with or without martial law.'

Two days later, on our flight to London, the newspapers gave us a poignant reminder of his words: 'One cop killed. Four dacoits die in major gunbattle in Karachi' was the headline in *Dawn,* one of Karachi's leading newspapers. The incident, described as 'the biggest street gunfight in Pakistan's history, was reported with the sensationalism of a cinema spectacular. It had begun after a tip-off as a pre-dawn raid by a dozen policemen on a house where four armed and wanted dacoits were hiding. An alarming escalation of events led to the involvement of several hundred policemen in a four-hour gun battle. According to the reporters:

'Smoke bombs, tear-gas shells and thousands of rounds fired from the sten-guns and the Soviet Klashnikovs [sic] carried by the dacoits and the Chinese rifles Sind Police shook the entire Block 'I' locality where the high noon thriller was witnessed by thousands of residents... The thrill-packed and suspenseful encounter ended with... crowds carrying the I.G.P. [Inspector General Police] Sind on their shoulders... policemen firing hundreds of rounds in the air in jubilation... until the I.G.P. Sind took a megaphone and pleaded with his jawans not to waste the ammunition.'

A photograph depicted a crowd of several hundred onlookers, eagerly watching the events like spectators at a bullfight. It was easy enough to imagine the outbreak of cheers and victory shots when the police had finally stormed the house and the dacoits were all dead. To us it was a disturbingly bloodthirsty form of entertainment, but then after the last week we had become peculiarly sensitive to violence. It seemed an appropriate day to be leaving Pakistan.

TRAVELS WITH A 2CV

BIBLIOGRAPHY

Brosnahan, Tom, *Turkey on $10 and $15 a Day,* Arthur Frommer, Inc. 1978

Clough, Neil, *Two-wheel Trek,* Hutchinson, 1983

Encyclopedia Britannica, 1971

Fraser-Brunner, Alec, *Danger in the Sea,* Hamlyn, 1973

Hawley, Donald, *Oman and its Renaissance,* Stacey Intl, 1980

Ici Commence L'Aventure, Relations Publiques Citroën, 1981

Jackson, Jack, and Crampton, Ellen, *The Asian Highway,* Angus and Robertson, 1979

Lawrence, T. E., *Seven Pillars of Wisdom,* Penguin Books Ltd., 1979

Moorhouse, G., *To the Frontier,* Hodder & Stoughton, 1984

Newby, Eric, *A Short Walk in the Hindu Kush,* Pan Books Ltd., 1974; *On the Shores of the Mediterranean,* Pan Books Ltd., 1985

H.R.H. Prince Philip and Fisher, James, *Wildlife Crisis,* Hamish Hamilton Ltd., 1970

Thubron, Colin, *Mirror to Damascus,* Heinemann, 1967

Traveller's Guide to the Middle East, 1C Magazines Ltd., 1978

Printed in Great Britain
by Amazon